THE BEDFORD SERIES IN HISTORY AND CULTURE

July 1914:
Soldiers, Statesmen, and the
Coming of the Great War

A BRIEF DOCUMENTARY HISTORY

Related Titles in
THE BEDFORD SERIES IN HISTORY AND CULTURE
Advisory Editors: Lynn Hunt, *University of California, Los Angeles*
David W. Blight, *Yale University*
Bonnie G. Smith, *Rutgers University*
Natalie Zemon Davis, *Princeton University*
Ernest R. May, *Harvard University*

THE BEDFORD SERIES IN HISTORY AND CULTURE

July 1914:
Soldiers, Statesmen, and the Coming of the Great War

A BRIEF DOCUMENTARY HISTORY

Samuel R. Williamson Jr.

University of the South

and

Russel Van Wyk

University of North Carolina at Chapel Hill

BEDFORD/ST. MARTIN'S   Boston ◆ New York

For Bedford/St. Martin's

Publisher for History: Patricia A. Rossi
Director of Development for History: Jane Knetzger
Developmental Editor: Louise Townsend
Editorial Assistant: Rachel L. Safer
Associate Editor, Publishing Services: Maria Teresa Burwell
Production Supervisor: Jennifer Wetzel
Marketing Manager: Jenna Bookin Barry
Project Management: Books By Design, Inc.
Text Design: Claire Seng-Niemoeller
Indexer: Books By Design, Inc.
Cover Design: Billy Boardman
Cover Photo: Austro-Hungarian Troops in Formation © Hulton-Deutsch/CORBIS
Composition: Stratford Publishing Services, Inc.
Printing and Binding: Haddon Craftsmen, an RR Donnelley & Sons Company

President: Joan E. Feinberg
Editorial Director: Denise B. Wydra
Director of Marketing: Karen R. Melton
Director of Editing, Design, and Production: Marcia Cohen
Manager, Publishing Services: Emily Berleth

Library of Congress Control Number: 2002110032

Manufactured in the United States of America.

8
f e

For information, write: Bedford/St. Martin's, 75 Arlington Street, Boston, MA 02116 (617-399-4000)

ISBN-10: 0-312-12010-9
ISBN-13: 978-0-312-12010-8

Acknowledgments

Reprinted from Luigi Albertini, *The Origins of the War of 1914, Volumes II & III,* translated and edited by Isabella M. Massey (1952–1957), by permission of Oxford University Press.

Reprinted with the permission of Simon & Schuster from *The Road to Sarajevo* by Vladimir Dedijer. Copyright © 1966 by Vladimir Dedijer. Copyright renewed © 1994 by Simon & Schuster.

Acknowledgments and copyrights are continued at the back of the book on page 273, which constitutes an extension of the copyright page.

Foreword

The Bedford Series in History and Culture is designed so that readers can study the past as historians do.

The historian's first task is finding the evidence. Documents, letters, memoirs, interviews, pictures, movies, novels, or poems can provide facts and clues. Then the historian questions and compares the sources. There is more to do than in a courtroom, for hearsay evidence is welcome, and the historian is usually looking for answers beyond act and motive. Different views of an event may be as important as a single verdict. How a story is told may yield as much information as what it says.

Along the way the historian seeks help from other historians and perhaps from specialists in other disciplines. Finally, it is time to write, to decide on an interpretation and how to arrange the evidence for readers.

Each book in this series contains an important historical document or group of documents, each document a witness from the past and open to interpretation in different ways. The documents are combined with some element of historical narrative—an introduction or a biographical essay, for example—that provides students with an analysis of the primary source material and important background information about the world in which it was produced.

Each book in the series focuses on a specific topic within a specific historical period. Each provides a basis for lively thought and discussion about several aspects of the topic and the historian's role. Each is short enough (and inexpensive enough) to be a reasonable one-week assignment in a college course. Whether as classroom or personal reading, each book in the series provides firsthand experience of the challenge—and fun—of discovering, recreating, and interpreting the past.

Lynn Hunt
David W. Blight
Bonnie G. Smith
Natalie Zemon Davis
Ernest R. May

Preface

"The greatest error of modern history." So one prominent historian described the First World War.[1] For nearly a century, historians have sought to explain how the assassination of the Archduke Franz Ferdinand and his wife, Sophie, in the Bosnian capital of Sarajevo on June 28, 1914, sparked the slide to war that summer. *July 1914: Soldiers, Statesmen, and the Coming of the Great War* uses original sources—memoirs, diaries, government documents, newspaper editorials, and other contemporary accounts—to introduce the reader to the decision makers and decision making of that summer. Focusing on the interaction between two leading participants—one civilian, one military—in each of the great powers and Serbia, the book explores how individuals, not monolithic governments and impersonal forces, actually contributed to the rapidly escalating crisis.

Readers will discover the impact that contextual factors, such as alliance structures and secret military arrangements, had on the range of options available to the key participants, and they will also come to understand how various other factors—the lack of information, miscommunication, individual ruthlessness, ambition, and fear of failure—affected the decision process. Each dimension will help students appreciate the making of the ultimate decision for any state: the decision to go to war.

In the period between the two world wars, historians of the Great War investigated the arms races, militarism, civil-military relations, and mobilization arrangements, but they did so with only limited access to archival files and personal papers. In the early 1960s, German historian Fritz Fischer reopened the debate, stressing domestic considerations behind Germany's drive to war. Since then, historians with access to nearly all of the archives have examined and reexamined almost every aspect of the July crisis. While Germany remains the government most blamed for irresponsible actions in 1914, Austria–Hungary, Russia, Serbia, and even Britain have been accused of escalating the crisis. Moreover, the Bosnian/Kosovo crises of the 1990s have altered attitudes toward Serbia, allowing for a less romantic assessment of Belgrade's actions in 1914. Yet despite the wealth of new research, there has been no comparative assessment of civil-military relations among the 1914 powers.

The tragic events of September 2001 have been a painful reminder of the power of terrorists to alter the national and international context. At the same time, the military actions taken by the United States and its allies against the terrorist operations in Afghanistan have once again brought issues of civil-military relations into public discussion. For the current generation, the questions posed by July 1914 have become vivid and familiar. This study therefore has both a historical and a contemporary relevance.

This book draws on the changing historical assessments of the twentieth century while introducing the student to a newer, comparative approach to the final decisions for war and peace in 1914. The introduction and chapter 1 set the framework for the discussion, establishing the comparative perspective and summarizing the July crisis itself. The subsequent narrative chapters, interlaced with a range of primary documents, prompt the reader to consider a series of questions about the role of the military and civilian leaders in the crisis. The book concludes with an epilogue that reflects on some of the lessons to be drawn from this study of civil-military relations during July 1914. By the end of the book, we hope that students may understand more clearly the decisions behind "the greatest error" of the twentieth century.

A NOTE ABOUT THE TEXT

This study draws on official documents, memoirs, diaries, collections of letters, and newspapers for Serbia and each of the great powers and their leaders. Since the range of printed sources on the origins of the First World War is enormous, a word about the selection of materials is required. The authors have consulted the published diplomatic document collections, now available with some gaps, for all seven countries covered in the study and other collections of documents that have appeared regularly since the end of the war in 1918. They have also reviewed the existing memoirs and published diaries written by the major participants in the decisions of 1914; the most significant gaps are for the Serbian leaders and for Italian Foreign Minister Antonino di San Giuliano. Collections of letters for some of the participants and memoir accounts of ministerial colleagues have also provided valuable information, especially on issues of personality. Williamson's extensive research in the British archives led to the use of the original texts to buttress the older, printed version of Henry Wilson's indiscreet diaries. Van Wyk's search of the Russian archives unfortunately produced no new material.

In selecting the documents, the authors have asked four questions: What does the material reveal about the nature of civil-military relations in the particular country? What does it tell about the personality of the individual decision maker and his conception of the issue of war or peace? What does the material say about how other key decision makers viewed the major personalities and the issue of war or peace? Finally, what does it tell us about how strategic war/peace decisions were made? With these selections, the authors have sought to show the state of public and private opinion on the critical issues of July 1914.

For documents in English, the authors have not modified the text, though some repetitive detail has been eliminated and explanatory notes have been added as needed. The authors and their research colleagues have translated the German, French, Italian, Russian, and Serbo-Croatian sources, striving for accuracy, clarity, and ease of reading. In instances where we have used other translations of these materials, that is noted in the footnotes. Russian texts that appeared in German translation have been translated into English by the authors; some Russian material is taken from other translations, as noted for each document. In the original documents, Russian names have been variously transliterated; the authors have left them as they have appeared in the texts rather than seeking uniformity across the book.

A final word about the dating of the material: With memoir accounts, we have given the date of the publication of the memoir as the date of the document, even though the document might refer, as in the case of a diary entry, to earlier events. In the case of the monumental study by Luigi Albertini, *The Origins of the War of 1914,* published initially in Italy during the Second World War, we used the publication dates of the individual volumes as published in English during the 1950s.

ACKNOWLEDGMENTS

The authors divided their tasks as follows: Williamson wrote the introduction, the summary of the July crisis, and the chapters on Serbia, Austria–Hungary, France, Italy, and Great Britain; Van Wyk wrote the chapter on Russia; and they collaborated on the German chapter. Each has contributed to the epilogue and to the bibliography.

Both authors want to thank Peter Coogan of Hollins University for his diligent, thoughtful comments, even if we did not always agree with them, and also those who reviewed the work for Bedford/St. Martin's, especially Ross Doughty of Ursinus College, David Herrmann of Fordham University, Dennis Showalter of Colorado College, and Christine White at Penn State. George Williamson of the University of Alabama has been an unsparing critic. Sam Williamson wishes to thank Temple Weiskopf, Cindy Burt, Teresa Smith, Minnie Raymond, and especially Kinion Asmus, whose diligence has made the permissions and production process much easier. He is also grateful to Inela Selimovic for help with the Serbian documents and Leslie Richardson, Maria Smith, and Brandon McInnis for help with the Italian documents. Russ Van Wyk wishes to thank Ivan Tyulin, Sergey V. Mironenko, and Dmitry Manakov for help with Russian sources. He would also like to thank Cary Academy, and Peter A. Coclanis and Richard H. Kohn for advice and support throughout the project. The librarians at the University of the South and the University of North Carolina at Chapel Hill have been patient and helpful with our unusual requests. At every point, Louise Townsend, our development editor, has worked to make this book a reality; we owe her more thanks than we can possibly give here. Rachel L. Safer of Bedford/St. Martin's has rendered invaluable assistance with the permissions and illustrations, and Emily Berleth and Nancy Benjamin with the final production arrangements. Finally, we want to thank Ernest May, Sam's Harvard mentor, colleague, and friend, for suggesting the topic initially and for his patience as we labored to complete it.

Samuel R. Williamson Jr.
Russel Van Wyk

NOTE

[1] Niall Ferguson, *The Pity of War: Explaining World War I* (New York: Basic Books, 1999), 462.

Contents

Maps and Illustrations

Introduction: Civil-Military Relations and July 1914

Europe is "militarism run wild." So reported special assistant Edward House to American President Woodrow Wilson in May 1914. Two months later, after the assassinations of the Archduke Franz Ferdinand and his wife in the Bosnian capital of Sarajevo, Europe plunged into what became the First World War. More than eight and a half million combatants died in the war, four empires disappeared, and European prestige suffered a decisive blow. The First World War, however judged, constitutes perhaps the seminal event of the twentieth century, since it prepared the way for so many of the century's later events: the Russian Revolution, the Second World War, the Holocaust, decolonization, and the cold war.

Because of the First World War's importance, historians have repeatedly analyzed the causes of the July 1914 crisis. One approach has centered on a fundamental constitutional issue: Who controls the military forces, and who makes the final, fateful decision to go to war with those forces? Some writers have argued that rampant militarism meant that the political leaders in July 1914 lost control of the situation, with the generals usurping power and thus preventing a diplomatic solution to the crisis. More recently, some historians have contended that the political leaders were themselves militarized by the culture of the time, so that they and the military leadership shared similar values. Yet other analysts, warning against easy generalizations, recognize that each of the prewar powers in Europe had developed its own approach to the control of the armed forces, ranging from democratic to absolutist to expedient.

The crisis of July 1914 certainly represented a major challenge to the different constitutional approaches for controlling the armed forces. Since the revolution of 1688, English parliamentary leaders were assumed to have control over the instruments of state power. In the next century, the American Constitution gave specific control to an elected president while leaving declarations of war to the Congress. But the Anglo-Saxon experience was not duplicated on the Continent, where monarchs controlled the military (except in France after the creation of the Third Republic in the 1870s). Yet even among the most conservative governments, such as Germany, the monarchs and their advisers could not wholly ignore elected parliamentary bodies, however weak they might be. These groups, in most cases, had to vote the taxes that supported ever-increasing defense expenditures, up by 50 percent across Europe from 1890 to 1914. The final decisions for war might rest with the monarchs, but public opinion and parliaments could not be ignored entirely.

The problem of controlling the military forces grew far more complicated in the years after the Franco-Prussian War of 1870–71. The substantial expansion of standing armies, coupled with a late-century surge in naval construction, posed new financial and logistic challenges, including the development of intricate mobilization plans. Moreover, the professionalization of the armed forces made their supervision by political leaders all the more difficult.

In the first place, the sheer growth of military forces necessitated the creation of systems to oversee them. Each of the continental powers, followed by Great Britain, had developed bureaucratic ministries, general staffs, and professional military schools to support the staffs. As armies and navies grew rapidly, civilian governments created elaborate bureaucratic procedures to support them. Increasing numbers of officers were recruited, trained, evaluated, promoted, and eventually retired. These staff officers developed mobilization plans, justified new defense expenditures, and formed important pressure groups for militarism.

At sea, technological progress had transformed the navies. Steam-powered vessels now moved at will. Heavily armored to prevent damage and heavily armed to inflict damage, the new battleships symbolized state power. Wireless communications ensured the control of the fleets from the central government, albeit often very poorly. The navies, moreover, like the armies, were now ready, once mobilized, to move immediately into operational status. This meant that by 1914 a wholly new dimension had to be considered by the leaders: when to mobilize. Time now became the enemy of calm decision making.

Two other factors were important to the growth of militarism in Europe. The first was the prevalence of universal military service before and after 1914. Even the fledgling Boy Scout movement was an example of societal militarization. Second, the rapid imperial expansion of the late nineteenth century had buttressed these militaristic impulses and had often been used to justify increasing military expenditures. Furthermore, the experience of imperial service, whether in India or Africa, often shaped military leaders' approach to the problem of a future war, possibly giving too much credence to the offensive, given the often easy victories over native forces.

Yet the military trends of the last half-century had never—before the summer of 1914—converged to confront the decision makers with their full impact. The British had fought a slow war against the Dutch Boers in South Africa and the Russians an inept war against the Japanese. But the carefully refined mobilization plans of the great powers had never been fully tested simultaneously, despite two Moroccan crises and repeated Balkan tensions. The statesmen appreciated some of the risks, but they did not comprehend the sheer force of time, the uncertainty of information, and the compelling arguments that their military staffs would make for the dangers of inaction.

Unlike nineteenth-century crises, the mobilization plans put into effect by Germany and France after 1905 ensured that there would be immediate war. This was not true for the other powers; in Russia and Austria–Hungary, for example, mobilizations were more leisurely affairs. Thus in July 1914, all of the political leaders confronted a series of decisions that were unprecedented, for the most part, in their experience: When did they have to agree to mobilization? Would mobilization mean war? Could diplomacy and mobilization continue in parallel and fighting thus be postponed? And most important, what were the risks of action or inaction?

This study focuses on the novel military and strategic issues that July 1914 posed for military and political leaders. This civil-military perspective leads to a series of interlocking questions: Did military considerations dictate political decisions in July 1914, and were governments forced to war because of military pressures? Second, how did the German military machine differ from its contemporaries? Was excessive militarism unique to Germany? Indeed, what are military values, and were these values shared across governmental boundaries by a group of warriors, or were they distinctly separate in each country? Third, could it be argued that some of the civilian leaders were themselves militarized, possessing values that differed very little from those of the professional soldiers? Finally, did the form of government influence the nature of the decision making?

The interaction of pairs of key decision makers—one political and one military—in each of the major powers and Serbia forms the crux of this study. This focus allows the reader to see how the crucial leaders interacted and how their responses shaped the final outcome. This semibiographical approach also serves as a reminder that individuals, not anonymous forces, make the decisions for war. These men held pivotal positions. Each, had he adopted a different policy, could have stopped the momentum toward war or altered the nature of his government's participation. Only the French leaders lacked options for avoiding war.

THE MAJOR ACTORS

Serbia: Prime Minister Nikola Pašić and Chief of Serbian Military Intelligence Colonel Dragutin Dimitrijević

Austria–Hungary: Foreign Minister Count Leopold Berchtold and Chief of the General Staff General Franz Conrad von Hötzendorf

Germany: Chancellor Theobald von Bethmann Hollweg and Chief of the Prussian General Staff General Helmuth von Moltke

Russia: Foreign Minister Serge Sazonov and War Minister General V. A. Sukhomlinov

Italy: Foreign Minister Antonino di San Giuliano and Chief of the General Staff General Luigi Cadorna

France: President Raymond Poincaré and Chief of the General Staff General Joseph Joffre

Great Britain: Foreign Secretary Sir Edward Grey and Director of Military Operations Major General Henry Wilson

A few generalizations about these leaders will enable the reader to compare them. All were men. All of the civilian leaders were veteran statesmen. Some had been active for more than thirty years, such as British Foreign Secretary Sir Edward Grey and Serbian Prime Minister Nikola Pašić. Of the leaders, Grey had held his position the longest (nearly nine years), and while Raymond Poincaré had served as president of France for less than two years, he had also been premier. Each of them, save Pašić, had surmounted the challenges of possible war during the recent Balkan upheavals; the Serbian leader had, arguably, emerged from the Balkan Wars in a much stronger domestic political position, or so it seemed.

These men represented the spectrum of social classes at a time when social standing still meant much in Europe. Though class played no part in the actual decision making, certainly the preservation of privileged position shaped the conceptual stances taken by many of the participants, especially those in Germany, Austria–Hungary, and Russia. Austrian Foreign Minister Leopold Berchtold stood at the top, an aristocrat with extensive land holdings. He was followed by the nobles, such as Grey and Italian Foreign Minister Antonino di San Giuliano. The group also included successful bureaucrats and lawyers, such as German Chancellor Theobald von Bethmann Hollweg, Russian Foreign Minister Serge Sazonov, and Poincaré. Each man had had ample exposure to issues of grand strategy and to the demands of his military associates. In sum, these civilian leaders represented experience, success, survival, and a determination to maintain their own standing and their country's position in the European arena.

The military leaders discussed here (and others as well) represented the new professionalism then increasingly pervasive throughout Europe. All were highly experienced in their respective governmental and military positions. All except Colonel Dragutin Dimitrijević were generals, and a number had actually been involved in recent wars. Ironically, only the German leadership, the alleged major culprit of 1914, had seen no significant military action after 1870.

These military men were the new professionals. By 1914, the concept of the professional military expert—a person whose expertise was unchallenged and to whom the civilian leadership owed deference—had gained currency in every state. All had actually seen fighting, which gave their advocacy still greater force. Each had faith in the efficacy of the offensive, believed the next war would be short, and regarded the decision to mobilize as the point of no return. Each general had climbed his way to the top of his profession, through his political skill and professional ability. These men, to use political scientist Samuel P. Huntington's expression, had become the professional managers of state violence. Their own and others' confidence in their alleged expertise would deeply influence developments in the July crisis.[1]

Put on a still larger canvas, the military and civilian leaders whom we shall meet as they confront the July crisis shared a number of assumptions about strategy, international politics, and the role of war. To a man, each of the leaders accepted war as a legitimate part of state policy and a necessary evil. Most of the military men believed war was inevitable, and all were influenced to some degree by a social Darwinian view of societies rising and falling, of some prospering and some falling by the wayside. By 1914, both the political and the military leaders had come, moreover, to accept the existence of the Triple Entente and Triple Alliance structures (see chapter 1) as given, without exploring the risks these groupings posed for expanding any local conflict into a European war.

This study introduces the reader to the key decisions that brought war in July–August 1914. The narrative analysis sets the framework for the documents that are incorporated into the text. These documents allow the reader to examine contemporary records and descriptions of and by the decision makers about their decisions. In many instances, we can see the policymaker groping toward a decision or justifying an action or finally making a choice. The documents also illustrate the values that the leaders brought to the crisis, as well as the fears, ambition, vanity, intrigue, and anger that motivated them. Finally, the documents and the questions posed in juxtaposition with them are designed to encourage students to think about how they would have responded to that most momentous of all political decisions: Should we go to war?

We want to add a concluding comment about the relevance of this study. Many who read this have never worn a service uniform, marched in a military parade, or seen a shot fired in anger. For many, the experiences of the army, navy, and air force are as foreign as a distant culture. But in a world altered by the terrorist attacks of September 11, 2001, these experiences now seem more immediate.

Recent military actions in the Balkans and in Afghanistan not only provide reminders of the dangers of war, they also raise anew the fundamental questions of who controls the military and what constitutes national security. Georges Clemenceau, who served as French prime minister during the First World War, once quipped, "War is too important to be left to the generals." Nothing in the intervening decades has changed the force or relevance of this remark. There remains the danger that a citizenry inexperienced with the military and too prone to deference toward all forms of expertise will forget Clemenceau's axiom.

The struggle between liberty and authority, between disciplined military forces responsive to civilian-political considerations and forces acting in their own self-interest, remains an enduring problem for all governments, not least that of the American people and more so after September 11, 2001. If future civilian leaders wish to control their military forces and to use them effectively, then they must understand their nature, their goals, their fears, their inadequacies, and their capabilities. The stories told in these chapters are designed to contribute to that end.

NOTE

[1]Samuel P. Huntington, *The Soldier and the State: The Theory and Practice of Civil-Military Relations* (Cambridge, Mass.: Harvard University Press, 1957). For a more recent discussion, see David Halberstam, *War in a Time of Peace: Bush, Clinton, and the Generals* (New York: Scribner's, 2001). Also see Eliot A. Cohen, *Supreme Command: Soldiers, Statesmen, and Leadership in Wartime* (New York: Free Press, 2002).

1

July 1914: The Crisis

Just after 11 A.M. on June 28, 1914, Gavrilo Princip fired two shots into the open touring car that carried the Archduke Franz Ferdinand and his wife, Sophie, through the streets of the Bosnian capital, Sarajevo. The Bosnian Serb youth was deadly accurate; within minutes, both the heir apparent to the throne of Austria–Hungary and his wife were dead. Exactly one month later, on July 28, the Habsburg monarchy, rulers of Austria–Hungary, declared war on the neighboring kingdom of Serbia; one week later, all of Europe was at war.

The assassinations set in motion a series of diplomatic moves, centering first on Vienna and Berlin, that soon involved all members of the Triple Alliance and of the Triple Entente. In 1879, Austria–Hungary and Germany had allied to meet any possible Russian threat; they were joined in 1882 by Italy, which wanted protection against France. The resulting Triple Alliance had a military component, with detailed arrangements for assistance if war came. But Italy was always a reluctant partner in the alliance, given its strong desire for parts of the existing Habsburg territory.

The Triple Entente of France, Russia, and Britain was more nebulous. At its heart was a Franco-Russian alliance signed in 1894; its military provisions were updated frequently. Only gradually had Britain moved toward the Franco-Russian group, fearful of German naval expansion after 1900 and worried about its own diplomatic isolation. In 1904, London negotiated a colonial settlement with France over Morocco and Egypt, followed in 1907 by a settlement with Russia over imperial issues in Middle Asia. Almost immediately, the Germans challenged this diplomatic alignment, helping to convert the Triple Entente into something resembling an alliance, but with London always asserting that it had no formal obligation to either France or Russia.

Should these alliance/entente groupings become engaged in an international crisis, military mobilization and possible war were not far distant. Yet in the years prior to the murders in Sarajevo, the two groups had survived a series of war scares, including major tensions during the Balkan Wars of 1912–13.

The Balkan events had been traumatic. The Ottoman Empire, which once ruled much of the Middle East, the coast of North Africa, and present-day Turkey, had also controlled the Balkan peninsula until the middle of the nineteenth century. The Ottomans had then been progressively pushed out of the Balkans, first by the Greeks, then by the Serbs, the Rumanians, and the Bulgarians. Still, in 1912, the Ottoman rulers controlled in the Balkans a sizable area known as Macedonia. During the Balkan Wars, the Turks were quickly driven from Macedonia, with its territory divided among the Serbs, the Greeks, the newly created state of Albania, and Bulgaria. Even Rumania got some territorial gains, as did the tiny kingdom of Montenegro.

During the wars, the leaders of the Triple Entente had negotiated with leaders of the Triple Alliance over Balkan matters. Indeed, the powers had forced Serbia to accept the peace arrangements. And while there had been sharp Austro-Serbian tension during this period, as well as Austro-Russian and German-Russian tensions, some observers in the late spring of 1914 believed the international scene to be uncharacteristically pacific. Then came Sarajevo.

The assassinations confirmed all of Vienna's worst fears. Twice during the preceding eighteen months Vienna had considered going to war with Serbia. The Habsburg leadership believed that Belgrade wanted to unite all of the South Slavs living in the Austro-Hungarian monarchy into a Greater Serbia or a "Yugoslav"—meaning "South Slav"—state. Seen from Vienna's perspective, Belgrade, encouraged by Russia, posed as the champion of the 7.3 million South Slavs who lived under Habsburg rule and wanted to expel the venerable monarchy from the Balkans. These Habsburg fears had taken on new urgency during 1913, after Serbia's military successes in the Balkan Wars doubled its territory and population.

Into this explosive atmosphere had come the murders at Sarajevo. From the start, Vienna believed, correctly but without conclusive proof, that the assassinations had been plotted in Belgrade. Tired of repeated taunts from the Serbs, the Vienna leadership now resolved to have a final reckoning with Serbia.

But Vienna could not act unless it had assurances of German help against possible Russian intervention on behalf of Serbia. Vienna could not ignore the much-publicized bonds of Slavdom between Saint Petersburg and Belgrade; indeed, Vienna assumed that an informal alliance existed between Russia and Serbia. In an earlier Balkan crisis, Russia had threatened to intervene on behalf of its fellow Slavs.

Thus on July 4, Count Alexander Hoyos, a senior official of the Habsburg Foreign Ministry, traveled to Berlin to seek German support. On July 5, the Habsburg ambassador to Germany met with Kaiser Wilhelm II at his palace in nearby Potsdam and received unequivocal pledges of help, even if it meant war with Russia. The German leader had been profoundly shaken by the death of Franz Ferdinand, with whom he and his wife had visited just two weeks before. The next day, German Chancellor Theobald von Bethmann Hollweg gave his concurrence to the kaiser's pledges. Germany had thus linked its fate to its Austrian ally.

On July 7, the Common Ministerial Council, the senior group of Habsburg ministers, met to address the Bosnian issue. All but Hungarian Premier István Tisza now supported the idea of a war with Serbia; a diplomatic victory alone would be insufficient. The ministers agreed, with Tisza the exception, to have an ultimatum drafted that could not possibly be accepted, chiefly because it would demand the participation of Habsburg officials on Serbian territory to investigate the assassination conspiracy. Once the Serbian government rejected the ultimatum, then Vienna would have the legal pretext for a war.

By mid-July, Foreign Minister Leopold Berchtold had won Tisza over, and Vienna was firmly headed toward a confrontation. The final details of the confrontation were approved on July 19 in a secret meeting of the council. The forty-eight-hour ultimatum was delivered on Thursday, July 23. It would have been presented earlier, but Berchtold was determined to wait until a French state visit to Russia by President Raymond Poincaré had ended, so that France and Russia could not coordinate their response. When the Serbians answered the ultimatum at 6 P.M. on July 25, the Austrian envoy judged their reply inadequate and broke diplomatic relations. Mobilizations started in both countries.

The presentation of the ultimatum in Belgrade prompted the Russians to take a series of preliminary military measures that constituted virtual mobilization in some areas. These steps accelerated the crisis. At the same time, British Foreign Secretary Sir Edward Grey sought to stop the momentum for war, trying to initiate further negotiations among the relevant powers. The Berlin government played a thoroughly unhelpful role, alternately supporting and thwarting attempts to find a diplomatic solution. But the real stumbling block was Berchtold, who, like his military colleague Franz Conrad von Hötzendorf, welcomed a military confrontation with Serbia and thus would not agree to negotiations. On July 28, Austria declared war on Serbia.

The escalation to general war came rapidly, as further attempts at negotiations came to nothing. Each hour saw the chances for a European war increase substantially; then events on July 30 guaranteed that outcome. First, the Russians moved to general mobilization, a step the German government considered tantamount to war and which they believed necessitated German mobilization. While Russia's slow-moving mobilization did not translate immediately into military action, the German mobilization did. Britain, France, and Belgium appreciated that German mobilization meant war—and quickly.

Still, there were more diplomatic exchanges, and the question of Belgium's neutral status emerged. With a guarantee of neutrality dating from 1839, Belgium lay in the path of the expected German invasion in the west. On July 30, Berlin tried to get Britain to remain neutral if Belgian neutrality was violated, promising to restore Belgium to its former sovereignty once the war had ended. Grey rebuffed this maladroit request and countered, asking Paris and Berlin to pledge respect for Belgian neutrality. Only Paris made the commitment. Germany's failure gave Grey a potent weapon in his efforts to convince a reluctant British cabinet to intervene in a continental war. For its part, the British navy was already mobilized and had moved to its battle stations.

On Friday and Saturday, July 31 and August 1, the Germans and the Russians took further steps toward war. The French too moved to mobilization status, reacting to various reports of German military activity along their common border. Amid this increasing tension, the chances to avert war had virtually vanished. Now each power sought to position itself for the clash. France stood by Russia, Russia stood by Serbia, Germany stood by Austria–Hungary, and Italy moved to declare neutrality.

London, however, had still not committed itself. Despite a decade of entente relations with Paris and detailed plans for military cooperation between the army and naval staffs, the British cabinet refused to pledge to assist the French. Throughout most of July, the British cabinet had confronted rising political tensions over the issue of Irish home rule; indeed, talk of possible civil war in Ireland was rampant. Furthermore, the more radical members of the cabinet had long been suspicious of the French because of their ties with tsarist, illiberal Russia. These sharp differences in the cabinet handicapped Grey's efforts to threaten the Germans.

Germany, however, soon took actions that ensured British participation, occupying Luxembourg on August 2 and demanding that German troops be allowed to move through Belgium. Ignoring Belgium's refusal, German troops moved into the neutral state on Monday, August 3.

On that same Monday, Grey told a cheering British parliament of the government's intention to demand that Germany respect Belgian neutrality. No one doubted that the two great naval antagonists were headed for war. The next day, Grey demanded that Berlin cease the attack on Belgium; Berlin did not respond. At 11 P.M. Greenwich mean time, the two countries were at war (Map 1).

During the next two days, the British government decided to send military forces to the Continent to help France. Meanwhile, Austrian forces, having gone south to fight Serbia, were retrained and headed back to the northeastern front to fight the Russians. By August 6, all of the allies and entente partners and Serbia, save Italy, were at war. Italy would later join with the entente. Peace would not come for more than four years.

In this slide to war, the statesmen made hard decisions, often based on fragmentary information and under intense pressure from their advisers and the military. Did the military force the political leaders to war, or did the pairs of individuals in each of the countries face these issues jointly, finding themselves confronted with few apparent options? And how had the pre–June 1914 relationships between the two actors—political and military—in each country defined their reaction to the crisis or, in the case of Serbia, helped to create the crisis in the first place?[1]

NOTE

[1]For more details, see Hew Strachan, *The First World War*, vol. 1, *To Arms* (Oxford: Oxford University Press, 2001), chap. 1; and Samuel R. Williamson Jr., "The Origins of the War," in *World War I: A History*, ed. Hew Strachan (New York: Oxford University Press, 1998).

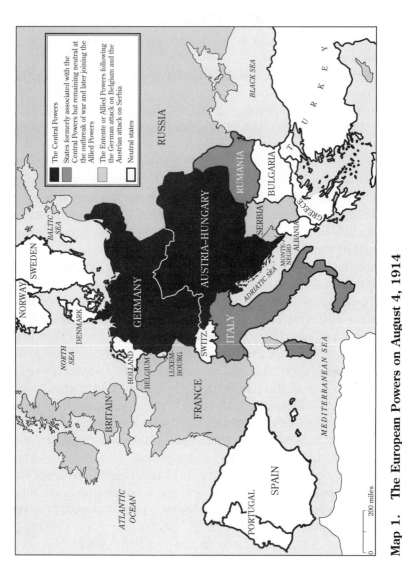

Map 1. The European Powers on August 4, 1914

From *Atlas of World War I*, 2/e, by Martin Gilbert, p. 12 (Oxford University Press, 1994).

2

Pašić, Apis, and the Battle for Serbia

The Kingdom of Serbia fell under Ottoman Turkish rule after its defeat in Kosovo on June 28, 1389. For more than four hundred years, the Serbs were ruled by the Ottoman Empire from Constantinople. But after the Napoleonic Wars, Serbia began to emerge as an autonomous state, and in 1878, the Congress of Berlin recognized Serbian independence. In the ensuing years, efforts to establish an effective parliamentary monarchy met with only modest success.

The first years of the twentieth century brought dramatic changes—changes that reflected growing Serbian nationalism, the treacherous nature of Balkan politics, and the further erosion of Ottoman power. First, there was the murder and ouster of the hated King Alexander Obrenović and his mistress turned wife and queen, Draga Mašin, by a group of young army officers in 1903. The Karadjordević dynasty, headed by the venerable Peter, became the ruling family and gradually shifted Serbia away from a pro-Habsburg foreign policy. Second, in 1908, Austria–Hungary formally annexed the provinces of Bosnia-Herzegovina, which it had administered since the Congress of Berlin, thwarting Serbian hopes to control these two provinces. The subsequent international crisis nearly resulted in Serbia at war with Vienna.

Finally, the third major event was Serbia's stunning military successes in the Balkan Wars of 1912–13, which elevated the prestige of Serbian military leadership and saw Serbia's population and territory almost double to 4.4 million people and 34,000 square miles (Map 2). But a major goal remained for Serbian nationalism: the unification of the 7.3 million diverse South Slavs of varying religions who still lived in the neighboring Habsburg monarchy—whether Slovenian, Serb, or Croat, Muslim, Catholic, or Orthodox Christian—into a greater Serbia. It was within this framework of recent events—the military coup of

15

Map 2. The Balkans, 1912–1913

From *Europe's Crucial Years: The Diplomatic Background of WWI, 1902–1914* by Dwight E. Lee (University Press of New England, pp. 314–15).

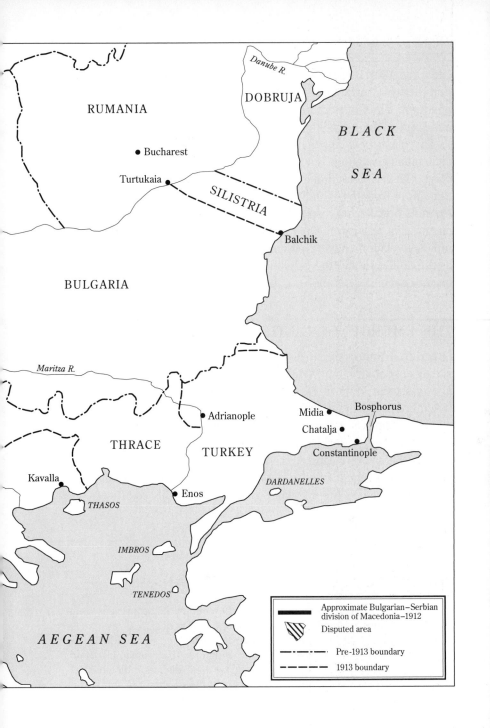

1903, the 1908 Bosnian crisis, and the victories of the Balkan Wars—that the two central figures of the Serbian drama of June and July 1914 operated: Chief of Serbian Military Intelligence Dragutin Dimitrijević and Prime Minister Nikola Pašić.

The clash between these two men defined the nature of Serbian civil-military relations, not just in 1914, but from 1903 through the July crisis. Their interaction provides the background to the conspiracy that murdered the Archduke Franz Ferdinand and his wife. It also explains how Serbia responded to Habsburg demands, thus helping to ensure that war came. Only in Serbia in the summer of 1914 did civil-military relations have a potentially lethal quality for the participants as the politician and the colonel struggled to control the direction and pace of Serbian aspirations.

THE EMERGENCE OF THE CONSPIRATOR

Dragutin Dimitrijević, nicknamed "Apis" (the bull) because of his sturdy appearance, entered the Serbian military academy in 1892 at the age of sixteen (Figure 1). After brief regimental service in Belgrade, he completed general staff training and soon began his conspiratorial career. A lifelong bachelor, he devoted his entire energies to the Serbian army and to Serbian nationalism. Apis was appalled by the subservient behavior of King Alexander toward Austria–Hungary. He soon became one of the leading conspirators in the 1903 plot to murder the king. He fashioned the following oath in 1902 for his co-officers.

The Conspirators' Oath

1902

Foreseeing the certain destruction of the country if the present situation continues even for the shortest time and proclaiming as chiefly responsible for all this King Alexander and his lover, Draga Mašin, we swear and obligate ourselves with our signatures that we will kill them. To the throne of Serbia, bathed in blood by these dishonorable ones, we shall bring Peter Karadjordević, grandson of the Chieftain [Karadjordje] and son of the legitimate prince, the late Alexander Karadjordević.[1]

Figure 1.   Dragutin Dimitrijević

Nicknamed "Apis" for his bull-like appearance, the head of Serbian military intelligence organized the 1914 assassination plot and evaded Pašić's efforts to stop it.

Friedrich Würthle, *Die Spur führt nach Belgrad* (Vienna: Molden Verlag, 1975).

Apis would be as good as his oath. Wounded three different times at the royal palace during the assassinations of the king and queen on the night of June 10–11, 1903, he survived to become both a feared and respected figure.

Over the next seven years, Apis advanced steadily in the Serbian army, forging links with senior military officers, keeping close ties with his fellow conspirators, and ingratiating himself further with the new Karadjordević dynasty. Two assessments of Apis—one by a professor friend of Pašić, the other by Apis's nephew—provide interesting insights into the Serbian leader's character.

STANOJE STANOJEVIĆ

Description of Apis

1923

Gifted and cultured, honourable, a convincing speaker, a sincere patriot, personally courageous, filled with ambition, energy, and the capacity for work, Dragutin Dimitrević exercised exceptional influence on those around him, in particular on his associates and junior officers who were all his inferiors in qualities of mind and character. He had the characteristics which cast a spell on men. His arguments were always striking and convincing. . . . Withal he was in every respect a remarkable organizer. He kept all the threads in his own hand, and even his most intimate friends only knew what was their own immediate concern. But at the same time he was extraordinarily conceited and thoroughly affected. Ambitious as he was, he had a taste for working in secret, but he liked it to be known that he was doing secret work and that he kept all the threads in his own hand. He was incapable of distinguishing what was possible from what was not and perceiving the limits of responsibility and power. He had no clear concept of civil and political *(staatlichen)* life and its requirements. He saw only his own aims and pursued them ruthlessly and without scruple. . . . He believed that his opinions and activities enjoyed the monopoly of patriotism. Hence anyone who did not agree with him could not in his eyes be either honourable or wise or a patriot.[2]

MILAN ZIVANOVIĆ

Assessment of Apis

1937

He was resolute and wise and had a shrewd political mind. He thought and acted by himself without seeking the advice of others, and once a decision was made, he went straight ahead with an iron will, without hesitation, without change of mind. He was a man of the utmost secrecy. He never spoke of his intentions nor of his share in events, even if these were long past. Many times my father said to him that he had the temperament and the ability of a politician rather than of a soldier and pressed him to write his memoirs or describe the part he played in the history of Serbia, my father being deeply interested in history. He always answered that he had no time. In reality he did not want to break silence. He was devoid of personal vanity.[3]

During the 1908 Bosnian crisis, the Serbian government had encouraged the creation of a Serbian patriotic society, the Narodna Odbrana (National Defense). It soon had 220 committees across Serbia and 5,000 volunteers ready for guerrilla war against Austria–Hungary. When the Belgrade government accepted diplomatic defeat in March 1909, it agreed to Vienna's demands that the Narodna Odbrana be curbed. Nevertheless, the organization continued to exist and provided inspiration for a more sinister undertaking.

Many of the same Serbian army officers who had participated in the 1903 murders of the royal couple were soon involved in the creation of a wholly new society: the Black Hand (Crna Ruka). Apis, a major force in the new group from the start, developed its structure and began its infiltration of Narodna Odbrana units, both in Serbia and in the neighboring Habsburg monarchy. By late 1911, the Black Hand had secret oaths and elaborate rituals, and its members pledged to use any means to advance Serbian dominance in the Balkans. No one— military or civilian—could afford to ignore the young officer or the new organization. Organized into cells, the Black Hand represented a protofascist approach to political life. The end justified all means, and the oath of the Black Hand graphically reflected this fact.

The Oath of the Black Hand
1911

Article 1: This organization is formed in order to achieve the ideal of unification of Serbdom; all Serbs, regardless of sex, religion, or place of birth, can become members, and anyone else who is prepared to serve this ideal faithfully.

Article 2: This organization chooses revolutionary action rather than cultural, and is, therefore, kept secret from the general public. . . .

[Article 4: This organization]:

1. In accordance with its essential nature, will influence Serbia, at official levels and throughout all classes of society, to become a Piedmont;*
2. undertakes the organization of revolutionary activities in all territories inhabited by Serbs;
3. will fight with all means available to it those outside the frontiers who are enemies of the ideal;
4. will maintain friendly contact with all states, organizations, and individuals who are friendly toward Serbia and the Serbs;
5. offers help to all peoples and organizations who are likewise struggling for liberation and ambition.[4]

By 1912, Apis had achieved a prominence enjoyed by no other young officer in prewar Europe. His energy, carefully cultivated network of conspirators, and his ambitious vision for Serbia all worked to his advantage. Already the Black Hand's newspaper, *Pijémont,* posed as the new voice of a group that would unite all Serbs. Apis had created a virtual web of power, with himself at the center, with contacts in the Black Hand, the foreign ministry, the Narodna Odbrana, and the army. He had, moreover, inserted the Black Hand into the guerrilla movements operating in Macedonia that were attacking Ottoman rule, helping to accelerate Serbia's role in the Balkan Wars.

Apis gained considerable recognition for his early efforts to prepare Serbia for the victorious conflict and in August 1913 was made chief of Serbian military intelligence with the rank of colonel. Thus, less than a year before the momentous events in Sarajevo, the dangerous Apis, whose intrigue and manipulation had already gained him legendary status, became the head of Serbian military intelligence. This position conferred a still broader mandate for conspiratorial activities against Austria–Hungary. The new director wasted no time.

At the center of Apis's intelligence network stood Rade Malobabić, an idealistic and zealous agent. He established procedures to move students and agents into and out of Bosnia while he visited Habsburg military installations for additional information. Like Apis, Malobabić

---

* The Italian kingdom that had united all of Italy and defeated the Habsburgs in the process.

would utilize members of both the Narodna Odbrana and the Black Hand for these intelligence and subversive activities.

By April 1914, Apis had established an apparatus for intelligence gathering and covert activity against Austria–Hungary. His status in the Serbian army had become even greater. Yet this success also made him more conspicuous when the so-called Priority Question erupted over who had priority at official receptions—soldiers or the civilians—in the newly occupied Turkish lands. This apparently trivial issue would bring Apis and Nikola Pašić into conflict in May 1914.

APIS'S IMPLACABLE ENEMY: NIKOLA PAŠIĆ

At age sixty-nine, Prime Minister Nikola Pašić was the second oldest of the key decision makers in the summer of 1914; only Habsburg emperor Franz Joseph, at eighty-four, was older. Pašić was initially trained as an engineer, but he entered parliament as a deputy in 1878, the year that Austria–Hungary gained administrative control of Bosnia-Herzegovina. He quickly became a central figure in the emerging Radical Party, promoting the national welfare and unification of all Serbs. A clever, wily tactician and a political survivor, Pašić brought uncommon zeal to his efforts to transform Serbia into a democratic, constitutional system (Figure 2).[5]

Pašić welcomed Serbia's victories in the Balkan Wars. He and his colleagues applauded the support given by the Russian government throughout the turmoil. Thanks to the additional population and territorial expansion, Serbia had become the major state in the Balkans. At the same time Pašić, now serving as prime minister, realized that Serbia had depleted its finances and military equipment and desperately needed time to incorporate its new gains. He also was keenly aware of the threat posed by Austria–Hungary.

Nor did Pašić ignore the political gains made by the Serbian military during the fighting. Always distrustful of the Serbian officers, and especially Apis, the minister kept a careful eye on the officers. Certainly, he worried about the pervasive presence of the Black Hand and was alert to the dangers posed by the new secret society.

The wary relations between the two men continued until 1914 and the political upheaval prompted by the Priority Question in New Serbia, as the recently acquired territories were called. Pašić had not

Figure 2. Nikola Pašić

A wily survivor of lethal Serbian politics, the Serbian prime minister knew of the assassination plot but failed to stop it. Hulton/Archive by Getty Images.

expected administering New Serbia to be easy, but he was astonished by the hostility of the Serbian military to civilian administrators in the newly conquered lands.

Pašić found himself drawn into this issue as he backed Interior Minister Stojan Protić, who in April 1914 proclaimed the priority of civilian officials over the military. The local army commander in New Serbia then refused to obey this order, only to be summarily retired by the Pašić government. Pašić's political opponents immediately sided with the army officers, throwing Serbian domestic politics into total upheaval.

No one watched these events more closely than Apis. Convinced that Pašić had to go, he sought army support as a way to pressure King Peter to call for Pašić's ouster. At this point, however, Pašić made a tactical decision to resign and thus forced a new election to which the king consented. Under pressure from the Russian minister in Belgrade, Nikola Hartwig, Peter reappointed Pašić to head the caretaker government. To everyone's surprise, the king also virtually turned the throne over to his son, Prince Alexander, who disliked Apis but worked well with Pašić. To ease the tension, the prime minister significantly modified the Priority order and thus mollified many of the army officers. On the other hand, he kept Protić as Minister of the Interior. Apis and his clique of officers had little reason for joy in mid-June 1914; Pašić had outflanked them.

THE PLOT TO ASSASSINATE
ARCHDUKE FRANZ FERDINAND

While Apis and his military colleagues struggled for power in Serbia, an unforeseen opportunity presented itself to the Serbian military intelligence chief. Some Bosnian Serb students told a Black Hand informant that they wished to assassinate the Archduke Franz Ferdinand when he visited Bosnia's capital, Sarajevo, in late June. These Serbs, like many others, regarded the Habsburgs as the hated oppressor of all South Slavs. Any blow against the Habsburgs was a blow for liberation, or so many South Slavs believed. When Apis learned of the students' desire for revenge, he arranged for weapons, funds, and the use of the Black Hand network to smuggle the conspirators—Gavrilo Princip, Trifko Grabez, and Nedeljko Cabrinović—into Bosnia in late May 1914.

Apis's support for the assassination effort is understandable. At the very least, it provided him with a chance to achieve a clear victory against the Habsburgs. If the murder succeeded, he would be a hero in Serbia; if it failed, he could disavow it. Either way, his political position would be strengthened, and Pašić and his civilian colleagues would be put on notice.

The conspiracy did not long go undetected. By early June, the authorities in Belgrade had their first intelligence that some plot was under way. On June 4, 1914, a border official near Šabac wrote the Ministry of the Interior: "I have information that the officers who are on duty on the border of this area have recently sought to get our people to transport a certain quantity of arms and bombs into Bosnia. I do not know if this is permitted, so I will stop it unless you tell me otherwise."

This information reached Belgrade on June 6, prompting the following reply on June 10: "In response to your letter of June 4 of this month, confidentially referred to the Royal Minister of the Interior, about the bombs and arms that were transferred to Bosnia, I wish to inform you that the Minister President [Pašić] commands that all similar cases should be stopped."[6]

At this point, Pašić may have informed one or more of his cabinet colleagues about this intelligence. After the Great War in 1924, when controversy about Serbia's role in the assassination flared anew, a former cabinet colleague of Pašić offered incriminating evidence about official Serbian knowledge of the plot.

LJUBA JOVANOVIĆ

On Belgrade's Knowledge of the Conspiracy

1924

I do not remember whether it was at the end of May or the beginning of June, when one day M. Pašić said to us . . . that there were people who were preparing to go to Sarajevo to kill Francis Ferdinand, who was to go there to be solemnly received on the Vidov Dan.* As they afterwards told me, the plot was hatched by a group of secretly organized persons and in patriotic Bosnia-Herzegovinian student circles in Belgrade. M. Pašić and the rest of us said . . . that [Stojan Protić, Minister of the Interior] should issue instructions to the frontier authorities on the Drina to deny a crossing to the youths who had already set out from Belgrade for that purpose. But the frontier "authorities" themselves belonged to the organization, and did not carry out Stojan's instructions, but reported to him (and afterwards he reported to us) that the order had reached them too late, for the young men had already got across.[7]

Jovanović also claimed that Pašić had attempted to warn Vienna of a possible attack. These revelations in the 1920s caused consternation in Belgrade. Pašić never effectively refuted them. Recently published

---

Vidov Dan: St. Vitus Day, marking the day in 1389 when the Turks had beaten the Serbs in Kosovo.

Serbian documents basically support Jovanović's statements about the efforts to thwart the plot. Moreover, there does appear to have been a vague attempt to alert Vienna to the dangers of an archducal visit.

During mid–June 1914, Protić became even more alarmed about the conspiracy, reporting to Pašić about the transportation of arms across the border from Serbia to Bosnia.

STOJAN PROTIĆ

Letter to Nikola Pašić

June 15, 1914

The head of the Podrinje District has informed me [Protić] about events mentioned earlier.

"I [the District Head: Tucaković] had informed you in my confidential letter on 22 May [4 June] 1914 that frontier officers in this area were trying through confidants to transfer a certain quantity of guns and bombs to Bosnia. In response to my report, I received coded commands from you and the head of the consular department of the Ministry of Foreign Affairs to prevent this.

"I took preventive measures but I failed eight days ago when . . . 4 revolvers and 400 bullets were transported into Bosnia.

"Yesterday I learned that one very heavy suitcase . . . probably had arms and bombs. Moreover, the section head . . . showed a written order which directed that this suitcase should be brought into Bosnia . . . and afterwards to Bjeljina to Rade Malobabić.

"I will explain about Rade Malobabić. When I was a secretary in the minister's office during the war and the chief of the intelligence department in the War Ministry was collecting reports, I learned that Rade was an agent for Austria–Hungary. Also I have found out that this same person was a Serbian agent in Austria. He said he had accepted this work [with Austria] because he wanted to get more confidential information and facts that we needed.

"So, as the above report indicates, it is obvious that Rade is working to transfer the arms to Bosnia. . . .

"As the above makes clear, arms have been transported into Bosnia by our border troops. Since neither you nor I was informed of this in advance, I conclude that somebody else has done this on his own without informing the royal government which is ultimately responsible if this is discovered or the persons caught. I am afraid that this will be

discovered because it has been done so openly. Unless this can be prevented privately, it could bring us to a conflict with Austria. This is a
problem that we really do not need."

Please, Minister, either stop the practice, or if it is continued, let it be
done with the government's consent and with knowledge of the Minister of the Interior since I already have your confidence. If you are
against this, please let me know so I can frame my orders.[8]

Pašić agreed entirely with Protić's alarmist reaction. He directed
immediately that the "War Minister should be asked to order that
such acts be stopped because they are very dangerous for us."[9]

Pašić now faced a difficult but common problem for civilian heads
of government: how to get accurate and reliable reports from their
intelligence services, and especially their military intelligence services. Fully aware of Apis's conspiratorial tactics and willingness to
use violence, the Serbian politician faced real personal danger if Apis
decided to move against him. Pašić believed that political leaders
should control the military and make the final policy decisions. But in
Serbia, the boundaries between domestic politics and the military
were virtually nonexistent; there was almost no constitutional tradition
that the minister could use.

Nonetheless, Pašić demanded an explanation from Apis, who—not
surprisingly—took his time to reply to the army commander.

APIS

Reply to the Army Commander
June 21, 1914

In response to a previous order, it is my pleasure to give you a report:

It is about the transportation of arms, bombs, and ammunition into
Bosnia for Rade Malobabić in order to arm our people in Bosnia. . . .
This is the information known to me:

Malobabić has been our agent for several years. . . . Since September
1913 Mr. Malobabić has worked with success as an agent of the General
Staff Office. His reports deserve praise. . . . Our people in Zagreb consider Malobabić a good and correct Serb and they trust him. Moreover,

it is known that Malobabić was one of those alleged Serbian traitors accused by the Agram process.*

By the way, the last time he was in Belgrade, he worked at the Narodna Odbrana office. . . . He handles his reports very carefully and reveals that he is a good Serb and patriotic, ready for any sacrifice for Serbia. I believe this information is necessary for you to understand this person and why he is so important.

*A 1909 trial of Serbs accused of plotting against the Habsburg monarchy.

With this explanation, Apis had neatly shifted the burden to Pašić and Protić: How could they challenge the qualities of one of the army's most patriotic intelligence agents? Nor did Apis stop there in his attempt to mislead the civilian leadership.

For on the question of the transportation of arms and bombs, I report:

Several days ago I invited Malobabić to Belgrade for introductions and reports. We discussed ways to get information from our agents, especially during a crisis. At that time Malobabić told me that the couriers should have guns for self-defense. He suggested that we arm them with revolvers. I agreed and allowed him to take four revolvers and a certain number of bullets.

We tried to keep his visit in Belgrade secret, and he decided to go back over the River Drina on a route which is known to him, and he hopes to organize a faster transfer of reports this way. At the time Commander Vulović [of the Black Hand] was also traveling in the same direction. I thus introduced them to each other so they could travel and work together. Also, I told both of them (Vulović and Malobabić) to keep their actions secret and only to inform the persons actually involved in the undertaking. . . .

As you can see, Malobabić's confidential trip to Bosnia was officially authorized. The transport of the four revolvers and bullets was allowed to help our agents in Bosnia, not to arm the Bosnian population. I only wanted the necessary people to be informed. I have no information about bombs, though it is possible that Malobabić wanted to take his own suitcase and the District officer thought bombs were in it.[10]

Neither Protić nor Pašić was misled by Apis's report. And on June 24, Protić wrote the war minister and urged him to control the army officers, warning that attacks on Austria–Hungary could bring war to Serbia: "All our allies would desert us if they learned what our officers and non-commissioned officers do, and besides that, the allies would agree with Austria–Hungary and let it punish its neighbor." The war minister did issue such orders, which of course came far too late to stop the Sarajevo conspiracy and attack.[11]

With the stakes very high, Apis may have chosen a foreign move to bolster his domestic political position, put Pašić on the defensive, and offer a potent reminder to the civilian leadership of the dangers posed by the powerful Black Hand. As for Pašić, his knowledge of the conspiracy left him completely trapped after the murders in Sarajevo on June 28. He could not be more flexible toward Vienna for fear of revealing his prior knowledge, nor could he move to punish Apis without compromising both Serbian security and possibly his own safety. In a Balkan state with only a modest history of parliamentary rule, with the 1903 regicides not forgotten, and with Serbian nationalists gleeful after the recent military successes, Pašić faced the most dangerous situation of all of the decision makers in 1914.

In Serbia, no history of constitutional practice enshrined the principle of civilian control of the military. The Serbian situation prompts three questions: Do governments of emerging states face special problems in controlling their military? Does the heroism of some military leaders make them less easy to control? And how does one block a terrorist attack when the secret intelligence service itself is the culprit?

One final comment about the terrorist plot is necessary. During April–June, the Austrian military attaché in Belgrade, Otto Gellinek, provided Vienna with a very accurate assessment of the civil-military struggle. He categorized the key issues, identified the key players, and noted the part played by Apis and the Black Hand in all the machinations.

OTTO GELLINEK

Report to Franz Conrad von Hötzendorf

June 21, 1914

The current crisis gives no occasion for any new conclusions; it can only confirm previous views about the internal political situation in Serbia.

1. The powerlessness of the Throne and the ever growing influence on one side of a group of conspiratorial officers *(Geheimbund der crna ruka)*.

2. The willingness of the officer corps in general to influence all internal and external political decisions; the lack of discipline which has been seen in the entirely unqualified attacks on the War Minister in the press organs of the officer party.

3. The all powerful current position of the extreme Russophile, old Radical party and its founder and thirty year leader, Nikola Pašić.

4. The influence of the Russian ministry on the Crown in all internal questions.

For the relations with the [Habsburg] monarchy, the recent events have little significance; in their Austro-phobia all of the parties of the country are united! (The so-called Austrophile, conservative party still possesses no mandate.)[12]

In short, Vienna had significant background intelligence about a serious power struggle under way in Belgrade. Yet after the Sarajevo assassinations, the Habsburg policy apparatus never used this information. The subsequent ultimatum never mentioned the Black Hand and failed entirely to blame Apis. Whether a Habsburg denunciation of Apis might have given Pašić more freedom to maneuver is an interesting question.

PAŠIĆ AFTER THE ASSASSINATION: THE CONFRONTATION WITH VIENNA

In July 1914, Pašić faced four interlocking policy issues: (1) how to soften Austria–Hungary's anger over the Serbian public's reaction to the murders; (2) how to conceal his knowledge of Apis's involvement in the plot; (3) how to secure foreign assistance if a denouement came; and (4) how to defend Serbian sovereignty and prevent Apis and others from retaliation against the civilian government. The minister succeeded on nearly every issue, though not without fateful consequences for peace and for the future of the Balkans.

In only one arena did Pašić fail: quelling Serbian press excesses over the deaths of the royal couple. From the moment that news of their assassinations reached Belgrade, the Serbian press trumpeted its delight. The *Pijémont,* closely aligned with the Black Hand, represented the tone of most of the Belgrade press.

The Pijémont

July 1, 1914

And Gavrilo Princip, born at Grahovo, district of Livno, in a small place which has kept the love of liberty and the memory that revolt always terminates in blood, which was a foyer of great national agitation in the second half of the nineteenth century, Gavrilo Princip became, according to all laws of probability, a terrorist and attacker, which would come from the pages of an anarchist brochure and his first encounter with young revolution. Although he is only nineteen years old, he had openly told the Sarajevo police that he had had for a long time the intention to kill some great person for national reasons. It is thus that he wanted to kill the Archduke Franz Ferdinand or some other personality who imposes his will upon the milieu of his brothers.

Consider that the act of Gavrilo Princip finds its explanation in the system which actually dominates Bosnia and Herzegovina and the moment in which it occurred.

The regime of Bosnia-Herzegovina is far from acceptable. The economic deprivation and the absence of national rights for our co-nationals must profoundly affect the heart of a young revolutionary. . . .

The death of Franz Ferdinand and his wife is deplored in all civilized countries. Even in our aggrieved country, no one wants to glorify the act of Princip. . . .

And while Gavrilo Princip, martyred according to the rules of the inquisition in his jail, before being taken to the gibbet, and while all the Courts and all of the diplomatic chancelleries manifest profound and sincere condolences at the tragic death of the heir to the Double Monarchy, there leaves from the world an infant of 19 years, loving to the fullest the earth where he had seen, for the first time, the light of day.[13]

The French minister in Belgrade, Léon Descos, reported to Paris on July 1 that "the press displays no regret at the surprising incident; only the *SamoOuprava* indicates slightly a sense of humiliation. . . . The other journals project any responsibility for what has happened on the Austrian regime of national repression. . . . [One paper] could not resist the exaltation of the young 'martyr' Gavrilo Princip."[14]

These enthusiasms continued despite Pašić's attempts to curb the worst offenses. Austro-German anger at the Serbian press mounted, and Austrian press accusations that the murders had been planned in Belgrade began to appear, further embittering relations with Vienna. This failure to temper the hostility of the Serbian press, which in turn fed that of Austria–Hungary and Germany, sharply limited Pašić's ability to maneuver diplomatically vis-à-vis Vienna.

Nor was Pašić helped by a June 30 press report alleging that Belgrade had in fact warned Vienna of a possible plot. Did Pašić, in fact, try to warn Vienna? The truth of this has never been discovered, but in 1914 he could not admit to such a step and did not; nor did he later in the 1920s when the matter was disputed.

In any event, in July 1914, Pašić could not afford for this assertion to remain current; he thus moved quickly to deny all prior knowledge of the plot. His rebuttal remained the government line for obvious reasons; any hint, as one historian writes, of "official Serbia's" involvement in the plot would have thoroughly compromised Serbia's international position. Any such admission might also have brought Apis and his military colleagues aggressively back into Serbian politics.[15]

The Serbian prime minister, meanwhile, had to gauge what Austria–Hungary might demand from Serbia. Pašić made no move to investigate any Belgrade connection with the plot, since he wanted no trouble from Apis. Nor, of course, did Pašić want to do anything to give Vienna's accusations any currency, though he also left no doubt that Serbia would defend its sovereignty against any unacceptable Habsburg demands.

As July progressed, the information Pašić received from Vienna was not reassuring. The Serbian minister in Vienna, Jovan Jovanović, reported that the political and military circles in Vienna were very excited. Still, as late as July 15, the Serbian envoy said that he did not anticipate Austria–Hungary taking decisive action against Serbia. In retrospect, it would appear that Jovanović may have been victimized by Foreign Minister Leopold Berchtold's careful efforts to conceal Austria's intentions, including manipulation of the monarchy's press.

Then suddenly, the situation changed dramatically. By July 17, Pašić was no longer confident. Reports from Budapest indicated a fiery speech by Minister President István Tisza to the Hungarian parliament, inferring that war might be unavoidable. A day later, the Serb minister received reports from Berlin of stock market panic and rumors of Habsburg troop activity. (There was none.)

This threatening information galvanized Pašić, who on July 18–19 sent a telegraphic dispatch to all missions except Vienna.

NIKOLA PAŠIĆ

Telegram to All Serbian Missions Abroad Except Vienna

July 18–19, 1914

Immediately after the Sarajevo assassination the Austro-Hungarian press began to attack Serbia and views of Serbian nationalism which are supported by different groups and associations such as the Narodna Odbrana and others. The press accused the Serbian government of tolerating these activities. The Serbian Government regrets the events in Sarajevo. It has asked for the punishment of the assassins. It also canceled all celebrations on the day of the deaths. But the Austro-Hungarian press has continued to charge Serbia with guilt and to give false reports which have prompted the Belgrade press to respond and defend Serbia.

The Serbian Government has asked the Belgrade press to remain calm, but daily news reports from Austria–Hungary revealed that the assassination would be used against Serbia, as well as against Serbians in the Austro-Hungarian monarchy.

The polemic between Austria–Hungary and the free Belgrade press has been aggravated by certain stories from the papers. They have spread the reports with only one goal—to make Serbia appear in European eyes as an unstable and arrogant country. Everyone who has followed this polemic knows that the Belgrade papers were simply defending against these attacks and lies. But foreign governments have not had time to note the tendency of the Austro–Hungarian press to spread alarms, not only in that country, but outside of it as well.

The Serbian government has been ready to turn over to the courts anyone connected with Sarajevo if there was evidence. The Serbian government has also been willing to change its law about explosives and has given this project to the Privy Council. The project has not been completed because the Parliament is dissolved. Serbia has shown that it is ready—like all European countries—to perform its neighborly duties. . . .

But Austria–Hungary constantly continues the press campaign against Serbia. The Austro-Hungarian government as well as the rest of Europe has become irritated with Serbia—an irritation seen by the actions of the political leaders who respond to questions in the Hungarian Parliament. This has prompted different discussions and demands for some answers from the President [István Tisza].

From all of these discussions we can see that the Habsburg government will act against Serbia; it is not possible to see in which direction. All measures, especially military ones, will depend upon the answers and cooperation of the Serbian Government. There has indeed been muted talk of armed conflict if the Serbian government does not give satisfactory answers.

The sudden death of [Russian Minister] Hartwig prompted another journalistic quarrel. . . .

Everything that has happened has been used against Serbia. In the Hungarian Parliament it has been asserted that conflict could have very bad consequences. Nor do they limit the attacks to the investigation of the assassins, but also Serbia and greater Serbian ideals.

The Serbian government has worked to keep peace and good relations with all of its neighbors. It has worked especially to improve relations with Austria–Hungary, which were not really good during the [Balkan] war. We have sought to settle all of the railroad issues, including security for the transportation of Austro-Hungarian products to Constantinople, Sofia, Salonika, and Athens.

The Serbian Government asserts that peace and calmness are vital interests. But Serbia is afraid that the angry people in the Austro-Hungarian government will take a step that could humiliate Serbia and that Serbia will not accept.

Serbia wants friendly governments to know that Serbia desires "friendly" relations with Austria–Hungary and has prevented attempts from our territory that would disturb the peace and security of the neighboring empire. The Serbian government would also accept any Austro-Hungarian request that demanded that the participants of the crime, if they could be found, be brought before an "independent court."

But Serbia cannot accept demands which would not be acceptable to any government that presumes its own independence and dignity.

We hope that the present situation will calm down. I ask that friendly governments take these reports seriously and help and work if there is need for it.[16]

With this set of dispatches, Pašić had defined his policy: He would appear flexible, concede nothing, and hope the great powers might deter the crisis.

This expectation was dashed at 6:00 P.M. on July 23, when Austrian minister Wladimir Giesl delivered a forty-eight-hour ultimatum to the Serbian Foreign Ministry.

The Habsburg Ultimatum to Serbia

July 23, 1914

The Royal Serbian Government further undertakes:

1. To suppress any publication which incites to hatred and contempt of the Monarchy and the general tendency of which is directed against its territorial integrity;
2. To dissolve immediately the society styled Narodna Odbrana, to confiscate all its means of propaganda, and to proceed in the same manner against the other societies and their branches in Serbia which engage in propaganda against the Austro-Hungarian Monarchy; the Royal Government will take the necessary measures to prevent the dissolved societies from continuing their activities under another name and form;
3. To eliminate without delay from public instruction in Serbia, both as regards the teaching body and the methods of instruction, all that serves or might serve to foment propaganda against Austria–Hungary;
4. To remove from the military service and administration in general all officers and officials guilty of propaganda against the Austro-Hungarian Monarchy and of whom the Imperial and Royal Government [Austria–Hungary] reserves to itself the right to communicate the names and deeds to the Royal Government;
5. To accept the collaboration in Serbia of organs of the Imperial and Royal Government in the suppression of the subversive movement directed against the territorial integrity of the Monarchy;
6. To take judicial proceedings against the accessories to the plot of 28 June who are on Serbian territory;

   Organs delegated by the Imperial and Royal Government will take part in the investigations relating thereto:
7. To proceed without delay to the arrest of Major Voija Tankosić and of a certain Milan Čiganović, a Serbian state employee implicated by the findings of the preliminary investigation at Sarajevo;
8. To prevent by effective measures the cooperation of the Serbian Authorities in the illicit traffic in arms and explosives across the frontier; to dismiss and severely punish the officials of the Šabac and Loznica frontier service guilty of having assisted the authors of the Sarajevo crime by facilitating their crossing of the frontier;

9. To furnish the Imperial and Royal Government with explanations regarding the unjustifiable utterances of high Serbian officials both in Serbia and abroad, who, notwithstanding their official position, have not hesitated since the outrage of 28 June to express themselves in interviews in terms of hostility towards the Austro-Hungarian Government, finally;
10. To notify the Imperial and Royal Government without delay of the execution of the measures comprised under the preceding heads.[17]

SERBIA AFTER THE ULTIMATUM

The ultimatum clearly challenged Pašić's intention to defend Serbia's sovereignty, and from the start, the prime minister indicated that Serbia could not accept all of Austria–Hungary's demands. While he and the ministers debated the answers on July 24–25, Pašić ordered a series of military measures, the first actually taken by any of the powers in 1914. Pašić possessed few illusions about the immediate future.

Although the Belgrade government hoped for more determined support from abroad during these critical days, no help was forthcoming from London and little from Paris. Still more surprising, Belgrade failed to get any ironclad assurances from its Russian patron. In contrast to earlier scholarship on the subject, Russia's stance was ambiguous and ambivalent in the forty-eight hours after the ultimatum.

The Serbian minister in Saint Petersburg, Miroslav Spalajković, sent the following telegrams during the night of July 24–25, after a long interview with Russian Foreign Minister Serge Sazonov.

MIROSLAV SPALAJKOVIĆ

Telegrams to Belgrade

July 24–25, 1914

The Russian Minister of Foreign Affairs sharply criticized the ultimatum of Austria–Hungary. Sazonov told me that the ultimatum contains demands that no state could accept. He said we could count on Russian help, but he did not explain what shape or form that help would take. Only the tsar could decide, and they have to cooperate with France as well.

Sazonov said he had done everything he could in Vienna and Berlin to help.

Sazonov had gotten a telegram from his chargé in Belgrade, who said that chaos prevailed and that Serbia cannot defend itself without arms and munitions. If this is true, the Russian Foreign Minister advised the following: inform all countries that Serbia condemns the crime in Sarajevo as an assassination and that it would bring to court any of her subjects for whom it could be proved he was a participant. But the Serbian government should refute all accusations which say Serbia ordered the events in Sarajevo and which makes Serbia responsible for them. Sazonov also wanted Serbia to say it had always been loyal to Austria–Hungary and that other European governments recognize this. . . .

That is why Serbia does not want to go to war with a country which is eleven times bigger than Serbia. Therefore, Sazonov advises us if we cannot defend ourselves then we must do like Bulgaria last year.* That would cause a protest from other states against Austria–Hungary. He has also sent this advice to the chargé in Belgrade.

I [Spalajković] told him [Sazonov] that his advice would be practical if we would be sure that Austria–Hungary only wanted to invade the border areas. But we cannot let her destroy the country. We have to organize the defense and accept battles in the interior. Sazonov answered that everything depends on our capability to defend ourselves. Money and valuables should be sent to Greece and the army retreat there if necessary. . . .

I have told Sazonov that the only way to prevent war is for Russia to tell Austria–Hungary that Russia will order general mobilization if the conflict between Serbia and Austria–Hungary is not put before the great powers to resolve as had been done in 1909. The Serbian government's response at that time was a part of the great powers decision, and they have a right to decide if Serbia did as it promised. Sazonov said that this would be done tonight.

*Presumably referring to Bulgaria's decision to make a quick peace after its defeat in the Second Balkan War.

Pašić wrote at the bottom of the cable, "I am gratified for this."[18]

But how could he interpret the Russian suggestions? Were the bonds of Slavic unity as strong as he had believed? And what would happen if he proclaimed a willingness to let the courts try anyone accused in the conspiracy? Perhaps more important, how could he convince the proud Serbian army to retreat? The Russian response touched on a range of diplomatic issues, and it inadvertently touched on a series of sensitive civil-military issues inside Serbia.

In any event, the Russian stance did not alter Pašić's intention to frame a reply that conceded on some points, evaded others, and ultimately defended Serbian sovereignty. Such a response was bound to be rejected by Vienna, and so it was. When Minister Giesl read the reply at 6:00 P.M. on July 25, he deemed it unacceptable and immediately left Belgrade, in effect breaking diplomatic relations in the process. War had moved much closer.

The Serbian Response to Vienna's Ultimatum

July 25, 1914

2. The Government possess no proof, nor does the note of the Imperial and Royal Government furnish them with any, that the Narodna Odbrana and other similar societies have committed up to the present any criminal act of this nature through the proceedings of any of their members. Nevertheless, the Royal Government will accept the demand of the Imperial and Royal Government and will dissolve the Narodna Odbrana Society and every other society which may be directing its efforts against Austria–Hungary. . . .

5. The Royal Government must confess that they do not clearly grasp the meaning or the scope of the demand made by the Imperial and Royal Government that Serbia shall undertake to accept the collaboration of the representatives of the Imperial and Royal Government upon their territory, but they declare that they will admit such collaboration as agrees with the principle of international law, with criminal procedure, and with good neighbourly relations.

6. It goes without saying that the Royal Government consider it their duty to open an inquiry against all such persons as are, or eventually may be, implicated in the plot of 15 [28] June, and who happen to be within the territory of the kingdom. As regards the participation in this inquiry of Austro-Hungarian agents or authorities appointed for this purpose by the Imperial and Royal Government, the Royal Government cannot accept such an arrangement, as it would be a violation of the Constitution and of the law of criminal procedure; nevertheless, in concrete cases communications as to the results of the investigation in question might be given to the Austro-Hungarian agents.[19]

Even as Pašić was working on his reply to the ultimatum, the Serbian army was mobilizing. General Radomir Putnik, on vacation in the Habsburg monarchy when the crisis deepened, was allowed by Vienna (in the gallantry of the age) to return to Serbia. Apis and his army colleagues began their military preparations in earnest.

The summary Austrian rejection of the Serbian response jolted Pašić, who still hoped for more negotiations. Within hours it became clear that Vienna did not intend to negotiate further unless Pašić would allow an Austrian investigation inside Serbia, a concession the prime minister had no intention of making. But if Pašić was rebuffed on the Vienna front, he was cheered by reports from Saint Petersburg.

After Sazonov's momentary ambivalence of July 24–25, the Russian position shifted forcefully. The Russian military were openly belligerent in their support of their Serbian Slav brothers, and popular enthusiasm for Serbia erupted throughout the Russian capital city. Then came still more reassuring information. Russia planned to mobilize 1.6 million men to deter a Habsburg attack. Unlike 1908 and 1912–13, it appeared that Russia would back Serbia to the limit in its confrontation with Vienna. These Russian military measures, as we shall see later on, virtually ensured a European-wide war.

By July 28, Pašić appeared to have survived the most dangerous challenge of his political career. He had kept Belgrade's role in the assassination concealed despite Habsburg accusations, and he had given Apis and the army no grounds for complaint. In the ensuing fighting of the world war, Pašić would have many reasons to wonder whether the ultimate goal of a Yugoslav state with all Serbs included would be possible. Still, he had accepted the Black Hand's creation of the "war option" as a way to achieve Serbian unity. If defeat came, it would be an honorable military defeat, not a diplomatic humiliation that left him and his radical ministers exposed to the dangers of Apis and his murderous colleagues.

In the end, neither the civilians nor the military controlled the decision for war in Serbia; that decision had been made in Vienna. But Serbia's chaotic political situation and the military's open involvement in politics meant that a faction of the Serbian military could be said to have defined the parameters for the ultimate answer of who actually ruled in Belgrade.

When Serbia's tumultuous war fortunes finally stabilized in 1916, Pašić moved to exploit his July 1914 success. Helped by Regent Alexander and with the collaboration of other officials, Pašić had Apis, Malobabić, and others arrested in late 1916 on spurious grounds of treason and an alleged plot against the regent's life. Almost none of the charges would stand the light of cross-examination. Nonetheless, Apis, Malobabić, and Ljubomir Vulović received death sentences that were carried out in June 1917. Pašić, the veteran Serbian politician, had no intention of allowing a government within a government to exist after the end of the war. Just as Apis had added a lethal dimension to Serbian public life, so now he bore the effects of it from his relentless civilian foe, Nikola Pašić.

No other civil-military relationship in 1914 would have this final, grim conclusion. But none of those relationships had endured so long or with such abiding passion. If Apis's part in the conspiracy to assassinate the Archduke Franz Ferdinand helped to start the First World War, his disappearance would make it possible for the newly emergent, postwar Yugoslavia to have a chance. Paradoxically, the same Serbian military pretensions that drove Apis would eventually lead to a virtual Serbian takeover of the Yugoslav government in the 1920s. These moves in turn set in motion the forces that would ultimately see post–World War II Yugoslavia split apart in the 1990s. This dissolution would come in part from the relentless political struggles between another volatile Serbian leader, Slobodan Milosević, and his Serbian military associates. Pašić and Apis would have felt right at home in the Belgrade of the 1990s.

NOTES

[1] David MacKenzie, *Apis, The Congenial Conspirator: The Life of Dragutin T. Dimitrijević* (Boulder, Colo.: East European Monographs, 1989), 35.

[2] Luigi Albertini, *The Origins of the War of 1914,* trans. and ed. Isabella M. Massey, 3 vols. (London: Oxford University Press, 1952–57), 2:28–29.

[3] Ibid., 29.

[4] Vladimir Dedijer, *The Road to Sarajevo* (New York: Simon & Schuster, 1966), 374.

[5] There is no adequate biography of Pašić in English, but Alexander Dragnich, *Serbia, Nikola Pašić, and Yugoslavia* (New Brunswick, N.J.: Rutgers University Press, 1974), is helpful.

[6] Tucaković to Protić, June 4, 1914, *Documents sur la politique exterieure du Royaume de Serbie, 1903–1914 (Dokumenti o spolnoj politici Kraljevine Srbije, 1903–1914),* book 7, vol. 2, ed. Vladimir Dedijer and Života Anić (Belgrade: Academy of Sciences, 1980), no. 155. (Hereafter cited as *Documents.*)

[7] Albertini, *Origins,* 2:90.

[8] Protić to Pašić, June 15, 1914, *Documents,* no. 206.

[9] Ibid.

[10] Dimitrijević to Chief of the Operations Section of the General Staff, June 21, 1914, *Documents,* no. 230.

[11] Protić to the War Ministry, June 24, 1914, *Documents,* no. 254.

[12] Barbara Jelavich, "Documents: What the Habsburg Government Knew about the Black Hand," *Austrian History Yearbook,* 22 (1991), 149–50.

[13] The French minister translated the press clippings; the author has translated these French versions of the Serbian press statements; see Descos to Viviani, July 1, 1914, *Documents diplomatiques français, 1871–1914,* 3rd ser., vol. 10 (Paris: Imprimerie Nationale, 1936), no. 469.

[14] Ibid.

[15] Mark Cornwall, "Serbia," in *Decisions for War, 1914,* ed. Keith Wilson (New York: St. Martin's Press, 1995), 60–68.

[16] Pašić to all missions except Vienna, July 18–19, 1914, midnight, *Documents,* no. 462.

[17] Albertini, *Origins,* 2:287–88.

[18] Miroslav Spalajković to Pašić, July 24–25, 1914, *Documents,* no. 527.

[19] Albertini, *Origins,* 2:367–69.

3

Berchtold and Conrad Push
Austria–Hungary to War

Foreign Minister Leopold Berchtold and Chief of the General Staff Franz Conrad von Hötzendorf were two of the key figures in the drama of July 1914. Indeed, it can be argued that no other individuals played so pivotal a role in the decisions leading to war. Since 1906, each had held major positions of responsibility and ranked among the elite decision makers of the Habsburg monarchy. The story of their interactions could shape an entire study. Their relationship was complicated, moreover, by their ties with the late Archduke Franz Ferdinand, who had served as sponsor, friend, and occasional enemy to both. The heir apparent's determination to maintain the peace from 1912 to 1914 had kept Conrad's bellicosity in check; for his part, Berchtold was committed to militant diplomacy but wanted to avoid any real fighting. But now the murder of Franz Ferdinand provided the pretext for a Habsburg reckoning with Serbia. A brief analysis of Habsburg policies before July 1914, especially of Conrad's and Berchtold's roles, exposes a major dimension to the subsequent decisions after Sarajevo. The Austro-Hungarian story forms the crux of the July crisis.

THE COMPLEX HABSBURG INHERITANCE

By 1914, eighty-four-year-old Emperor Franz Joseph had ruled over the Habsburg monarchy for nearly sixty-six years. His rule had seen persistent military defeats but also the acquisition of administrative control over Bosnia and Herzegovina, followed by their formal annexation in 1908. Since 1867, Austria and Hungary had existed as two virtually independent governments with a common monarch (Franz Joseph), a common foreign policy, and a common military structure.

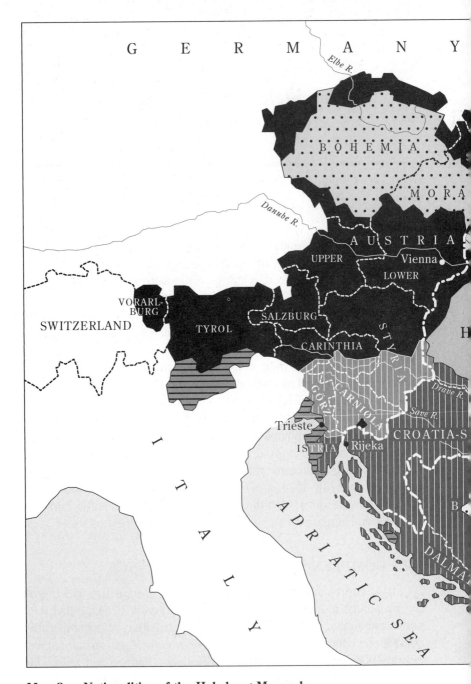

Map 3.   Nationalities of the Habsburg Monarchy

Used by permission of Professor and Mrs. A. J. P. Taylor, *The Habsburg Monarchy, 1809–1918* (Hamish Hamilton, Ltd.).

■	Germans	▦	Slovenes
	Magyars	▤	Italians
∴	Czechs	▦	Rumanians
⧄	Slovaks	▦	Poles
▥	Croats	⦀	Little Russians
∴	Serbs		

RUSSIA

GALICIA

BUKOVINA

Danube R.

Tisza R.

Budapest

HUNGARY

TRANSYLVANIA

Maros R.

RUMANIA

SERBIA

HERZEGOVINA

The 1867 *Ausgleich* agreement left Vienna and Budapest with indepen-dent functions and each with a de facto veto over war/peace decisions.

Uneasily, these three governmental arrangements—monarchical, Austrian, Hungarian—ruled over the third largest European state. Containing nearly fifty million people of eleven nationalities, the monarchy was effectively controlled by the Magyars (native Hungari-ans) and the German-Austrians (Map 3). In Hungary, the Magyars governed sternly, oppressing the rights of the Rumanians, Croats, and other South Slavs. In Austria, the German-Austrians controlled the central political apparatus. Together, the two governments provided the funds for the common army and navy that were administered by a common war minister under Emperor Franz Joseph's direct super-vision. In addition, each state had its own military force.

The demands of its disparate nationalities threatened repeatedly to tear the Habsburg Empire apart. The Slavs wanted formal political recognition like that enjoyed by the Magyars, which neither the Aus-trians nor the Magyars would grant. More dangerously, some South Slavs were increasingly attracted by talk of creating a new Yugoslav (South Slav) state or a greater Serbia, ideas encouraged by Russia's Pan Slavic propaganda. The monarchy's formal annexation of Bosnia-Herzegovina had created further difficulties, given the significant reli-gious differences among the Roman Catholic Croats, Muslims, and Orthodox Serbs living there. Adding still more confusion were the demands of Austria–Hungary's Italian ally for a part of the Tirol (and Dalmatia), demands that strained relationships within the Triple Alli-ance. And because the domestic nationality issues had their inter-national counterparts, the Habsburg neighbors—Rumania, Serbia, Russia, and Italy—created potential strategic problems. It was within this uncongenial international configuration that General Conrad von Hötzendorf had to operate after his appointment in 1906 as chief of the Austro-Hungarian general staff.

CONRAD AND BERCHTOLD BEFORE SARAJEVO: THE STRUGGLE FOR CONTROL

Conrad's entire life was centered in the Austrian military system. The son of a Napoleonic War veteran, he had entered a military academy at the age of ten in 1862. Thereafter, he served in uniform until 1917

**Figure 3.
Franz Conrad
von Hötzendorf**

A prime advocate
of war in July 1914,
Conrad hoped mili-
tary victory would
allow him to marry
his beloved Gina.
He married Gina;
he won no other
victories.
Photo: AKG London.

(Figure 3). After brief fighting in the occupation of Bosnia-Herzegovina
in 1878–79, he served in Galicia, where he met and married his wife,
the daughter of a senior army officer. A published writer on infantry
tactics, Conrad ranks among the most interesting of the pre-1914 generals who decided for peace or war in July 1914. He loved to sketch
and paint. He detested parade-ground drills, hiked whenever he could
in the Tirol, and dabbled in philosophy.[1]

Few other general officers had Conrad's energy, strategic grasp,
and sheer force of personality. In his assumptions and actions he
espoused the late-nineteenth-century theory of social Darwinism. This
theory applied the teachings of Charles Darwin about natural selection and survival of the fittest to human societies, arguing that progress resulted from relentless competition among humans in which the

strongest survived and prospered and the weak died out. Conrad believed that the Habsburg monarchy faced a life-or-death struggle for survival. To prevent its decline, he advocated an aggressive, preventive imperialistic policy in the Balkans. His incessant demands for war after 1912 made him largely responsible for the bellicose atmosphere in Vienna both before and after the Sarajevo murders. Conrad can be called the general most responsible for war in 1914.

But there was another dimension to Conrad. While he discharged his duties as chief of the general staff, he also carried on a prolonged love affair with Gina von Reininghaus, who was twenty-eight years his junior, married, and the mother of six. Gina refused to divorce to marry Conrad, who had been widowed in 1905. He continued his amorous pursuits to the outbreak of the war, and he, Gina, and her husband often appeared together in public. Finally in 1915, after Gina secured a divorce, they were married, to the scandal of Austrian society, and she accompanied him to the army's field headquarters in Teschen. The scarcely concealed affair titillated Habsburg society and had offended the prudish Franz Ferdinand.[2]

In his capacity as chief of staff with final responsibility for military planning and training, Conrad systematically began to develop new war plans against Italy, Serbia, and Russia after 1906. Strongly supported by Franz Ferdinand in his early years as chief, Conrad enlarged the monarchy's intelligence apparatus and tried to improve the military's weapons and technical support.

Vienna's decision to formally annex Bosnia-Herzegovina had provoked a major international crisis in 1908–09. Eventually, Britain and France made it clear that neither would fight to undo the Austrian act, even though it meant a major diplomatic humiliation for Saint Petersburg and for Russia's client, Serbia. Conrad, for his part, vehemently insisted on attacking Serbia while Russia, still recovering from its 1905 defeat by the Japanese, could not help. But his pleas were turned aside. Still, he continued to hope, as he wrote Gina von Reininghaus.

FRANZ CONRAD VON HÖTZENDORF

Letter to Gina von Reininghaus

December 26, 1908

Midnight.

Gina! Should I share with you the great despair, should I describe for you the great suffering, should I share with you the great pangs which I have endured, should I tell you that I have been half conscious of each heart throb? No, I prefer not. But I tell you directly and candidly: "I have only one thought—and that is: To make you my wife." The bonds which foolish men have created must be torn asunder—You must become mine, entirely and forever. Why has fate put this growing fire in my heart if it did not want you to be mine? Do not resist being mine—never have you been so loved as by me, never is a man so given to a woman as I for you. I belong to you alone with furious, boundless love. I want to treat you with great tenderness, I want to worship you, you and only you, that is everything that I want in this world.

You must be my adored, idolized wife. I hold firmly that it cannot be otherwise.

The times are serious, and the coming year will in all probability bring war. I go physically well, since you have saved me. If I return with failure, then I will disappear as nothing into loneliness, if I have survived these battles. But if I come, as I can only self-consciously hope, crowned with success, then Gina, I will break all restraints in order to achieve the greatest success in my life, having you as my dear wife.

But if things go otherwise and everything continues in rotting peace, Gina, what then? In your hands rest my fate, entirely in your hands. Grasp the entire seriousness of the situation, as I have you steadily before my eyes!

Conrad[3]

Italy—Vienna's erstwhile ally—always remained Conrad's preferred target. He persisted so vigorously in his call for an attack on Italy that he was removed from his post in November 1911. Franz Joseph made it clear that he favored peace and that Conrad had inappropriately crossed into the political arena. For the next thirteen months, Conrad served as an army inspector in the Tirol.

While Conrad was away from Vienna during most of 1912, Count Leopold Berchtold returned in February 1912 at the behest of

Emperor Franz Joseph to become Habsburg's foreign minister and de facto chancellor of the Empire. His return climaxed a career unusual for both its rapid success and its aristocratic hue. A noble landowner of enormous holdings in both halves of the empire, his marriage to Nandine Karolyi had given him additional Hungarian estates (Figure 4). Entering the Habsburg bureaucracy in the late 1880s, he had transferred to the foreign service in 1893. He served in London, among other places, and in 1906, at the age of forty-three, became ambassador to Russia, arguably the second most important diplomatic post after Berlin. He stayed in Saint Petersburg until early 1911, returning to his estates at Buchlau, where he remained until the emperor's summons.

Because of his role in the July crisis, Berchtold's historical reputation has until recently been a tattered one. While not brilliant, Berchtold managed during 1912 and 1913 to secure the Habsburg monarchy's minimal interests during the kaleidoscopic changes in the Balkans. After Sarajevo, he clearly dominated the decision process—for the worse.

In the months from February to the start of the First Balkan War in October 1912, Berchtold successfully negotiated an increase in the size of the Habsburg standing army. But he was less fortunate in thwarting the Serbian-led Balkan League after its emergence in early 1912 under Russian sponsorship. The league sought to oust the Ottoman Empire from the Balkans, and there were hints that it might also act against the weakened Habsburg monarchy.

In October 1912, the Balkan League—consisting of Serbia, Bulgaria, Greece, and Montenegro—went to war against Turkey, pushing Turkish troops from all of Macedonia. In the ensuing diplomatic chaos, Berchtold managed to prevent Serbian access to the sea by creating an independent Albanian state. Meanwhile, Austro-Russian tension increased dangerously as Saint Petersburg kept tens of thousands of extra troops on duty along the Habsburg frontier, forcing Vienna to make countermobilization moves. Anxious to have a more experienced general in charge if war came, Franz Joseph and Franz Ferdinand recalled Conrad as chief of the general staff in December 1912. His return ensured that Berchtold was kept busy defending a diplomatic approach to issues instead of a military confrontation.

Not surprisingly, upon his return Conrad began his repeated demands for military action against Serbia. His first confrontation with Berchtold came in late December, when he wanted to push ahead with

Figure 4.   Antonino di San Giuliano and Leopold Berchtold

These two aristocrats, shown here in a meeting in April 1914, ran the foreign policies of Italy and Austria–Hungary. Urbane and rich, they represented governments that were allies but usually at odds over most issues.

From *Diario fotografico del marchese di San Giuliano,* ed. Giuseppe Giarrizzo.

more troops and mobilization against Serbia. Conrad left no doubt of his goals.

FRANZ CONRAD VON HÖTZENDORF

Letter to Leopold Berchtold

December 23, 1912

The results of a halting, purely peaceful policy in the Balkan crisis can only be:

The loss of prestige and with it the loss of political and economic power and prestige;

Mistrust of the allies in the force of the monarchy and with it the worth of the alliance;

Already now but more in the future: the vehemence in the demands of the enemies of the monarchy, the vehemence that would lead to further concessions by the monarchy to these demands in conjunction with ever more aggressive demands by the momentary chief enemy of the monarchy, Serbia;

The flare-up and growth of revolutionary sentiments among the Slavic populations of the greater Serbia aspirations;

The collapse of the patriotic sentiments of the remaining nationalities of the monarchy as a result of the state's impotence;

The sinking of the military spirit and of the confidence of the army in itself, because of the inaction;

A deep upset among the officer corps;

Danger of the final destruction of the South Slav areas in the monarchy and the loss of the seapower position;

The economic ruin of private businesses because of the crisis conditions;

The economic ruin of the state because of the cost of the preparations without any positive gain;

The enduring worsening of the situation in the future.

The only means to the problem: a military defeat of Serbia without shying from the possible consequences of such a step, with the consideration that further passivity will lead to the ruin of the monarchy, while energetic, active measures can lead to a favorable outcome. If the entente powers seek to help Serbia against the monarchy, they create the choice of giving these states a general war which these states fear. If we do not solve the question of the monarchy's existence now, then it will be decided in the future under worse circumstances.[4]

Berchtold resisted Conrad's demands, as did Franz Joseph and Franz Ferdinand. Nor did the German allies show any disposition to help. Conrad backed off the demands during January 1913 but continued to insist that war offered the only solution for the monarchy's long-term situation. In late April 1913, Montenegro's continued defiance of the European concert led to an ultimatum. But the Montenegrins retreated so quickly that Conrad could not go to war.

The Second Balkan War of July 1913 occurred before all of the Habsburg troops had been demobilized from the first struggle. But Conrad made few demands to intervene. Within weeks, the rapid fighting saw Bulgaria defeated by its former allies: Serbia, Greece, Montenegro, and now Rumania.

Something else kept Conrad in check. He and Franz Ferdinand had nearly parted company over a spy scandal involving Colonel Alfred Redl. Former head of Austrian counterintelligence until 1911, Redl had been compromised by his homosexual behavior, which the Russians, once they discovered it, used to blackmail him. He had been betraying plans to Saint Petersburg since at least 1906. Upon discovering the treachery, Conrad had allowed (or had persuaded) Redl to commit suicide. This act deeply offended the Catholic Franz Ferdinand and made it impossible to assess the damage caused by the treason. In July 1913, the archduke ignored Conrad's calls for action, and thereafter personal relations between the two were uneasy. Had Franz Ferdinand lived, Conrad's days as chief clearly would have been numbered.

In October 1913, the monarchy and Serbia had a further confrontation, this time over Belgrade's failure to evacuate territory allocated to the new Albanian state. When the ministers met to discuss the situation, the following exchange took place between Berchtold and Conrad.

Extract of Ministerial Meeting
October 13, 1913

Count Berchtold declared that he was convinced of the necessity for action against Serbia, that the monarchy could do nothing else, but there is still the question of what consequences a move against Serbia would have: relations with Rumania, the possible involvement of Russia! There is also room for doubt whether Germany and Italy would support the monarchy.

I: I have for seven years in writing and with the kaiser stressed that the monarchy is at a turning point, to undertake an active Balkan policy, and that the Balkan question, that is the Serbian question, must be solved. Since we cannot count upon a peaceful resolution with Serbia, we must consider them as the enemy, and we cannot wait until all the circumstances are against us.

In 1908 we had a wonderful chance. I pressed with all means to use the occasion, but we did not.
In 1913 I have again pressed. . . .

[Conrad then argued that no diplomatic victory would suffice.]

We must under all circumstances have a military success, unconcerned about the views of the other powers.

The tactic of mobilizing must be avoided since it hurts the army and the population. If after an ultimatum Serbia does not yield, no later opportunity for concessions must be given—then there remains only mobilization and war.

Count Berchtold: If it comes to war, then it can only last three weeks! How can that happen?

I: That cannot be changed for it is in the nature of things. We can resolve it if we have the necessary firmness.[5]

This time Berchtold did send a seven-day ultimatum, and military action seemed probable. But Belgrade and the Pašić government relented, evacuating the territory. Again Conrad was thwarted in his chance for action. On the other hand, the Serbian retreat ratified for the Habsburg policymakers the utility of militant diplomacy. This militarization of attitudes may have been Conrad's most significant contribution, as force appeared the only instrument that brought Serbian compliance. And in this instance, Russia had again tolerated a rebuff to Serbia.

In the remaining months before Sarajevo, Conrad and Berchtold saw each other occasionally, usually to discuss military spending. Nearly a year's regular budget had gone into the militant diplomacy, so much that Conrad proclaimed that he would never again agree to mobilization unless war followed. War, he argued, could not be much more expensive than the diplomacy of mobilization.

Berchtold, meanwhile, surveyed the wreckage to the monarchy's foreign policy caused by the Balkan Wars. Serbia had doubled in size and population. Montenegro and Serbia talked about a possible union that would give Belgrade access to the sea. Vienna's frictions with its Italian ally had increased as each ally clamored for position in Albania. More dangerously, Rumania, a secret partner with the Triple Alliance since 1883, now appeared to be drifting toward the Triple Entente. Nor could Berchtold be happy about Germany's repeated demands that Vienna and Belgrade reach a détente.

Closer to home was a further complication for Berchtold. István Tisza had once again become Hungarian prime minister in July 1913, demanding and getting a major voice in the formation of Habsburg foreign policy. Tisza, who viewed the German alliance as the sine qua non of Habsburg diplomacy, became a new personality with whom Berchtold now had to reckon.

By June 1914, the foreign minister had become convinced that Vienna should seek to recapture the initiative in the Balkans and to isolate Serbia through diplomacy. In a major policy memorandum in late June, he did not mention military action. But the document had an urgency of tone that betrayed a sense of desperation in Vienna. Clearly, Berchtold was prepared to be more assertive and less compliant.

On Sunday, June 14, Berchtold and his wife visited Franz Ferdinand and Sophie at the archduke's Bohemian estate at Konopischt. The two women were friends; the men held some political discussion and relaxed. Exactly two weeks later, the royal couple were dead.

VIENNA RESOLVES TO ACT

The heir apparent's death radically transformed the decisionmaking process in Vienna. Since 1906, ministers had treated Franz Ferdinand with respect; if he were not yet the emperor, one day he would be. And despite contemporary reports to the contrary, the archduke generally favored a cautious Habsburg foreign policy. Increasingly suspicious of Conrad's repeated demands for military action, Franz Ferdinand together with Emperor Franz Joseph had supported Berchtold in his repeated confrontations with the aggressive general. Now, suddenly, the chance for a military solution had strongly increased. The absence of Franz Ferdinand made the decision for war far more likely, even as his death would be the pretext.

When news of the Sarajevo murders reached the Habsburg deci-
sionmakers, Berchtold returned to Vienna that Sunday evening, June
28, from his Buchlau estate, as did Franz Joseph, who traveled from
his hunting lodge at Bad Ischl. Conrad, already en route from the
Bosnian maneuvers, arrived in Vienna on the 29th. On his way, he
wrote to Gina von Reininghaus.

FRANZ CONRAD VON HÖTZENDORF

Letter to Gina von Reininghaus

June 28, 1914

Karlstadt

Highly honored Frau!

Yesterday evening I left Sarajevo with Metzger and Kundmann [two
key aides]. This afternoon at 2 in Agram [now Zagreb] I learned from
the corps commander of rumors of the sad event. Later we came to
Karlstadt, where I received the official telegram which contains details
of the awful attack.

In the first attack Boos and Merizzi [two officers with Franz Ferdi-
nand] were slightly wounded by a bomb, while in the second attack the
heir apparent and the archduchess were killed with shots from a Browning pistol. Both were dead within fifteen minutes. The attackers have
been arrested; one is a printer, the other a Serbian student.

The attack comes from the outspoken Serbian-nationalist character
and is the result of the political agitation which has undermined our
South Slav areas. Therein lies, entirely apart from the purely human
side, the deep political significance of this repugnant crime. Energetic
action in 1909 would have sent these developments in an entirely different direction—so punishes indecisiveness and neglect.

I immediately asked His Majesty [Franz Joseph] whether I should
continue this trip or return at once to Vienna; I have received a telegraphic order for the latter. I thus will leave here tonight and reach
Vienna on the 29th at 9 A.M. . . . .

What consequences the attack will have cannot now be seen. Whether
this was a single action or a part of a greater action cannot yet be judged.

Unfortunately I have gained the impression that for the future of the
monarchy and indeed for the immediate future that nothing good will
come of this. Serbia and Rumania want to put the nails into our coffin;

Russia will support both actively. It will be a hopeless fight; nevertheless it must be waged, since an old monarchy and a glorious army must not perish without glory.

So I see a desperate future and confront a sad fading away of my life.

I love you my dear woman; God knows when and how we will meet again.

Conrad[6]

As the senior officials gathered, three assumptions dominated their discussions. First, each held the Serbian government responsible for the attack. Second, the Habsburg leadership was inclined to believe that monarchical solidarity would prevent Russia from supporting Serbia. Finally, each Habsburg policymaker realized that German support would be required for any military encounter with neighboring Serbia.

Berchtold and Conrad first met on Monday evening, June 29. Berchtold wavered about immediate military action, while the general was unequivocal in his desire for an immediate attack on Serbia. Berchtold described the sessions in his diary notes.

LEOPOLD BERCHTOLD

Notes on His Meeting with Franz Conrad von Hötzendorf

June 29, 1914

On the evening of 29 June, even before the details of other conversations could be known, Franz Conrad von Hötzendorf appeared and spoke very directly about need for immediate military action.

The Chief of the General Staff talked about the failures in the past, especially that Count Aehrenthal [Berchtold's immediate predecessor as foreign minister] had not drawn the final consequences of his policy at a time when the power relations for the monarchy were still relatively favorable. Now we must face the consequences.

"On 1 July we must mobilize without further negotiations with Serbia. If someone meets a poisonous viper in his tracks, one did not wait for a bite." With a trace of melancholy in his fine, pale countenance, he concluded with these words full of meaning: "War, war, war!"[7]

Conrad gave a slightly different version.

FRANZ CONRAD VON HÖTZENDORF

Notes on His Meeting with Leopold Berchtold

June 29, 1914

On the evening of 29 June, prior to an 8 o'clock meeting of the ministerial staff, I spoke to Count Berchtold. I greeted him with these words:

"We meet again under very different circumstances than when we left each other before."

Count Berchtold observed that Kaiser Wilhelm would come for the funeral ceremonies [of Franz Ferdinand] and that would provide an opportunity to discuss the situation. I responded that I certainly hoped so, since the attack against the monarchy must bring an immediate response. In my opinion, there must be mobilization against Serbia. It appeared to me unavoidable and the least we could do right now.

The minister replied that the foreign situation had some gaps and that public opinion must be prepared.

Count Berchtold: Don't you believe a revolution might break out?
I: Where?
Berchtold: In Bohemia.
I: But don't you have something to propose?
Berchtold: I have other proposals. We must demand that Serbia dissolve the associations, dismiss the police minister, and so forth.
I: The police minister might calm the Serbs, but the only effective method is power. . . .

Even Count Berchtold believes, to be sure, that the moment to solve the Serbian problem had now come, and he would speak to His Majesty [Franz Joseph] about it. Above all, however, we had to await the outcome of the investigation.[8]

When Berchtold saw the Emperor Franz Joseph the next day, he found him shaken but inclined to military action. Nevertheless, both men had to confront Hungarian Prime Minister István Tisza, who preferred a diplomatic confrontation and no military action. Tisza realized that a military victory over Serbia might bring still more Slavs into the monarchy, a position that he, as a Hungarian leader, strongly resisted. He thus disliked any talk of an immediate attack upon Serbia and wanted a clarification of Germany's position before any decision.

Conrad, meanwhile, continued to press for a showdown, taking his case directly to Franz Joseph on July 5.

FRANZ CONRAD VON HÖTZENDORF

Notes on His Audience with Emperor Franz Joseph

July 5, 1914

The conversation came quickly to the political situation.

His Majesty surveyed it entirely and clearly understood its seriousness. I expressed to His Majesty my belief in the unavoidability of war with Serbia.

His Majesty: "Yes, that is entirely correct, but do we want a war, if everyone is against us, especially Russia?"

I: "Don't we have our flank covered by Germany?"

His Majesty glanced at me questioningly and said: "Are you sure about Germany?" He knew that at Konopischt, the heir apparent, Franz Ferdinand, had sought to get the German kaiser to promise unconditional support for the future. The German kaiser had evaded the question and left the answer uncertain.

I: "Your Majesty, we must however know where we stand."

His Majesty: "Last night a note was sent to Germany in order to get an answer."

I: "If the answer says that Germany stands on our side, could we go to war against Serbia?"

His Majesty: "Then yes. (After a short pause His Majesty continued): If Germany does not give the answer, then what?"

I: "Then we stand, to be sure, alone. We must have the answer soon, for the greatest decision depends on it."

His Majesty: "The German kaiser is on a North Sea cruise. In any case we must await the answer."

[Their discussion then turned to personnel matters and to Franz Joseph's questions to Conrad about his relations with the late archduke and the maneuvers in Bosnia which the archduke had attended.]

While the audience continued, there came an excited exchange with His Majesty, when I proclaimed the need to take certain measures to protect against Serbian attacks in the monarchy and suggested that measures be taken elsewhere in the monarchy, as had been done in Bosnia, to protect persons, command positions, important objects like bridges and so forth.

His Majesty: "That could wait till mobilization."
I: "That is too late."
His Majesty: "No—that is impossible."
I: "There remains nothing else to do."
His Majesty: "But I do not authorize it."
I: "As Your Majesty orders—but I must as a matter of duty propose it."
[Conrad got Franz Joseph to agree only to let him search for bombs.][9]

The general also spent early July reviewing the details of his war plans. One plan that was clearly excluded was Plan I, his scheme to attack his Italian ally. In this instance, the most he expected from Rome, despite a flurry of recent Triple Alliance military staff talks, was neutrality.

Conrad's other two war plans represented the crux of his military strategy. He feared that, should Austria–Hungary attack Serbia, Russia would attack in the north once Habsburg forces were committed in the south. To address this contingency, Conrad divided his forces into three separate cohorts. Plan B (Balkan) called for a group of eight divisions in the south to defend against any Serbian move. Plan R (Russia) called for twenty-eight and a half divisions in the north to defend against any projected Russian attack. The remainder of his force, twelve divisions, was his offensive force. If these divisions went south, Plan B became an offensive operation against Serbia. If these divisions went north, Plan R became a two-pronged offensive operation against Russia, while the southern forces contained the Serbs (Map 4). In July 1914, the crucial questions for Conrad were what would Russia do, when should the swing forces be committed, and in which direction? In July–August 1914, General Franz Conrad von Hötzendorf, the assumed great strategist, did not answer any of these questions correctly.

Conrad's review of the plans also revealed a further complication. By July 6, he realized that he could not launch an immediate attack

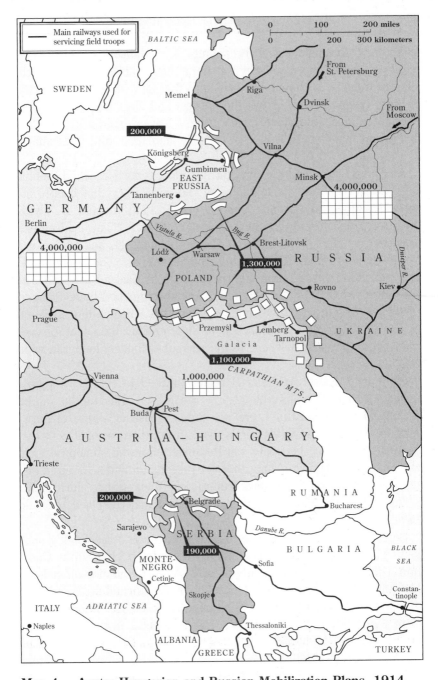

Map 4. Austro-Hungarian and Russian Mobilization Plans, 1914

From *Suicide of the Empires: The Battles on the Eastern Front, 1914–1918,* by Alan Clark (American Heritage Press, 1971).

under any circumstances. Large numbers of Habsburg troops were scattered across the monarchy on the annual "harvest leave," which allowed them to go home and help with the harvest. A sudden recall of these troops would disrupt the harvest and alert Europe to Habsburg intentions. And since most of these leaves expired by July 25, this meant that Conrad could not possibly launch an immediate attack in early July.

As Conrad surveyed the strategic situation, reports reached Vienna from Sarajevo about the tentacles of the conspiracy that clearly involved members of a Serbian political organization. Indeed, by July 3, Emperor Franz Joseph had heard enough about Serbian involvement to accept a military resolution of the Serbian threat, and he agreed with Berchtold's plan to approach Berlin for support. The foreign minister had Franz Joseph draft a personal letter to Kaiser Wilhelm II requesting German support. The letter was accompanied by a stronger version of Berchtold's June memorandum that left few doubts about Vienna's belligerent intentions. The foreign minister then sent Alexander Hoyos, the most bellicose of his key subordinates, to Berlin with these messages.

On July 5, Kaiser Wilhelm II readily agreed to Habsburg action against Serbia. Although he clearly recognized that Russia might become involved and that there was thus the risk of a general European war, his only reservation involved the need to consult with the German chancellor, Theobald von Bethmann Hollweg, a step he took later that same day. The chancellor, for reasons to be discussed in the next chapter, agreed. In stark contrast to their stance during the Balkan Wars, the German political apparatus had resolved to back Vienna come what may.

Berchtold, buttressed by German assurances and thoroughly supportive of Conrad's desire for a military showdown, chaired the Common Ministerial Council on July 7, 1914. All of the senior officials of the monarchy, save Franz Joseph, who had returned to Bad Ischl, attended the lengthy sessions. Most were veterans of previous discussions about going to war against Serbia or Russia. In fact, the group had actively considered the question of peace or war three times in the last twenty months. But this time, the stakes were infinitely higher, for each participant realized that military action would almost certainly result from their discussions.

Minutes of the Common Ministerial Council

July 7, 1914

[Those present: Austrian Premier Count Stürgkh, Hungarian Premier Count Tisza, Common Finance Minister Biliński, Common Minister of War Krobatin, Chief of the General Staff Conrad, the Deputy Chief of the Naval Staff, Rear-Admiral von Kailer, Count Berchtold as chair.]

The Agenda: Bosnian concerns. Diplomatic action against Serbia.

Foreign Minister Berchtold opened the meeting, saying that the Council had been called to advise on the measures to be taken for restoring the situation which the catastrophe in Sarajevo had unleashed on the internal situation in Bosnia and Herzegovina. In his opinion a number of internal measures were desirable given the critical state of Bosnia. But first they should also decide whether the moment had come when a show of force might put an end to Serbia's intrigues once and for all. Such a decisive blow could not be done without diplomatic preparation; therefore he had contacted the German Government. The conversations in Berlin had led to a very satisfactory result. Kaiser Wilhelm and Herr von Bethmann Hollweg had strongly promised Germany's unconditional support in case of war complications with Serbia. We must still take into account Italy and Rumania; he agreed with the Berlin cabinet that it would be better to act first and wait for eventual claims for compensation afterwards.

He recognizes that an armed conflict with Serbia could mean war with Russia. But Russia's present policy, taken in the long view, sought to create a league of Balkan states, including Rumania, which could be turned against the Monarchy at a favorable moment. He believed that they had to take this into account, since our situation in view of this policy would grow worse and an unpunished deed will be seen by our South Slavs and the Rumanians as a sign of weakness. This would also make them more willing to listen to our neighbors across the frontiers.

The logical result of what has been said would be to get ahead of our foes and through a timely reckoning with Serbia stop the development of the current process which it might not be possible to do later.

Hungarian Prime Minister Tisza agreed that the situation in recent days had changed because of the results of the investigation and the attitude of the Serbian press. He also stressed that the possibility of military action against Serbia seemed closer than he had believed just after Sarajevo. But he could never agree to a surprise attack on Serbia without diplomatic preparations, a step which had been discussed earlier. . . . He could not agree because in his opinion it would create a very bad impression in the eyes of Europe and create hostility throughout the Balkans. . . .

We must formulate unconditional demands against Serbia and give an ultimatum if Serbia does not fulfill them. If Serbia accepts them, we will have a striking diplomatic success, and our prestige will rise in the Balkans. If our demands are not met, then it would be time for military action. But I must stress that we could only reduce Serbia, not fully annihilate her, because on the one side Russia would never allow this without a life-and-death struggle, on the other because Hungary would never agree to an annexation of a part of Serbia.

War Minister Krobatin believed that a diplomatic success would have no value. Such a success would only be seen as weakness. From a military standpoint he had to stress that the moment was more favorable for war now rather than later, since the power relationships would in the future be still more unfavorable. As to the mode of starting the war, he noted that in the last two wars, the Russo-Japanese and also the Balkan Wars, there had been no declaration of war. He believed that they should mobilize only against Serbia and wait for general mobilization until it was seen what Russia would do.

We have already neglected two opportunities to resolve the Serbian question and each time had postponed it. If now, after new deeds, we do not act given these new provocations, then the South Slav provinces will regard this as a sign of weakness, and we will confront even stronger agitation against us.

In military terms it would be desirable to mobilize immediately and have a summation against Serbia as soon as the mobilization was complete. That would also be favorable vis-à-vis the Russians, since the Russian border corps were just now away on harvest leave.

A general discussion then followed about the goals for a war against Serbia. During that discussion everyone adopted [Tisza's] view that Serbia might be reduced but not annihilated given considerations about Russia. The Austrian prime minister [Stürgkh] also recommended that the Karageorgevich dynasty be removed and that one of the European princes be given the crown; further that the small Serbia be dependent on the monarchy, certainly from the military point of view. . . .

A lengthy debate on the question of the war followed. The result of the discussion may be summarized as follows:

1. That all present wished for a speedy decision of the controversy with Serbia, whether decided in a warlike or a peaceful manner;
2. That the Common Ministerial Council is prepared to adopt the view of . . . [Tisza] that mobilization would only take place after the precise demands had been made to Serbia and when those had been refused, an ultimatum would be sent.

All present except the Hungarian prime minister believed that a purely diplomatic success, even if it brought a striking humiliation of

Serbia, would be worthless. Thus the most far-reaching demands must be made of Serbia in order to assure a rejection, which would then open the way to the radical solution of a military attack. . . .

Berchtold stated that while there were still differences between all of the participants and Tisza, still they had narrowed their differences, since in all probability his proposals and those of the other members would lead to military action against Serbia.

Count Berchtold then told the Council that he intended to go to Ischl on the 8th of the month to report to His Apostolic Majesty. The Hungarian prime minister asked the minister to give His Majesty a memorandum from him on the situation.

After a communication to the press had been agreed upon, the presiding minister closed the sitting.[10]

In the ministerial discussions, Berchtold left no doubt of his conversion to the military option. He had now become a "hawk." Without the death of Franz Ferdinand, Berchtold probably would have remained committed to a policy of militant, threatening diplomacy, everything short of actual war, an approach he had used during the Balkan Wars. But with the archduke dead, Conrad's calls for direct military action against the troublesome Serbs had a clarity and appeal that he had earlier resisted. Berchtold's and Conrad's convergent views meant that Franz Joseph now faced united advice from his two most senior advisers on strategic matters.

The only obstacle was Tisza, the leader of the Magyars, who had grave reservations about a military venture and preferred a diplomatic attempt to humiliate Serbia. The Hungarian feared that victory would complicate the monarchy's problems with the South Slavs, especially if more Slavs were added to the monarchy. Berchtold's most immediate task was then to gain Tisza's support for war. First, he traveled to Bad Ischl, where he got Franz Joseph's backing, thus managing to outflank Tisza, who only communicated in writing with Franz Joseph. Eventually, by July 14, Berchtold had won the Magyar's consent, stressing German support and, perhaps most effectively, the possibility of a Serbian-Rumanian alignment over Transylvania. This nationality issue, a continuing source of Rumanian-Hungarian conflict to the present, involved three million Rumanians living under less than benevolent Magyar rule. Any threat to Magyar supremacy in this key area guaranteed Tisza's attention — and it worked.

On July 19, the senior Habsburg officials gathered again to finalize the war-peace decision. To escape attention, they met at Berchtold's private residence, and Conrad arrived in civilian clothes. Plans were reviewed, and the ultimatum discussed.

Minutes of the Common Ministerial Council
July 19, 1914

[Those present: Austrian Premier Count Stürgkh, Hungarian Premier Count Tisza, Common Finance Minister Biliński, Common Minister of War Krobatin, Chief of the General Staff Conrad, the Deputy Chief of the Naval Staff, Rear-Admiral von Kailer, Count Berchtold as chair.]

Subject: Forthcoming diplomatic action against Serbia.

Before the Council formally started, there was an informal discussion about the text of the note to be sent to Serbia, and the text was definitively settled.

Foreign Minister Berchtold then opened the Common Ministerial Council and proposed that the note be presented to the Royal Serbian Government on 23 July at five in the afternoon, so that the term of forty-eight hours would expire on Saturday, the 25th at five in the afternoon. The order for mobilization could be published in the night from Saturday to Sunday. Count Berchtold believed that it is improbable that word of our step would be publicly known before [Poincaré] had left Saint Petersburg. But even if this happened, he did not think that it would cause any harm. . . . He would object to any further delay on diplomatic grounds. Already Berlin was getting nervous, and news of our plans had already reached Rome, so that unexpected developments could not be prevented if there were further delays. . . .

The Council voted that the note would be presented on the 23 inst. at five in the afternoon. . . .

Conrad said that for military reasons the speedy initiation of action was highly desirable. Recent military reports suggested three emerging situations in Serbia.

First, large numbers of [Serbian] troops were assembled along the Bulgarian and Albanian frontiers. Next, there were reports of soldiers moving to Old Serbia. He disregarded these moves since these were only exchanges of reservists. During the last three days, however, he had received more serious news. First, two regiments . . . had been transferred from new Serbia to Old Serbia; and yesterday from trusted intelligence from Bulgaria he learned that three divisions had been ordered north. Of course he would have to get these reports verified.

If they proved true, he must ask to be allowed to take speedy counter-measures.

[The Council discussed a declaration of martial law in all of the monarchy's territories where South Slavs lived; they decided not to do it.]

[War Minister Krobatin then discussed various mobilization issues.]

[At Tisza's request, Conrad gave him secret information and assurances that Transylvania would be protected adequately from any possible Rumanian attack.] . . .

Tisza then asked the Council to vote on the conclusion, discussed at the last meeting and on which the agreement of the Royal Hungarian Government depended. The Common Ministerial Council must declare unanimously that the monarchy had no plans of aggrandizement against Serbia and that no part of Serbia would be annexed except for frontier areas for military reasons. He must unconditionally insist that such a resolution be voted unanimously by the council.

Berchtold declared that he could agree with [Tisza] but only with certain reservations. He was of the opinion, given the current political situation, that in case of a victory over Serbia, that the monarchy should annex no territory. But they might consider surrendering large portions of Serbian territory to Bulgaria, Greece, and Albania, and eventually to Rumania, thus reducing its size so it would cease to be dangerous. Given the foreign situation, he must, as manager of the foreign affairs of Austria–Hungary, reckon with the possibility that after the war there could be circumstances that made it impossible for us to renounce all annexation if we are to improve our frontiers.

Tisza said he could not accept Count Berchtold's reservations and insisted that the Council vote his point of view unanimously. He requests this not only for domestic political reasons but because he believes that Russia would resist to the end should the monarchy insist upon the full annihilation of Serbia. He asserted that the monarchy's best card for improving the international situation is to declare to the Powers as soon as possible that we have no intention of annexing any territory whatever.

Berchtold stated that even before this discussion he had the intention of making such a declaration to Rome.

Austrian Premier Stürgkh expressed his belief that even if annexation of Serbian territory was impossible, Serbia could be made dependent upon the Monarchy by replacing the dynasty, by a military convention, and by other corresponding measures. Certainly he did not want the Council to take action that would prevent strategic border changes. . . .

The Common Ministerial Council voted, on the proposal of the Royal Hungarian Premier (Tisza), that as soon as the war begins the Monarchy will declare that no war for conquest is intended, nor is the annexation of the kingdom contemplated. Of course the strategically necessary corrections of the frontier lines, or the reduction of Serbia's territory to the advantage of other states or the unavoidable temporary occupation of Serbian territory would not be precluded by this resolution.[11]

On July 21, Berchtold again traveled to Bad Ischl to get Franz Joseph's final consent to proceed. Though perennially unlucky in war, the emperor now accepted the argument that Serbia represented a genuine menace to the monarchy's future; military action had apparently become a necessity. But by the time of his death in November 1916, Franz Joseph would realize anew that he remained unlucky in war, for Conrad's strategic dreams had brought scant victory and much defeat.

Conrad and Berchtold were in Vienna when the ultimatum was delivered on July 23. When the Serbian reply was deemed unsatisfactory on July 25, Franz Joseph that same day ordered partial mobilization of two-fifths of the Habsburg forces, with the first day of mobilization coming on July 28. No moves were taken along the Russian frontier.

In the case of Austria–Hungary, the most senior ruler in Europe agreed to a dangerous course of action and one with only a limited chance of success. Had the failure of earlier diplomatic victories against Serbia convinced Franz Joseph and his advisers that only war would resolve the Serbian problem? And why had they ignored the real danger of Russian intervention?

THE LAST STEPS TO WAR

From July 26 to August 2, Berchtold and Conrad were in nearly continuous contact. It was not easy to go to war. During these days each man made decisions that proved wrongheaded, both for the preservation of the monarchy and for the conduct of the looming war. That individuals who had been under intense stress for over a month made errors of judgment should not be surprising. Nevertheless, it remains astonishing that such experienced leaders failed to perceive fully the implications of their decisions.

Berchtold attempted to shore up the monarchy's diplomatic position. Thanks to German help, Vienna won Bulgarian and Rumanian pledges of neutrality. Berchtold, after his initial disdain for Italy, urgently sought Italian neutrality as well. Berlin demanded that Vienna offer Italy some territorial concessions. The Habsburg minister reluctantly agreed to concede Valona in Albania to Italy if Rome fulfilled its alliance obligations and if Austria–Hungary actually occupied Serbia, but beyond this he would not go.

More dangerously, Berchtold frustrated Sir Edward Grey's efforts to repeat his 1912–13 success as Balkan peacemaker. Grey's persistence complicated Berchtold's timetable, for the British foreign secretary managed to prompt some minimal German reconsideration about its support for Vienna. (See chapter 4.)

Detecting the subtle atmospheric changes in Berlin and fearing that his war plans would be jeopardized, Berchtold urged Conrad to accept an immediate declaration of war against Serbia. The general preferred a more gradual approach, one that did not alarm Russia, but Berchtold prevailed. Berchtold now pressed Franz Joseph at Bad Ischl to declare war. On July 28, Austria–Hungary declared war on Serbia. Berchtold had forestalled any foreign interference on the road to war. Yet, as Conrad feared, this step heightened Russian fears, making a two-front war far more likely.

The Habsburg declaration of war accelerated the international crisis. On the night of July 28, there was some fighting near Belgrade and some shelling of the city. Though the damage was not significant, the Serbian government portrayed the incident as a massive attack on an "open" city. The Russian leaders scrapped their partial-mobilization arrangements and opted instead for full mobilization on July 30, a move that guaranteed German mobilization with all of its fateful consequences.

On July 28, Berchtold and Conrad met, with others, to discuss the strategic situation. The foreign minister pressed Conrad about the Russian danger. He wanted specifically to know at what point a Russian move might upset the confrontation with Serbia. Conrad responded definitively: "I answered, that I must know by 1 August whether the war would go against Russia, since if it were not determined, all of the transports toward Serbia would start to move. If Russia mobilized, then Germany must attack as soon as the Russians mobilize and not abandon us."[12]

Meanwhile, the German leadership continued to hesitate. At one point, Berlin talked of a "Halt in Belgrade" plan for Austria–Hungary, yet simultaneously Conrad heard from the German military that it expected the Habsburgs to mobilize against Russia and be ready for war. These ambiguities worried both Conrad and Berchtold, prompting the foreign minister to exclaim about Berlin: "Who rules: Moltke or Bethmann?" Not surprisingly, Conrad and Berchtold fretted that in view of Berlin's new hesitation, the Emperor Franz Joseph might have a change of heart and block the implementation of their plans. But after the two men met with the emperor on July 30, 1914, Conrad recorded that Franz Joseph had reached the following decisions: "The war with Serbia would continue; the English proposals would receive an obliging answer without taking any position; general mobilization would be ordered on 1 August with the 4th of August the first day."[13]

By late on that same day, Thursday, July 30, Conrad had unequivocal evidence that the Russians were taking extensive military measures. Despite this intelligence, the general ordered his reserve troops southward, as mandated by Plan B—two days ahead of his own timetable. Conrad later alleged that his railway experts had said that if the troops were sent south and then had to return immediately to the north, that this could be done without much trouble. The validity of this explanation has been much debated. The fact remains that Conrad sent the troops in the wrong direction at the wrong time and in the process exposed the monarchy to the very danger that he had so long anticipated.

Conrad's failure owes less to issues of civil-military relations than to his own judgment, but Berchtold's inaction may have played a role. As a former ambassador to Russia, Berchtold understood much of the political milieu in Saint Petersburg. He was aware of a strong split inside the Russian foreign office between "hawks" and "doves," but made no attempt to exploit these differences.

Perhaps Berchtold clung to the earlier images of a weakened Russia that would not intervene in any crisis. He certainly did not appreciate that the Russian cabinet realignment in the spring of 1914 had brought new decisiveness to a Russian government prone to indecision. (See chapter 5.)

*   *   *

Although his blunders have been variously explained or excused, recent critics have been less than kind to Conrad. Some have blamed his incompetence; others his determination to have a war at all costs and his belligerent zest for the offensive, which robbed him of perspective in the actual moment of crisis. However explained, his decisions effectively damaged the monarchy's overall strategy and severely reduced its ability to meet the greater Russian threat.

Historians have been even less kind to Berchtold. A blunderer, unequal to his task, an elite dandy, a diplomat outmaneuvered by an aggressive general—these are characterizations of his performance as Habsburg foreign minister in 1914. Why, critics ask, did he abandon the policy of militant diplomacy that had worked well in late 1912 and 1913? More recently, historians have given him credit for salvaging important gains from the wreckage of the two Balkan Wars and for winning German support early on. And he clearly outmaneuvered Tisza, for good or ill, in July 1914 and thus retained full control (and thus responsibility) for the eventual outcome. Had he become so militarized that only war seemed feasible, or was he afraid that Austria–Hungary would forfeit its international position if it did not avenge the death of Franz Ferdinand? Did similar conversions to a militant attitude take place in Berlin and Saint Petersburg among other civilian leaders?

In July 1914, the Habsburg leadership, deprived by the murders at Sarajevo of the more cautious Archduke Franz Ferdinand, resolved to punish Serbia once Berlin agreed. The constitutional arrangements of the monarchy left the final decisions in the hands of a very few men who gave the aged emperor unified advice to go to war. He did so.

Conrad and Berchtold jointly went to war. If Berchtold failed to control the military, his failure matched that of the other civilian leaders who neither understood the details of the military plans nor grasped that the carefully devised plans rested upon dubious assumptions about the nature of the new warfare. Conrad was the professional; he got the deference the new professionals expected.

In July 1914, Conrad and Berchtold resolved early that only a military defeat of Serbia would ensure the monarchy's survival. The earlier Balkan crises, Serbia's continuing subversive activity, and its magnetlike appeal to many South Slavs prompted the decision to go to war. Thus, Austro-Hungarian desires for military action, along with those of the Germans who backed them, must be considered as principal contributors to the start of the Great War.

In August 1914, Conrad finally got his war. A year later, he would get Gina von Reininghaus as well, but he never got his military victories and would finally be forced out in early 1917. He spent the postwar years writing his memoirs, distorting his military record, and blaming Germany for the death of the monarchy.

Berchtold resigned as foreign minister in 1915. Although he made some efforts to salvage his reputation, he ultimately accepted responsibility for the decisions of July 1914 and defended the integrity of the old emperor. In an era in which war was still considered a viable policy option, Berchtold had taken that option. He did not anticipate that war would lead to mass destruction, nor did his civilian counterparts elsewhere. Berchtold had hoped to rescue the monarchy's fortunes; instead, the war destroyed the dynasty and monarchy. The disappearance of Austria–Hungary did not resolve the problems that led to the war; their presence remains painfully vivid to a world in which the word *Sarajevo* no longer means 1914 but rather the 1990s.

NOTES

[1] See Lawrence Sondhaus, *Franz Conrad von Hötzendorf: Architect of the Apocalypse* (Boston: Humanities Press, 2000).

[2] Samuel R. Williamson Jr. *Austria–Hungary and the Origins of the First World War* (New York: St. Martin's Press, 1991), 49–50.

[3] Gina Conrad von Hötzendorf, *Mein Leben mit Conrad von Hötzendorf* (Leipzig: Grethlein, 1935), 30–31.

[4] Franz Conrad von Hötzendorf, *Aus meiner Dienstzeit, 1906–1916,* 5 vols. (Vienna: Rikola Verlag, 1921–25), 2:395–96.

[5] Ibid., 3:464–66.

[6] Gina Conrad von Hötzendorf, *Mein Leben,* 113–14.

[7] Hugo Hantsch, *Leopold Graf Berchtold: Grandseigneur und Staatsmann,* 2 vols. (Graz: Verlag Styria, 1963), 2:558. [Based on Berchtold's notes.]

[8] Conrad, *Aus meiner Dienstzeit,* 4:33–34.

[9] Ibid., 4:36–38.

[10] *Österreich-Ungarns Aussenpolitik von der bosnischen Krise 1908 bis zum Kriegsausbruch 1914,* ed. Ludwig Bittner and Hans Übersberger, 9 vols. (Vienna: Österreichischer Bundesverlag, 1930), 8, no. 10118.

[11] Ibid., 8, no. 10393.

[12] Conrad, *Aus meiner Dienstzeit,* 4:137.

[13] Ibid., 4:151.

4

Bethmann, Moltke, and German Support for Vienna

In the early summer of 1914, German political and military leaders escaped Berlin for more comfortable environs. Not a single major decision maker was left in the German capital on Sunday, June 28, when the Sarajevo assassinations occurred. Exactly one week later, the German kaiser and some of his key advisers made one of the most important decisions in German history: to give Vienna a so-called blank check to deal with the problem of Serbia. After these discussions, many of the leaders returned to their vacations. For his part, the kaiser embarked on his traditional summer cruise on July 6, only a day after wholeheartedly supporting, perhaps even encouraging, the Habsburg government's confrontation with Serbia. How could the German leaders decide to run the risk of war with such apparent casualness in July 1914?

Many historians assert that Germany eagerly accepted war in 1914. To support this conclusion, scholars point to the technical military plan bearing the name of its initial creator, Count Alfred von Schlieffen, chief of the Prussian general staff from 1891 to 1905. With the Schlieffen plan and the substantial changes made to it by his successor, Helmuth von Moltke, Germany had virtually locked itself into mobilization and attack on France through Belgium if Russia or France ever mobilized. Indeed, some military leaders had already advocated war with France during the Moroccan crises of 1905 and 1911 before Russia could rebuild its military forces after its disastrous loss to Japan in 1904–05. Moreover, these views were certainly present in the spring of 1914 among senior German military planners, who thought it better to strike now rather than later. What made these attitudes so dangerous, some contend, was Germany's inability to control civil-military relations and the inappropriate influence of German military leaders and military attitudes in a governing structure reluctantly evolving toward a more regularized, constitutional monarchy.[1]

Whether Germany's leaders wanted war or the political structure failed, fundamental questions arise over the relationship between civilian and military leaders. Did they fulfill their constitutional duties during the July crisis? Did the German constitution and established practices virtually ensure the supremacy of military plans over civilian policies? What alternatives were explored or even pursued? To evaluate these and other questions, this chapter focuses on two of the central figures in the July crisis: Imperial Chancellor Theobald von Bethmann Hollweg and Army Chief of Staff Helmuth von Moltke. Before examining the part played by these two individuals in the July crisis, it is necessary to understand the background of recent German history within which they operated.

BISMARCK, KAISER WILHELM II, AND GERMANY'S *WELTPOLITIK*

The French Revolution and the Napoleonic Wars greatly simplified the political landscape of Germany, which traditionally had been fragmented among kingdoms, duchies, free cities, and religious jurisdictions. While kingdoms and free cities still existed, they were far fewer, and German unification was now a real possibility. But Napoleon's defeat and the ensuing surge of German nationalism brought no unity. Both Vienna, with its long tradition as head of the now-defunct Holy Roman Empire that had once covered most of Germany, and the newly assertive German state of Prussia wanted to dominate any unified country and managed to thwart early efforts at unification.

Then in the 1860s, the Prussian king, Wilhelm I, installed the Prussian diplomat, landowner, and noble Otto von Bismarck as the minister president of Prussia. The new minister had two tasks: (1) to prevent the liberals in the Prussian Landtag (lower house of parliament) from blocking modernization of the Prussian army and (2) to unify Germany under Prussian control. In a series of quick, limited wars, the Prussians defeated Denmark (1863), Austria (1866), and then France in the Franco-Prussian War (1870–71). Austria was thus excluded from the question of German unity, and France lost its provinces of Alsace and Lorraine to Prussia. Prussia's stunning successes left the other German kingdoms no choice but to join the new political structure. Bismarck had achieved German unity while besting the liberals. He later bragged, "Not by speeches and majority votes are the great questions of the day decided . . . but by blood and iron."

The new German empire, or *Reich,* reflected Prussian values and conservative constitutional practices, but with Bismarck's personal stamp on it. The Prussian king became the hereditary German kaiser and the wartime commander in chief of the predominantly Prussian German military forces. The kaiser also controlled German foreign policy and appointed the German chancellor.

The sovereignty of Germany rested not with the people but with the Bundesrat (upper house of the new German parliament), composed of delegates from the kingdoms, the remaining free cities, and duchies. Prussia had enough votes to block any future change in the German constitution. In addition, the newly created German Reichstag (lower house of parliament), found its powers carefully circumscribed. The chancellor was not answerable to it, nor was the Prussian minister of war. Furthermore, to make sure that the Reichstag did not interfere with the army, its power to vote for the military budget was limited to once every seven years. The size of the army and the powers of the kaiser on military matters were enshrined in two key articles, numbers 60 and 63, of the new constitution.

CONSTITUTION OF THE GERMAN REICH

Articles 60 and 63

1871

Article 60

The peacetime standing strength of the German army will be set, as of the 31st of December 1871, at 1% of the population and will be increased pro rata by the individual federal states. Any later peacetime strength of the army will be determined by Reichstag legislation.

Article 63

The total land forces of Germany will form one unified Army, in peace and war under orders of the emperor.

Regiments will be numbered successively throughout the entire army. The basic colors and cut of the Prussian Army uniform will determine dress. Respective army leaders may determine badges.

The emperor has the responsibility and the right to ensure that all troops within the German army are complete and war-ready and that unity is maintained in organization, formation, in armament and command structure, in the training of units as well as in officer qualification. To this end the emperor is authorized to ascertain for himself by inspection the state of the individual contingents and to order measures to address any shortcomings found.

The emperor will determine the strength, organization and structure of the contingents in the imperial army, as well as the organization of the provincial armies, and he has the right to determine the garrisons within federal borders as well as to order the mobilization of any part of the imperial army.[2]

Bismarck had thus ensured that the strength of the Prussian army would match Germany's population growth, that its administration would be firmly Prussian, and that the authority of the kaiser was unambiguous. He had also created a set of constitutional arrangements that would make the Reichstag's ability to intrude into military matters very difficult. As we shall see later in this chapter, Kaiser Wilhelm II would further strengthen his hold over the army and over his ministers and the Reichstag after he came to power in 1888.

Bismarck had achieved German unity, retained royal control of the army, and kept Prussian military values intact. But the chancellor also realized that Germany needed time to adjust to the fact of unity, while the rest of Europe needed reassurance that Germany had become a satiated power. Thus he established the Dual Alliance (1879) with Austria–Hungary and sought good relations with Russia to frustrate any French attempt to avenge the military and political defeats of 1870 and 1871. He added Italy to the alliance in 1882 to create the Triple Alliance, while seeking to remain on good terms with Britain.

While Bismarck's system largely kept the peace, his dominance came to an end after 1888 and the accession to the Prussian throne of Wilhelm II. The young, insecure kaiser, a grandson of Queen Victoria, wanted to be the kaiser in title and in fact; he did not wish to share power with the older man. When, in March 1890, Wilhelm II asked Bismarck to resign, the diplomatic consequences were almost immediate. Unwisely, Wilhelm allowed Bismarck's carefully constructed relationship with Russia to end, prompting Russia to negotiate an alliance with France during 1893–94. Germany now found itself surrounded by a potentially hostile alliance.

Wilhelm's determination to embark on a global policy of *Weltpolitik* (expansionist world policy) also offended Britain and later most of the rest of Europe. But a more significant strategic threat came with the passage of the German naval law of 1898. Berlin now embarked on a policy of constructing battleships, a move that challenged British naval supremacy. After 1900, the rate of construction and the number of ships increased. The destabilizing Anglo-German naval race had begun. Not surprisingly, there was now incentive for London to draw closer to Paris and Saint Petersburg and to create, after 1907, the Triple Entente.

The belligerent tone of *Weltpolitik* and navalism can be seen in some of Kaiser Wilhelm's remarks in 1900, comments that tell much about his new policies and about his ego.

WILHELM II
Comments on Weltpolitik
1900

And as My grandfather [did] for the Army, so I will, for My Navy, carry on unerringly and in similar manner the work of reorganization so that it may also stand on an equal footing with My armed forces on land and so that through it the German Empire may also be in a position abroad to attain that place which it has not yet reached. . . .

No great decision may now be made without the German Empire and the German Emperor. . . .

The Crown sends its rays through "Grace of God" into palaces as well as huts and—pardon me, if I dare say so—Europe and the world listen intently in order to hear "what says and thinks the German Emperor?," and not, what is the will of his chancellor! . . . For ever, and ever there will only be one true Emperor in the world, and that is the German Kaiser, without regard for his person or his traits, alone by right of thousand-year tradition and his chancellor has to obey![3]

Although the government funded three generations of battleships, navalism and *Weltpolitik* actually brought few gains. Instead, their pursuit saw two near war crises and a series of humbling diplomatic defeats. Disturbed by the rapid growth of German naval power, the

British began to expand their own fleet and strengthen their ties with France and Russia. These developments in turn increased Germany's fear of encirclement and made it consequently more dependent upon its alliance with Austria–Hungary.

In the decade before the First World War, Wilhelm and his advisers successively alarmed the other European governments. Surprised by the creation of the Anglo-French entente in 1904, Berlin decided to test its relevance for Morocco, unaware that London had pledged the north African country to France as a part of the arrangement. On March 31, 1905, the kaiser landed at Tangier, Morocco, and announced German support for the country's independence. The resulting international crisis strengthened, not weakened, the entente. Then in March 1909, Berlin belligerently ended the crisis provoked by Austria–Hungary's annexation of Bosnia-Herzegovina, issuing a virtual ultimatum to Russia to stop its support of the Serbian government. Saint Petersburg retreated but did not forget. And on July 1, 1911, the Germans provoked still another crisis over Morocco, this time sending a gunboat to the port of Agadir and blatantly seeking some colonial compensation in return for agreeing to total French control of Morocco. Once more the Anglo-French relationship held firm, and the Germans retreated. This diplomatic defeat, as we shall see later in this chapter, prompted a major debate in Germany about its army's readiness for war.

In the last two years before July 1914, the German government was more circumspect. It restrained Vienna during the Balkan Wars when the Habsburg leadership seriously considered war with Serbia, and the frantic race with Britain for naval supremacy eased somewhat. Since 1904, German diplomacy had often rattled European chancelleries, but it had always drawn back before an actual conflict. In the July 1914 crisis, that did not happen. Why it did not is a central question for understanding the origins of the Great War.

MILITARY INFLUENCE IN PRE-1914 GERMANY

In pre-1914 Europe, no country exemplified the influence of militarism more than Germany. Foreign observers commented on the degree to which military values appeared to dominate every feature of German life, from the kaiser's two hundred uniforms, to civilian reserve officers' penchant for wearing their uniforms whenever possible, to the acclaim given military leaders. The Prussian values of the great landowners, with their feudal pasts, were also associated with this militarism: blind obedience to the state, the role of the aristocracy, the need for order, the absolute power of the Hohenzollern dynasty of which Wilhelm II was the current representative. Reinforcing these values was the respect given the Prussian general staff, seen by many as the epitome of a professional military organization, with its annual military maneuvers designed to impress all with German power. The military values were also inculcated by the conscription that every German male faced. Not surprising, the new policy of *Weltpolitik* drew upon these values and in turn buttressed them, as did the new navalism, which coopted industry and labor grateful for the economic benefits of naval construction. The kaiser, for his part, frequently appeared with his generals, all of them wearing dazzling rows of medals, though almost none of them had experienced war since 1870.

The role of military values in German life and culture can be seen from the enthusiastic reception given to the lectures and writings of two apparently very different individuals: Professor Heinrich von Treitschke of the University of Berlin and General Friedrich von Bernhardi. Treitschke, a former academic liberal whose views had been transformed by Bismarck's success, supported a policy of militarism and power. For years, his rousing nationalistic lectures rallied generations of impressionable German students, future leaders, military officers, and government officials.

HEINRICH VON TREITSCHKE

Politics

1897–1898

The next essential function of the State is the conduct of war. The long oblivion into which this principle had fallen is a proof of how effeminate the science of government had become in civilian hands. In our century this sentimentality was dissipated by Clausewitz,* but a one-sided

Karl von Clausewitz: legendary Prussian military theorist and writer.

materialism arose in its place, after the fashion of the Manchester school* seeing in man a biped creature whose destiny lies in buying cheap and selling dear. It is obvious that this idea is not compatible with war, and it is only since the last war† that a sounder theory arose of the State and its military power.

Without war no State could be. All those we know of arose through war, and the protection of their members by armed force remains their primary and essential task. War, therefore, will endure to the end of history, as long as there is multiplicity of States. The laws of human thought and of human nature forbid any alternative, neither is one to be wished for. The blind worshipper of eternal peace falls into the error of isolating the State, or dreams of one which is universal, which we have already seen to be at variance with reason.[4]

* *Manchester school:* refers to the British free trade, laissez-faire approach to economics.
† *The last war:* the Franco-Prussian War of 1870–71.

After the turn of the century, General Friedrich von Bernhardi assumed the departed Treitschke's mantle. Recognized as an outstanding military writer, the general's work, *Germany and the Next War,* drew wide public attention, going through nine editions by July 1914. Completed after the Second Moroccan Crisis, Bernhardi's book reflected the military's dismay at the peaceful outcome of the crisis. His writings stirred German nationalists who accepted the necessity, even the urgency for war. Borrowing from the theory of social Darwinism, that societies could only advance through relentless competition with one another, Bernhardi praised the aggressive pursuit of an offensive war.

FRIEDRICH VON BERNHARDI

Germany and the Next War

1914

Everyone will, within certain limits, admit that the endeavors to diminish the dangers of war and to mitigate the suffering which war entails are justifiable. It is an incontestable fact that war temporarily disturbs industrial life, interrupts quiet economic development, brings widespread misery with it, and emphasizes the brutality of man. It is therefore a most desirable consummation if wars for trivial reasons should be rendered impossible. . . . But it is quite another matter if the object is to abolish war entirely and to deny its necessary place in historical development.

This aspiration is directly antagonistic to the great universal laws which rule all life. War is a biological necessity of the first importance, a regulative element in the life of mankind which cannot be dispensed with, since without it an unhealthy development will follow, which excludes every advancement of the race, and therefore all real civilization. "War is the father of all things." The sages of antiquity long before Darwin recognized this.

The struggle for existence is, in the life of Nature, the basis of all healthy development. All existing things show themselves to be the result of contesting forces. So in the life of man the struggle is not merely the destructive, but the life-giving principle. "To supplant or to be supplanted is the essence of life," says Goethe,* and the strong life gains the upper hand. The law of the stronger holds good everywhere. Those forms survive which are able to procure themselves the most favorable conditions of life and to assert themselves in the universal economy of Nature. The weaker succumb. This struggle is regulated and restrained by the unconscious sway of biological laws and by the interplay of opposite forces. In the plant world and the animal world this process is worked out in unconscious tragedy. In the human race it is consciously carried out and regulated by social ordinances. The man of strong will and strong intellect tries by every means to assert himself, the ambitious strive to rise, and in this effort the individual is far from being guided merely by the consciousness of right. The life-work and the life-struggle of many men are determined, doubtless, by unselfish and ideal motives, but to a far greater extent the less noble passions— craving for possessions, enjoyment and honor, envy and the thirst for revenge—determine men's actions. Still more often, perhaps, it is the need to live which brings down even natures of a higher mold in the universal struggle for existence and enjoyment.

There can be no doubt on this point. The nation is made up of individuals, the State of communities. The motive which influences each member is prominent in the whole body. It is a persistent struggle for possessions, power, and sovereignty, which primarily governs the relations of one nation to another, and right is respected so far only as it is compatible with advantage. So long as there are men who have human feelings and aspirations, so long as there are nations who strive for an enlarged sphere of activity, so long will conflicting interests come into being and occasions for making war arise.[5]

*Johann Wolfgang von Goethe: German Romantic writer, 1749–1832.

Invoking the science of Darwin, the literary prowess of Goethe, and *Weltpolitik,* Bernhardi encouraged a generation to embrace the merits of war. Implicit in his call, of course, was the belief that Germany would prevail in any future conflict. That conflict was not long in coming.

BETHMANN HOLLWEG AND THE STRUGGLE TO CONTROL THE MILITARY

Theobald von Bethmann Hollweg became chancellor of Germany in June 1909. For the next eight years, he struggled almost continuously to restrain the German military leadership, with limited success. His decisions in July 1914 would be fateful for the onset of war and for the future of Germany (Figure 5). When Bethmann Hollweg was born in 1856, his family had a newly acquired 7,500-acre estate at Hohenfinow near Berlin. His father, though aspiring to noble status, was actually a first-generation landowner, and his independent, reflective attitudes were shared by the younger Bethmann. In 1869, the future German leader went to the famous Schulpforta, which counted among its alumni Leopold von Ranke and Friedrich Nietzsche, and then he did almost a year of military service before starting his legal education. Self-doubting and intensely introspective during these years, Bethmann read copiously, including Darwin. In 1878, he moved to Berlin and soon entered the Prussian bureaucracy and began a rapidly ascending career.

In 1899, at the age of forty-three, Bethmann became the youngest ever governor of Brandenburg, the central Prussian province. Six years later, he became the Prussian minister of the interior, overseeing all of the Prussian bureaucracies. In this office, he learned how to be the practical politician, seeking compromise, winning respect for his moderate policies, and recognizing that the regressive electoral laws in Prussia needed change. He understood that the success of the German economy was altering the character of Prussia, causing new social and political alignments. Just two years later, Bethmann moved to the Imperial Ministry of the Interior. Again his reputation for hard work and moderate views served him well, though others thought he lacked imagination and had limited horizons. Nonetheless, his experience made him chancellor when Chancellor Bülow and Wilhelm had exhausted each other's patience. Kaiser Wilhelm later wrote of Bethmann in his memoirs.[6]

**Figure 5.
Theobald von
Bethmann Hollweg**

His stern appearance
concealed an often
melancholy, self-
doubting personality.
His decision to back
Kaiser Wilhelm II's
desire to support
Austria–Hungary in
July 1914 virtually
guaranteed a war.
Hulton/Archive by
Getty Images.

WILHELM II

Memoirs

1922

I had been well acquainted since my youth with Herr von Bethmann Hollweg. When I was in active service for the first time in 1877, as Lieutenant in the Sixth Company of the First Infantry Guard Regiment, it was quartered once at Hohenfinow, the home of old Herr von Bethmann, father of the Chancellor. I was attracted by the pleasant family circle there, which was presided over by Frau von Bethmann, a most worthy lady, born of Swiss nationality, amiable and refined.

Often, as Prince and later as Emperor, I went to Hohenfinow to visit the old gentleman, and I was received on every occasion by the young head of the rural district administration; at that time neither of us imagined that he would become Imperial Chancellor under me.

From these visits an intimate relationship sprang up little by little, which served to increase steadily my esteem for the diligence, ability, and noble character of Bethmann, which were much to my liking. These qualities clung to him throughout his career.

As Chief President and as Imperial Secretary for the Interior Bethmann gave a good account of himself, and, while occupying the last-named post, made his appearance successfully before the Reichstag.

Co-operation with the Chancellor was easy for me. With Bethmann I kept up my custom of daily visits whenever possible, and of discussing fully with him, while walking in the garden of the Chancellor's palace, on politics, events of the day, special bills, and occurrences and of hearing reports from him. It was also a pleasure for me to visit the Chancellor's home, since Bethmann's spouse was the very model of a genuine German wife, one whose simple distinction earned the esteem of every visitor, while her winning kindness of heart spread around her an atmosphere of cordiality. During the Bethmann régime the custom of holding small evening receptions, instituted by Prince Bülow and most enjoyable to me, was continued, and this enabled me to keep on associating informally with men of all circles and walks of life.[7]

In discussing Bethmann's appointment with the kaiser, Prince Bülow later wrote, "'For domestic policy Bethmann is certainly, all things considered, the best. He will keep the left on the string and bring back the Centre, and the Conservatives, as far as I know, are well disposed to him. Only he does not understand anything about foreign policy.' The Emperor brushed this aside. 'Foreign policy,' he said gaily, 'you can leave to me.'"[8] Bülow's summation proved very accurate. The kaiser had chosen Bethmann to help Germany through domestic difficulties, and the chancellor's initial reform program served conservative goals. This pleased the kaiser, who also appreciated Bethmann's loyalty. His willingness to negotiate with political parties that demanded greater participatory government and reduced military "presence" should not obscure his fundamental conservatism. Moreover, his pragmatic political program perpetuated the conflicting tensions of the German Reich, tensions that increased with the growing political presence of the Social Democratic Party in the Reichstag after the 1912 elections.

But it was in the realm of foreign and defense matters that Bethmann would face his greatest challenges. He sought repeatedly but in vain to constrain German naval expenditures and reach some political understanding with Britain. Nor were his efforts to restrain the army more successful. Making all of this more difficult was the Second Moroccan Crisis, since the conservatives and the military resented the diplomatic concessions to the French and demanded (and got) still larger forces to thwart such a defeat in the future. And, as the Balkan Wars developed, the military establishment began to talk about the need to check the Russian threat.

Not only did the kaiser's leadership style make controlling the military difficult, so also did the constitutional arrangements that had evolved since 1870. The Prussian minister of war no longer had to answer more than cursory questions in the Reichstag. The chief of the Prussian general staff reported directly to the kaiser, and thus the war minister had no reason to answer operational questions about the army in any political forum. To complicate matters further, the kaiser's military cabinets controlled all officer personnel matters, resulting in a constant coterie of military officers around the monarch. The militarism that pervaded the imperial court flowed over into all aspects of public life.

His political career dependent on the will of the kaiser, Bethmann often found himself unable to assuage public rancor and the parliament's frustration over increasing military spending, and the Reichstag finally overwhelmingly supported a vote of no confidence in him in 1914. Although the chancellor remained in office, he now avoided the Reichstag as much as possible because cooperation with political parties could cause him to lose the kaiser's backing. Thus in the spring of 1914, Bethmann felt in no position to challenge Wilhelm and the military. Given this constitutional background, the army's role in the July crisis takes on special importance, not least because of the assertion that the army pressed for preventive war. Was this another case when the monarchical structure favored a military outcome?

MOLTKE PREPARES FOR WAR

If Bethmann's family had recent noble roots, the Moltke family represented the tenacious tradition of almost feudal noble ancestry. Born in 1848, Moltke distinguished himself as a young lieutenant during the Franco-Prussian War. Of all the military leaders in 1914, he had had the most significant leadership role as a very young officer. It did not hurt, of course, that his uncle was Field Marshall Helmuth von Moltke ("the elder"), whose victories had united Germany. From 1882 until 1891, Moltke the younger served as his uncle's adjutant; then in 1891, Kaiser Wilhelm made him his personal aide-de-camp. In 1896, he became a colonel, and within six years he had achieved the rank of lieutenant general, all the while serving as the kaiser's aide. He and Wilhelm were in such frequent contact that the kaiser called him by the familiar *Du* as a sign of their friendship (Figure 6).

But as Moltke's critics noted at the time of his appointment as Prussian chief of staff in 1905, he had never commanded an army corps or even been the chief of staff of a corps. In fact, in 1904, then Chancellor Bülow worried about the kaiser's appointing Moltke, commenting, "His Majesty can afford to have a bad Reich-Chancellor some time; . . . He can also have a bad Minister of War some time. . . . But under all circumstances the Kaiser must always have the best man as Chief of the General Staff, because the outcome of a war, that we may face any day, depends on the choice of leader for the army."[9] But the kaiser appointed him anyway, not least because of their friendship.

Moltke mirrored many of the traits of his age. Cultured and philosophical, he played the cello, like Conrad, was a painter, discussed the newest books with his wife, carried a copy of Goethe's *Faust* with him, and dipped into the writings of nationalist historian Treitschke. His letters suggest that he was an anti-Semite and a rabid nationalist and was given to bouts of pessimism mixed with bellicosity. More suspect to many was the couple's fascination with the world of the occult and spiritualism. One of his detractors asserted that "above all, he [Moltke] was a religious dreamer . . . [who] believed in guardian angels, faith-healing, and similar nonsense."[10] Interestingly, upon his appointment, the new chief moved away from any public association with spiritualism, perhaps mindful of his new position. He was also aware that his military colleagues were constantly comparing him with his famous uncle.

Moltke had succeeded General Alfred von Schlieffen, the chief from 1891 until late 1905, when the latter retired at the age of nearly seventy-five. The 1905 Schlieffen "plan," drafted during the Russo-Japanese War when Russia appeared unable to help France and when Schlieffen wanted a preventive war against France, was not intended to be a final product. Staff procedures called for a complete reworking of military

Figure 6.   Wilhelm II and Helmuth von Moltke
These two friends were often at army maneuvers. The kaiser's decision to
support Austria–Hungary set Moltke's inflexible war plans into operation.
Despite all of his militant talk, Moltke's nerves failed in September 1914,
and he was the first of the leaders to be sacked.
SV-Bilderdienst.

plans each year. Schlieffen produced a working draft for a two-front
war, calling for Germany to attack and defeat France first in the west,
then turn east and remove the Russian threat. This remained the overall strategy in 1914. The bulk of German forces would be on the right
flank (northern side) and sweep through Belgium and Holland on their
way to France. Schlieffen viewed the risk of British intervention in
defense of Belgium as acceptable. Moltke inherited this offensive military strategy from Schlieffen, but he and his general staff revised elements of the plan over the next eight years (Map 5). Many German
military critics erroneously single out Moltke's weakening of the right

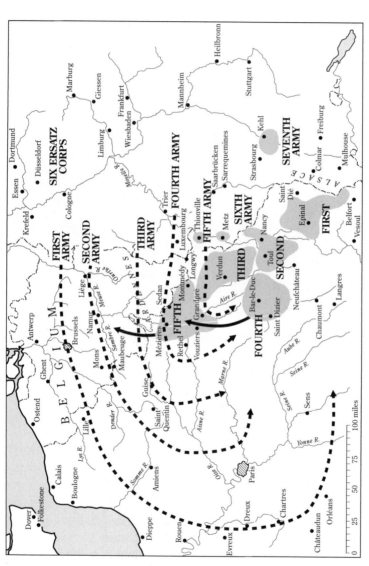

Map 5. Plan XVII and the Schlieffen-Moltke Plan

From *The Politics of Grand Strategy: Britain and France Prepare for War, 1904–1914*, Second Edition, by Samuel R. Williamson Jr., p. 225. (The Ashfield Press, 1990; publication copyright now held by Humanities Press of Prometheus).

flank for the failure of the German offensive in 1914 and ignore the larger reworking of the plan by Moltke's staff. General Schlieffen, even in retirement, encouraged his own lionization by his critiques of Moltke's adjustments while steadfastly defending the original concept.

ALFRED VON SCHLIEFFEN

Memorandum

December 28, 1912

The *whole* of Germany must throw itself on *one* enemy—the strongest, most powerful, most dangerous enemy: and that can only be the Anglo-French!

Austria need not worry: the Russian army intended against Germany will not invade Galicia before the die is cast in the West. And Austria's fate will be decided not on the Bug* but on the Seine!

Against Germany, the French intend to hold a position extending from the frontier at Belfort along the Upper Moselle as far as Toul, from there following the course of the Meuse to Verdun and leaning on neutral Belgian territory as far as the neighbourhood of Montmédy. In front of this position they will further occupy the passes across the Vosges, the fortified city of Nancy, Manonvillers, the heights right of the Meuse between Toul and Verdun, and also Longwy. Should the Germans succeed in breaking through the left wing of this position, they will still find the enemy behind the Meuse between Verdun and Mézières. Below the latter the river is not easily accessible. The first important crossing, farther north, is blocked by the fortress of Givet. The Germans cannot therefore count on crossing the Meuse without serious fighting so long as it runs through French territory. Beyond the Givet the rivers enter Belgium. This country is regarded as neutral, but in fact it is not. More than thirty years ago it made Liège and Namur into strong fortresses to prevent Germany from invading its territory, but towards France it has left its frontiers open. The French will therefore be free to send as many reinforcements as they wish into the position which the Belgians apparently intend to occupy between these two fortresses. The English may also be present. In 1911 they threatened to land with 180,000 men in Antwerp.† On its landward side the latter is heavily fortified. It is unlikely that the Dutch will bring their Scheldt batteries into action

---

* *The Bug:* river in southwestern Poland, then a part of Russia.
† No such plan ever existed in London.

against the English, upon whose goodwill they depend for their colonies. Therefore via Antwerp, or if need be Dunkirk, the English can join up with the Belgians and French in the position of Liège-Namur. From there the three, or two, of them will be able not only to prevent the Germans crossing the Meuse between Givet and Liège, but also most effectively to flank a German attack on the French position Belfort-Mézières.

Unless, therefore, the Germans are prepared to suffer a serious defeat, they are obliged to attack the offensive flank which the Belgians have added to the French position. This can be done if at an early stage a German army crosses the Meuse below Liège, wheels left and invades Belgium and France left of the Meuse and Sambre, while a second army supports the attack between Givet and [Namur on] the right of those rivers, a third advances on the sector Mézières-Verdun, and a fourth advances on the front Verdun-Belfort. . . .

A successful march through Belgium on both sides of the Meuse is therefore the prerequisite of a victory. It will succeed beyond doubt, if it is only the Belgian army which tries to obstruct it. But it will be very difficult if the English army, and perhaps even part of the French, is present. The area between Namur and Antwerp is so confined that it can easily be blocked by the English and Belgian corps, supported if necessary by a few French corps. In this case, the advance of the second army on the right of the Sambre must create a breathing space. If they, too, find the Meuse blocked between Namur and Mézières, help can come only from an attack on the whole front, with a breakthrough at some point after large-scale heavy artillery preparation.

But in general we must put our trust in an overwhelming right wing, which will progressively bring the whole line forward.[11]

An essential component of the final Schlieffen-Moltke plan was that once Germany mobilized, war followed. The overwhelming German thrust would be the northern flanking attack, violating Belgian neutrality, and then invading northern France. Unlike Schlieffen, Moltke would not violate Dutch neutrality, and he strengthened German defenses southward to meet a substantial French threat. Later critics blamed this allocation of forces for fatally weakening the northern flank. In retrospect, his actions appear prudent, given early French successes in this sector in 1914.

Moltke's revised plan made three critical assumptions. First, that the British would intervene, and thus German violation of Belgian neutrality as a trigger for British involvement was a moot point. Second, in 1909, after a series of discussions about war plans with his Habsburg counterpart, General Conrad von Hötzendorf, Moltke assumed that Austria–Hungary would launch its initial attacks against the Russians, relieving pressure on Germany while it attacked France. Conrad, however, concluded that Germany would intimidate the Russians long enough for Austria–Hungary to launch its first attack against Belgrade, not against the Russians. This misunderstanding surfaced during the implementation of the war plans in 1914, with disastrous results. Third, by 1914, Moltke worried that the idea of modest German forces holding the Russians in the east had become a strategic risk because of ongoing improvements in Russian mobilization efforts. Thus in late July, Moltke urgently pleaded for German mobilization when the Russians initiated "premobilization" measures.

For his part, Moltke always believed the German armies were ready for war. His bellicosity thus marked him as an aggressive and ambitious general. A letter to his wife during the Second Moroccan Crisis reveals much about the man and his readiness for combat.

HELMUTH VON MOLTKE

Letter to Eliza von Moltke

August 19, 1911

I am thoroughly fed up with this wretched Morocco affair. . . . If once again we crawl out of this affair with our tail between our legs, if we cannot pluck up the courage to take an energetic line which we are prepared to enforce with the sword, then I despair of the future of the German empire. Then I shall quit. But before that I shall propose that we do away with the army and place ourselves under the protection of Japan; then we can concentrate on making money and become country bumpkins.[12]

After the Moroccan crisis, Moltke pressed for, and got, sizable increases in the strength of the Prussian standing army. An additional 140,000 troops were added to the army after 1912, so that it reached 782,000 men. In December 1912, when the kaiser and some of his senior military advisers discussed war, the general argued the sooner the better. These remarks, which matched those of some of his counterparts elsewhere, became a bit more urgent in early 1914, as Russian manpower continued to expand and signs appeared that the French, Russian, and British general staffs had been working on joint plans. Although Sir Edward Grey had denied such reports in the past (and would continue to do so, as we shall see), a German spy in the Russian embassy in London said otherwise. Fear of these developments heightened Germany's sense of danger, and no one was more alarmed than Bethmann, as is clearly shown in the following exchanges with the German ambassador in London and his staff's reactions to them.

THEOBALD VON BETHMANN HOLLWEG

Letter to Prince Lichnowsky

June 16, 1914

It will not have escaped your Excellency that the article in *Birchewija Wjedomosti*, which is known to stem from the [Russian] Minister of War, General Suchomlinow, caused a considerable stir in Germany. As a matter of fact, probably no officially inspired article has ever revealed the warlike tendencies of the Russian military faction as recklessly as this press statement does. It is probably written too clumsily to strengthen French chauvinism permanently. On the other hand, one cannot fail to note its considerable repercussion on German public opinion.

Hitherto only the most extreme Pan-Germans and militarists insisted that Russia was deliberately scheming to attack us, but now calmer politicians are also beginning to incline to that view. The first result is a demand for renewed, immediate, extensive strengthening of the Army. As things are now, this will produce competition with the navy, which refuses to be shortchanged when anything is done for the army. I mention *very confidentially* that since His Majesty the Kaiser is already quite set in these views, I fear that the summer and autumn will see a fresh outburst of armaments fever.

Although the uncertainty of conditions in Russia makes it hard to discover the real aims of Russian policy with any precision, and although, disposed as we are politically, we must consider that Russia, more than all the Great European Powers, is prepared to run the risk of a great warlike adventure, nevertheless I still do not think that Russia is planning to make war on us soon. She wishes rather—and we cannot reproach her—to be secured with more extensive military armaments than during the last troubles in the Balkans, presuming a new outbreak there. A European conflagration—if there is to be one—will be determined entirely by the attitudes of Germany and England. If we act together as joint guarantors of peace in Europe (in doing so we are hampered neither by the engagements of the Triple Alliance nor of the Triple Entente, *so far as we pursue that aim from the start according to a jointly conceived plan*), war may be averted. Otherwise any minor conflict of interests between Russia and Austria–Hungary may kindle the war-torch.

It is obvious that more violent agitation by German chauvinists and armament fanatics will hamper such Anglo-German cooperation quite as much as any secret pressure from French and Russian chauvinism upon the British Cabinet. Germany will never be able to give up growth of her army in relation to the growth of her population. There is no thought of extending the Naval Law; but within the limits of that law the commissioning of extra cruisers for foreign service, the arming and manning of battleships, etc., will demand ever-increasing expenditures. Yet it does make a great difference whether such measures come forward as the result of gradual and quiet development or are undertaken in panic under pressure from public opinion that is excited and full of war fears.

It is very gratifying that Sir Edward Grey firmly denied in the House of Commons those rumors of an English-Russian naval agreement and that his denial was emphasized in the *Westminster Gazette*. Had these rumors had substance, even if only to the extent that the English and Russian navies planned cooperation in a future war against Germany (similar to the agreements which England made with France at the time of the Morocco crisis), it would have highly agitated Russian and French chauvinism, and public opinion here would have reacted in justified alarm that would have stimulated a 'navy scare' and renewed poisoning of nervous tension which Europe has experienced in the last few years, the further consequences would have been unforeseeable. In any case, the idea of a common English-German effort to foster peace would have been fatefully endangered from the very beginning by threats of emerging complications.

I most respectfully bid Your Excellency to express my special gratitude to Sir Edward Grey for his open and straightforward declarations and with it to express in an informal and cautious manner those general observations which I mentioned above.

I await with particular interest your report on the reception you encounter with Sir Edward Grey.[13]

PRINCE LICHNOWSKY

Letter to Berlin

June 24, 1914

I took the opportunity on my visit today to express to Sir Edward Grey the thanks of Your Excellency for the frank and honest statement he made in the Lower House disavowing the rumors of an alleged Anglo-Russian naval convention. I stated in addition that Your Excellency welcomed his explanations so much the more gladly inasmuch as they tended not immaterially to dissipate the fears to which of late a large portion of the German people had been subject in connection with the state of our foreign relations. It was principally Russia that was supplying the food on which these fears fed, and was responsible for the resulting efforts for increases of our armed strength, and, in this connection, I could point particularly to the article in the *Nowoje Wremja,* which had aroused an unpleasant sensation in Germany. In view of the possibility that a new war in the Balkans might break out and that Russia might then decide to conduct a somewhat more active foreign policy, it seemed to us to be of the greatest importance that the intimate contact which had existed between us during the last crisis should be maintained in the face of all future occurrences, in order that we might successfully encounter any warlike policy on the basis of a common understanding. I further called the attention of the Minister to the fact that only by the maintenance of the German-British intimacy, coupled with our conviction that he too would endeavor in the future, by the use of his extensive influence at Paris and Petersburg, to oppose all adventurous impulses, would it be possible for the Imperial Government to check the armament fever that was on the rise in our own country at the present time, and to keep our defensive measures within their present compass. . . .

The Minister took cognizance of my remarks with visible pleasure, and stated that he, too, was endeavoring to move forward with us hand in hand and to remain in close touch with us concerning all matters that came up. With this in mind, he had just discussed the present eastern situation, and believed that this was the way best adapted to our mutual aims. So far as Russia is concerned, he had not the slightest reason for doubting the pacific inclinations of the Russian Government. He did not need to begin now by assuring me that Count Benckendorff was pursuing no anti-German policy here. The Emperor Nicholas and Mr. Sazonoff always expressed themselves toward Sir George W. Buchanan in the most peaceable manner; though it could not be denied that Mr. Sazonoff had the desire that the Triple Entente should make a somewhat more robust appearance as a counterweight to the solid block of the Triple Alliance. But so far as concerned the article in the *Nowoje Wremja,* to which I had referred, he, the Minister, knew absolutely nothing. He added, smilingly, that just last evening he had seen in the specified paper a fierce attack on Great Britain on account of the Persian oil agreement. And so far as France was concerned, he knew from reliable sources and was furthermore strengthened in his opinion by foreign— for instance, American—reports, that the French felt not the least inclination toward a war.

There existed, so Sir Edward told me, no agreements between Great Britain and her Entente companions that had not been made public. He could reassert this to me as he had stated it in Parliament, and he was glad to be able to add that nothing would ever occur at his instigation to turn the head of this combination offensively against Germany. He also believed that in our country of late, a more satisfied view of this matter had begun to take hold. He wished, however, to be quite frank with me, not desiring that I should be led in any way to misunderstand him, so that he would take this occasion to tell me that in spite of the facts mentioned above, his relations with the other two allies were today, as always, most intimate, and that they had lost none of their earlier cohesion. He stood in permanently close touch with the Governments concerned on all important matters.

I thanked the Minister for his confidential explanations, which he made in an agreeable and friendly manner, and replied that they offered us no ground for objection, as long as he made use of his powerful influence in favor of peace and moderation.

Lichnowsky[14]

ARTHUR VON ZIMMERMANN

Letter to Theobald von Bethmann Hollweg

June 27, 1914

In this conference [the meeting in London on June 24, 1914], as was to be expected, Lichnowsky was once again put completely into swaddling-clothes by Grey, and allowed his conviction that he was dealing with an honorable and truth-loving statesman to be strengthened anew. There is nothing left to do but to give Lichnowsky some naturally very cautious hints concerning the secret but absolutely reliable reports we are getting from Petersburg, which permit no doubt at all to arise as to the existence of permanent political and military agreements between

England and France or concerning the initiation already in progress
of transactions between England and Russia directed toward similar
results.[15]

These exchanges did little for Grey's reputation in Berlin. For
months, Bethmann had hoped that he might ease Anglo-German tensions. But the French pressure on London to start Anglo-Russian
naval conversations, thus matching the military and naval ones with
Britain, had backfired. The German spy had incontrovertible proof of
what some in Berlin had long suspected. This new information had a
thoroughly unsettling effect on Bethmann and his associates, while
reinforcing the fears of Moltke and his colleagues as well. In this
already feisty atmosphere came the sudden news from Sarajevo of the
murder of the archduke and his wife.

BERLIN AND THE JULY CRISIS

The deaths in Sarajevo confronted Berlin with a major foreign policy
crisis. Bethmann and Moltke were two of the key participants along
with Kaiser Wilhelm II. As the crisis unfolded, did the chancellor seriously consider diplomatic options, or did military interests and pressures dictate Germany's response? Or is it more appropriate to argue
that the civil-military relationship changed once war became likely in
late July with the ominous threats of Russian mobilization?

The deaths of Franz Ferdinand and Sophie were repugnant to a
monarchist like Bethmann. Like his colleagues in Austria–Hungary,
Conrad and Berchtold, Bethmann viewed the assassins' defiance as
symptomatic of rising nationalism and dangerous democratic influences. The German leadership thoroughly agreed that the assassinations threatened the integrity of Austria–Hungary and that Vienna had
a right, even a duty, to resolve the persistent Serbian challenge to the
territories it controlled. Both civil and military leaders in Germany
believed that failure to punish the Serbs this time risked diminishing
the prestige of Germany's only reliable ally and further threatening
the German empire.

In early July, the civilian leadership and the kaiser made the first,
fateful decisions. As we saw in chapter 3, the Habsburg leaders sent

Alexander Hoyos from the Foreign Ministry to Berlin with Emperor Franz Joseph's letter requesting support and with Berchtold's memorandum about Habsburg plans. Veteran Habsburg ambassador Count Ladislaus Szögyény-Marich met with Wilhelm II on Sunday, July 5, at the New Palace in Potsdam, just outside Berlin. After a frank lunchtime discussion, the kaiser assured the ambassador that Berlin would support Vienna in any action against Serbia, even at the risk of a wider war, pending Bethmann's agreement. The ambassador's report conveys the tone of the discussion.

LADISLAUS SZÖGYÉNY-MARICH

Telegram to Vienna

July 5, 1914

When I had informed Kaiser Wilhelm that I had an autograph letter from His Imp. and Roy. Apostolic Majesty, which Count Hoyos had just brought and which I was to give to him, I received an invitation to lunch with Their Majesties at noon in the Neues Palais. I gave the autograph letter and the enclosed memoir into the hands of His Majesty. In my presence the Kaiser read both with the greatest attention. The first thing he assured me was that he had expected some serious step on our part towards Serbia, but that at the same time he must confess that the detailed statement of His Majesty made him regard a serious European complication possible and that he could give no definite answer before having taken council with the Imperial chancellor.

After lunch, when I again called attention to the seriousness of the situation, the Kaiser authorized me to inform our gracious Majesty that we might in this case, as in all others, rely upon Germany's full support.

He must, as he said before, first hear what the Imperial Chancellor has to say, but he did not doubt in the least that Herr von Bethmann Hollweg would agree with him. Especially as far as our action against Serbia was concerned. But it was his (Kaiser Wilhelm's) opinion that this action must not be delayed. Russia's attitude will no doubt be hostile, but [for] this he had been for years prepared, and should a war between Austria–Hungary and Russia be unavoidable, we might be convinced that Germany, our old faithful ally, would stand at our side. Russia at the present time was in no way prepared for war, and would think twice before it appealed to arms. But it will certainly set other powers on to the Triple Alliance and add fuel to the fire in the Balkans. He understands perfectly well that His Apostolic Majesty in his well-known love of peace would be reluctant to march into Serbia; but if we had really recognised the necessity of warlike action against Serbia, he (Kaiser Wilhelm) would regret if we did not make use of the present moment, which is all in our favor. Kaiser Wilhelm intends leaving tomorrow morning for Kiel, whence he starts for his northern tour; but before leaving, His Majesty will discourse with the Imperial Chancellor on the subject in question.[16]

Later that Sunday afternoon Chancellor Bethmann, with Arthur von Zimmermann (the undersecretary for foreign affairs) accompanying him, arrived at Potsdam to meet with the kaiser and discuss the Austrian request. At length, and fully cognizant of some (though certainly not all) of the risks, they resolved to support the Habsburg monarchy, whatever it decided. Attitudes of "now or never" and a sense that "the time was ripe" to crush Pan-Slavism resonated in Berlin. The Prussian war minister, General von Falkenhayn, the chief military figure present in Berlin and at the meeting, wasted no time in reporting in a confidential letter the kaiser's decision to General von Moltke, who was on vacation in Carlsbad.

ERICH VON FALKENHAYN

Letter to Helmuth von Moltke

July 5, 1914

This afternoon H.M. the Kaiser and King sent for me at the Neues Palais to inform me that Austria–Hungary seemed resolved no longer to tolerate the hatching of intrigues against Austria on the Balkan Peninsula and therefore, if necessary, to march into Serbia as a beginning; if the Russians refused to tolerate this, Austria would not be disposed to give way.

H.M. felt justified in drawing this inference from the words of the Austrian Ambassador, when the latter this afternoon delivered a memorandum from the Government in Vienna and a hand-written communication from Emperor Franz Joseph.

I was not present during this conversation, so am unable to permit myself to form any opinion in this matter. On the other hand, H.M. read aloud both the autograph letter and the memorandum. Insofar as the hurriedness of the proceedings gave one a chance to arrive at any opinion, these documents did not succeed in convincing me that the Vienna Government had taken any firm resolution. Both paint a very gloomy picture of the general situation of the Dual Monarchy as a result of Pan-Slav agitations. Both consider it necessary that something should be done about this with the greatest urgency. But neither speaks of the need for war. . . .

The Chancellor, who was also in Potsdam, appears to have as little faith as I do that the Austrian Government is really in earnest, even though its language is undeniably more resolute than in the past. . . . Certainly in no circumstances will the coming weeks bring any decision. . . . Your Excellency's [Moltke's] stay at the Spa will therefore scarcely need to be curtailed. Nonetheless, although I have not been authorized to do so, I considered it advisable to inform you of the gravity of the situation so that anything untoward which could, after all, occur at any time, should not find you wholly unprepared.[17]

The next day, July 6, Chancellor Bethmann Hollweg confirmed his support for the kaiser's assurances to Austria–Hungary when he met the Habsburg ambassador. These assurances, known infamously as the "blank check," gave Vienna the free hand that Berlin had so carefully withheld during the Balkan Wars. Bethmann had either taken a very calculated "risk" or had been unable to resist the kaiser and still believed that Vienna would fail to act. However explained, and historians are sharply divided on his rationale and motivation for agreeing to this support, Bethmann had set the Reich on a course from which retreat soon proved impossible. He duly informed his ambassador in Vienna about what would prove to be his momentous decision.

THEOBALD VON BETHMANN HOLLWEG

Telegram to Vienna

July 6, 1914

The Austro-Hungarian Ambassador yesterday delivered to the Emperor a confidential personal letter from the Emperor Franz Joseph, which depicts the present situation from the Austro–Hungarian point of view, and describes the measures which Vienna has in view. A copy is now being forwarded to Your Excellency.

I replied to Count Szögyény today on behalf of His Majesty that His Majesty sends his thanks to the Emperor Franz Joseph for his letter and would soon answer it personally. . . .

. . . As concerns Serbia, His Majesty, of course, cannot interfere in the dispute now going on between Austria–Hungary and that country, as it is a matter not within his competence. The Emperor Franz Joseph may, however, rest assured that His Majesty will faithfully stand by Austria–Hungary, as is required by the obligations of his alliance and of his ancient friendship.[18]

Germany's infamous "blank check" can be variously interpreted. Strong German support for Vienna to take decisive action, though a departure from past restraint on Vienna, should not necessarily be equated with the ultimate victory of aggressive German military ambitions in July 1914. For some, like German historian Fritz Fischer, the decision demonstrated Germany's desire to solve diplomatic problems by military means, a natural outcome of the desire for a preventive war. But it must be remembered that Vienna initiated this exchange, actively seeking German support. During the first weeks after the assassinations, Bethmann regularly counseled calm and continued his efforts for cooperation with the British. The diplomatic initiative against Serbia, he believed, as his letter to the German ambassador in Vienna makes clear, lay with Austria–Hungary.[19]

The request from the Habsburg leadership revealed the changed international situation for both Berlin and Vienna. In 1879, Germany and Austria–Hungary were both dominant powers with little to fear. By 1914, Berlin faced diplomatic encirclement by the Triple Entente, confronted an increasingly assertive France and Russia, had learned of Britain's secret military ties with the French, and faced considerable domestic turmoil. Austria–Hungary's image as an empire in decline was further tarnished by the assassinations. Bethmann and others in Berlin thus confronted the decision of whether to stand by their chief ally. On this they believed they had no choice. Berlin's messages to Vienna were consistently supportive, urging a rapid response and leaving no doubt about its willingness to risk a broader war. But although Bethmann and Moltke supported Vienna, the chancellor almost immediately began to worry about the risks of their support. Kurt Riezler, his aide, recorded some of Bethmann's musings.

KURT RIEZLER

Diary Entries

July 7, 1914

Traveled out with the imperial chancellor yesterday. The old palace, the wonderful, enormous linden trees, the alleys like a gothic vault. Everywhere the death of the woman still weighs heavily.* Melancholy and domination in the countryside and people.

In the evening on the veranda under the night sky a long discussion about the circumstances. The secret news that he confides in me shows a shocking scene. He takes seriously the English-Russian negotiations about a naval agreement—a landing in Pomerania—the last link in the chain. Lichnowsky† is much too gullible. He lets himself be taken in by the English. Russia's military power is growing fast; with Poland's strategic buildup, the situation is unstoppable. Austria is becoming weaker and weaker and more immobile; the undertow from the north and southeast has advanced greatly in this direction. In any case it is impossible for a German cause other than our allies to go to war. The Entente knows that consequently we are completely paralyzed.

I was totally shocked, because I did not consider it [the circumstances] to be so bad. One certainly does not get secret news when one does not belong to just the right club—and everything highly political and, on top of that, military is "completely secret."

The chancellor speaks of difficult decisions. The assassination of Franz Ferdinand. The Serbian officials participated. Austria wants to pull itself together. Franz Joseph's mission to the Kaiser with an inquiry about the *casus foederis*.‡ Our old dilemma with every Austrian action in the Balkans. We talk to them, so they say, as if we put them up to it; we agree, so it is said, that we have left them in the lurch. Then they fuel themselves on the western powers, and we lose our last mediocre ally. This time it is worse than 1912; because this time Austria is on the defensive against the Serbo-Russian plot. A campaign against the Serbs can lead to world war. The chancellor expects a war, and it will result in an upheaval of everything that survives. That which survives is surviving, unimaginative. "Everything has gotten so old." Heydebrand§ has said that a war would lead to the strengthening of the patriarchal order and mentality. The chancellor is outraged at such nonsense. Blinded all

---

*Bethmann had recently lost his wife.
†*Prince von Lichnowsky:* German ambassador to London.
‡*Casus foederis:* cause of war.
§*Ernst von Heydebrand:* leader of the German Conservative party in the Prussian Landtag.

around, a thick fog over the people. In all of Europe, the same. The future belongs to Russia, it grows and grows, and it weighs heavier and heavier on us.

The chancellor is very pessimistic about Germany's state of mind. Dreadful collapse of the superficial political image. Individuals as such are smaller and smaller and less meaningful, nothing is ever said that is somewhat important or honest. Failure of intelligence, of professors. My objection: time of the special development, but of the collective magnitude. The new beauty has not yet been realized.

The chancellor is a child of the first half of the 19th century and of a better cultivation. Strange that he, with his old humanitarian mentality, his seriousness and, for all appearances, his incompetence, could come to power in the new German milieu and maintain himself against parliamentarians and racketeers. Nevertheless, he is in no way straightforward. His craftiness is certainly equally as large as his ineptness. Both are blending and alternating.[20]

Bethmann remained at his country estate until July 25, when he returned to Berlin; Moltke came that night. Both men had to prepare for the European repercussions of the Habsburg ultimatum to Belgrade. Initially, the first reactions seemed promising, then on July 26, the British proposed a four-power mediation effort, which Bethmann rejected as premature.

At this point, Bethmann made two decisions that provide evidence for his will to go to war. Possibly fearful that the kaiser might decide to seek a negotiated settlement, the chancellor pressed Vienna to declare war even though Habsburg military forces would not be ready for action before August 12. Berchtold, who wanted war, concurred and got General Conrad to agree. Thus Vienna declared war on July 28. That night, shots were fired from Habsburg positions on Belgrade, a step that galvanized the Russian military, as we shall see in the next chapter.

The Habsburg declaration of war came just as Bethmann dealt with a kaiser now ready for peace. For Wilhelm now believed the Serbs' response to Vienna's ultimatum was sufficient. He thus proposed that Bethmann get Vienna to agree to halt in Belgrade and take no further military action. For reasons that are unclear, the chancellor delayed in instructing the German ambassador to make this overture to Berchtold in Vienna. This fact, coupled with indications of Russian military measures, made it easy for Berchtold to evade the idea of a "halt in Belgrade."

General Moltke, meanwhile, also confronted the expanding crisis. On July 27, he thought the situation might take weeks to clarify. But the very next day, he advocated war, and the following day, he gave the chancellor a long memorandum that summarized the military's attitude to the crisis and why mobilization was needed.

HELMUTH VON MOLTKE

Memorandum to Theobald von Bethmann Hollweg

July 29, 1914

It goes without saying that no nation of Europe would regard the conflict between Austria and Serbia with any interest except that of humanity, if there did not lie within it the danger of general political complications that today already threaten to unchain a world war. For more than five years, Serbia has been the cause of a European tension which has been pressing with simply intolerable weight on the political and economic existence of nations. With a patience approaching weakness, Austria has up to the present borne the continuous provocations and the political machinations aimed at the disruption of her own national stability by a people which proceeded from regicide at home to the murder of princes in a neighboring land. It was only after the last despicable crime that she took to extreme measures, in order to burn out with a glowing iron a cancer that has constantly threatened to poison the body of Europe. One would think that all Europe would be grateful to her. All Europe would have drawn a breath of relief if this mischief-maker could have been properly chastised and peace and order thereby restored to the Balkans; but Russia placed herself at the side of this criminal nation. It was only then that the Austro-Serbian affair became the thundercloud which may at any moment break over Europe.

Austria has declared to the European cabinets that she intends neither to make any territorial acquisitions at Serbia's expense nor to infringe upon her status as a nation; that she only wants to force her unruly neighbor to accept the conditions that she considers necessary if they are to continue to exist side by side, and which Serbia, as experience has proved, would never live up to, despite solemn assurances, unless compelled by force. The Austro-Serbian affair is a purely private quarrel in which, as has been said, nobody in Europe would have a profound interest and which would in no way threaten the peace of Europe but, on the contrary, would establish it more firmly, if Russia had not interfered with it. This only was what gave the matter its menacing aspect.

Austria has only mobilized a portion of her armed forces, eight army corps, against Serbia—just enough with which to be able to put through her punitive expedition. As against this, Russia has made all preparations to enable her to mobilize the army corps of the military districts of Kiev, Odessa, and Moscow, twelve army corps in all, within the briefest period, and is providing for similar preparatory measures in the north also, along the German border and the Baltic Sea. She announces that she intends to mobilize when Austria advances into Serbia, as she cannot permit the destruction of Serbia by Austria, though Austria has explained that she intends nothing of the sort.

What must and will the further consequences be? If Austria advances into Serbia, she will have to face not only the Serbian army but also the vastly superior strength of Russia; thus she cannot enter upon a war with Serbia without securing herself against an attack by Russia. That means that she will be forced to mobilize the other half of her Army, for she cannot possibly surrender at discretion to a Russia all prepared for war. At the moment, however, in which Austria mobilizes her whole Army the collision between herself and Russia will become inevitable. But that, for Germany, is the *casus foederis.* If Germany is not to be false to her word and permit her ally to suffer annihilation at the hands of Russian superiority, she, too, must mobilize. And that would bring about the mobilization of the rest of Russia's military districts as a result. But then Russia will be able to say: I am being attacked by Germany. She will then assure herself of the support of France, which, according to the compact of alliance, is obliged to take part in the war, should her ally, Russia, be attacked. Thus the Franco-Russian alliance, so often held up to praise as a purely defensive compact, created only to meet the aggressive plans of Germany, will become active, and the mutual butchery of the civilized nations of Europe will begin.

It cannot be denied that the affair has been cunningly contrived by Russia. While giving continuous assurances that she was not yet "mobilizing," but only making preparations "for an eventuality," that "up to the present" she had called no reserves to the colors, she has been getting herself so ready for war that, when she actually issues her mobilization orders, she will be prepared to move her armies forward in a very few days. Thus she puts Austria in a desperate position and shifts the responsibility to her, inasmuch as she is forcing Austria to secure herself against a surprise by Russia. She will say: You, Austria, are mobilizing against us, so you want war with us. Russia assures Germany that she wishes to undertake nothing against her; but she knows perfectly well that Germany could not remain inactive in the event of a belligerent collision between her ally and Russia. So Germany, too, will be forced to mobilize, and again Russia will be enabled to say to the world: I did not want war, but Germany brought it about.

After this fashion things must and will develop, unless, one might say, a miracle happens to prevent at the last moment a war which will annihilate for decades the civilization of almost all Europe.

Germany does not want to bring about this frightful war. But the German government knows that it would be violating in ominous fashion the deep-rooted feelings of fidelity which are among the most beautiful traits of German character and would be setting itself against all the sentiments of the nation, if it did not come to the assistance of its ally at a moment which was to be decisive of the latter's existence.[21]

That same day, Wednesday, July 29, Bethmann's illusory hopes that Britain might stand aside were shattered. While the kaiser fulminated about Grey's declaration that an attack on the west would bring London to war, Bethmann suddenly reversed course and sought to pressure the Habsburg leadership to give assurances to Russia and to negotiate. This belated peace effort went nowhere. It was too late to sway Vienna and too late to reassure the Russians, who were that same day discussing partial mobilization.

Although a frightened kaiser and tsar exchanged frantic telegrams urging each other to save the peace (see chapter 5), the mobilization timetables demanded action. The most decisive day came on July 30, with Russia's decision for general mobilization. Word of this reached Berlin just before noon on July 31, the date Bethmann and Moltke had set for a German decision about mobilization. The news meant that the chancellor could no longer resist Moltke and the general staff. Until this point, civilian control had held, more or less; now military necessity took over. In one last effort to avert the wider war, Berlin sent Saint Petersburg an ultimatum that demanded the Russians stop their mobilization. Russia did not.

Moltke and Bethmann now fully recognized the enormity of their situation. While the chancellor could blame the Russians for accelerating the war and thus secure strong public support at home, Moltke had clear forebodings, as Hermann von Santen of the general staff reported on July 31.

HERMANN VON SANTEN

Memoirs

ca. 1920s

The words that he directed toward us were sober and simple: the Reich probably stood facing the greatest war that world history had ever seen. We were entering a war on two fronts, for, even though the same news of mobilization measures as had been received from Russia had not yet been received from France, there could be no doubt regarding France's ultimatum position. Then Moltke declared in a loud voice: "Gentlemen! I trust the army! I know that its soul is healthy. And now, gentlemen, go to your posts and do your duty, as His Majesty and your country expect from you." . . . We parted under the impression that the man who had just spoken to us was fully aware of the difficult task . . . that fate had confronted him with.[22]

The next day, Saturday, August 1, represented one of the worst in Moltke's career and forecast his eventual dismissal as chief of staff in September. At 5 P.M., the kaiser signed the mobilization order with Moltke present. Later, a telegram came from Ambassador Lichnowsky in London suggesting that Britain might stand aside if Germany guaranteed neutrality in the west. Both the kaiser and the chancellor, now desperate to avoid war, summoned Moltke back to the palace. When he arrived, Wilhelm told him bluntly that the whole army should be deployed in the east and that actions in the west should stop. To the astonishment of all, Moltke indicated that there were no plans for an attack just in the east and that it was too late to stop the mobilization in the west.

To this comment, the kaiser barked, "Your uncle would have given me a different answer," and "It must be possible, if I order it." Orders were given to postpone the immediate attack in the west, and Moltke became exceedingly distraught. But later that same night, a further clarification came from London; new demands were made of Berlin that were unacceptable. The weary kaiser now told Moltke to resume the attack in the west. On August 2, Luxembourg was occupied; the next day, the attack began on Belgium; and the next day, Britain declared war on Germany.

*　*　*

In July 1914, the Austro-Hungarian government wanted a local war with Serbia, even at the risk of a larger war with Russia. In July 1914, the German government, already worried about the pace of Russian military expansion, resolved to support its longtime ally. In this decision the kaiser, his civilian officials, and his military commanders all recognized the chance of a world war, yet none believed it inevitable. Nevertheless, the German leadership did not shy away from confrontation after July 28. As one historian has written, the concepts of honor and loyalty came into play; the German leaders felt bound to honor their commitment to the Emperor Franz Joseph.[23] Nor did the civilian, constitutional leadership lose control of the situation until news of Russia's mobilization reached Berlin. Upon that news, Moltke and the military authorities had a constitutional role to play. Their demands for countermeasures, hence mobilization and attack, followed logically.

For five years, Moltke and Bethmann had worked together. Their previous international crises had seen peace prevail, even if the general had preferred otherwise. The chancellor had backed army increases while seeking to ensure that the constitutional position of the civilian authorities was not compromised. In this struggle, despite the German left, the public's strong support for military might and nationalism, and its scorn for parliamentary governments, all worked against Bethmann. A graphic commentary on the public mood in Germany in early August 1914 by leading German socialist Philip Scheidmann illustrates the problem that any civilian authority faced.

PHILIP SCHEIDMANN
Memoirs
1929

Critical Days

At express speed I had returned to Berlin. Everywhere where a word could be heard the conversation was of war and rumors of war. There was only one topic of conversation—war. The supporters of war seemed to be in a great majority. Were these pugnacious fellows, young and old, bereft of their senses? Were they so ignorant of the horrors of war? I only heard voices advocating peace in the circle of my own Party friends, apart from the few Social Democratic newspapers. Yet the vast majority of the people were opposed to war, without a doubt. Vast crowds of demonstrators paraded "Unter den Linden."* Schoolboys and students were there in the thousands; their bearded seniors, with their Iron Crosses of 1870–71 on their breasts, were there too in huge numbers.

Treitschke and Bernhardi (to say nothing of the National Liberal beer-swilling heroes) seemed to have multiplied a thousand-fold. Patriotic demonstrations had an intoxicating effect and excited the war-mongers to excess. "A call like the voice of thunder." Cheers! "In triumph we will smite France to the ground." "All hail to thee in victor's crown." Cheers! Hurrah!

The counterdemonstrations immediately organized by the Berlin Social Democrats were imposing, and certainly more disciplined than the Jingo† processions, but could not outdo the shouts of the fire-eaters. "Good luck to him who cares for truth and right. Stand firmly round the flag." "Long live peace!" "Socialists, close up your ranks." The Socialist International cheer. The patriots were sometimes silenced by the Proletarians; then they came out on top again. This choral contest, "Unter den Linden," went on for days."[24]

* *Unter den Linden:* the main street of Berlin, approaching the Brandenburg Gate and with the Royal Palace fronting on it; the linden were trees that lined the street.

† *Jingo:* a term of reference for extreme nationalists; used disparagingly for rabid nationalists.

In July 1914, it could be argued, Germany saw the civilian-military balance play out more or less according to a constitutional schedule. But the German failure in civil-military relations began much earlier than the last days of peace. The military's failure to share information with civilian officials (even with the kaiser) and the fact that Moltke had developed a plan so inflexible that it left little room for maneuver both contributed to the disaster. The cumulative impact of German militarism and its vaunted military professionalism meant that in one defining sense no one controlled the German military: not the kaiser, not the chancellor, not the generals. The state created by "blood and iron" was now doomed to fight a two-front war with an ineffective ally against a formidable coalition. Four more years of fighting lay ahead, with a total of nearly nine million military casualties across the world. The kaiser's *Weltpolitik* brought defeat, a short-lived democracy, and eventually a corporal of that war, Adolf Hitler, to power.

NOTES

[1] For recent assessments of Germany and the coming of the war, see Hew Strachan, *The First World War,* vol. 1, *To Arms* (Oxford: Oxford University Press, 2001), chap. 1.

[2] Johannes Hohlfeld, ed., *Deutsche Reichsgeschichte in Dokumenten, 1849–1926* (Berlin: Deutsche Verlagsgesellschaft für Politik und Geschichte, 1927), 103–4.

[3] Holger H. Herwig, *"Luxury" Fleet: The Imperial German Navy, 1888–1918* (London: Ashfield Press, 1987), 17–18.

[4] Heinrich von Treitschke, *Politics,* ed. Hans Kohn (New York: Harbinger, 1963), 37–38.

[5] Friedrich von Bernhardi, *Germany and the Next War,* trans. Allen H. Powles (New York: Longmans, Green, 1914), 18–19.

[6] For an excellent summary of Bethmann's career, see Gordon Craig, *Germany, 1866–1945* (Oxford: Oxford University Press, 1978), 286–88; see also Konrad Jarausch, *The Engimatic Chancellor: Bethmann Hollweg and the Hubris of Imperial Germany* (New Haven, Conn.: Yale University Press, 1973).

[7] Wilhelm II, *The Kaiser's Memoirs,* trans. Thomas R. Ybarra (New York: Harper and Brothers, 1922), 124–25; for a balanced study of the kaiser, see Christopher Clark, *Kaiser Wilhelm II* (New York: Longman, 2000).

[8] Craig, *Germany,* 287.

[9] Annika Mombauer, *Helmuth von Moltke and the Origins of the First World War* (Cambridge: Cambridge University Press, 2001), 50.

[10] Ibid., 52.

[11] Gerhard Ritter, *The Schlieffen Plan: Critique of a Myth,* trans. Andrew and Eva Wilson (New York: Praeger, 1958; reprint, Westport, Conn.: Greenwood Press, 1979), 172–73, 176.

[12] Helmuth von Moltke, *Erinnerungen, Briefe, Dokumente* (Stuttgart, 1922), 362, as quoted in Fritz Fischer, *War of Illusions,* trans. Marian Jackson (New York: W. W. Norton, 1975), 88.

[13] Henry Cord Meyer, ed., *The Long Generation: Germany from Empire to Ruin, 1913–1945* (New York: Harper and Row, 1973), 54–56.

[14] Max Montgelas and Walther Schücking, eds., *Outbreak of the War: German Documents Collected by Kaul Kautsky* (New York: Oxford University Press, 1924), no. 5. (Hereafter cited as *Kautsky Documents.*)

[15] Ibid., no. 6.

[16] Imanuel Geiss, ed., *July 1914: The Outbreak of the First World War—Selected Documents* (New York: Charles Scribner's Sons, 1967), 76–77.

[17] Ibid., 77–78.

[18] *Kautsky Documents,* no. 15.

[19] Strachan, *The First World War,* chap. 1; see also James Retallack, *Germany in the Age of Kaiser Wilhelm II* (New York: St. Martin's Press, 1996), 80–83.

[20] Kurt Riezler, *Tagebücher, Aufsätze, Dokumente,* ed. Karl Dietrich Erdmann (Göttingen: Vandenhoeck and Ruprecht, 1972), 181–84.

[21] *Kautsky Documents,* no. 349.

[22] Mombauer, *Moltke,* 212.

[23] Avner Offer, "Going to War in 1914: A Matter of Honor?" *Politics and Society,* 23 (June 1995), 213–41.

[24] Meyer, *The Long Generation,* 56–57.

5

Sazonov, Sukhomlinov, and the Russian Escalation of the Crisis

In Russia, civil-military decisions ultimately rested with the tsar of all Russians, Nicholas II. For the tsar and his family, however, 1914 had been a difficult year. In particular, Tsarina Alexandra felt overburdened by duties of state and the hemophilia that plagued her son, Alexis, heir to the Russian throne. Deeply devoted to his wife and family, the tsar took them south to enjoy springtime warmth in the Crimea at one of the Romanovs' magnificent palaces. A month later, the royal family embarked for their annual two-week cruise. While aboard ship, they learned of the assassinations in Sarajevo and the attempted murder of Rasputin—the reputed holy man whom the tsarina believed had healing powers for Tsarevitch Alexis. The archduke was dead, but Rasputin, after suffering multiple stab wounds, clung to life.

The Sarajevo news, and even the Austro-Hungarian ultimatum to Serbia that followed almost a month later, at first struck the tsar as little cause for alarm. As the perpetually optimistic Nicholas noted, previous Balkan crises had been resolved by great power negotiations, and he expected a similar pattern to follow once again. Nicholas's optimistic assessments exasperated his advisers. Conservative by nature, the tsar did not want to be the first to mobilize his troops and risk precipitating a conflict. Would Russia, however, be defenseless against a German invasion, as his advisers warned, if Nicholas tarried in making a decision? He hesitantly authorized preliminary measures to facilitate mobilization; indeed, his government would be the first among the great powers to do so. Persuaded by his ministers, Nicholas ordered general Russian mobilization on July 29, only to rescind his order upon receiving a personal telegram from his cousin, Kaiser Wilhelm II, who appealed to their kinship to help preserve European culture and warned that Russian mobilization would necessitate a German counteraction.

Foreign Minister Serge Sazonov and the military leaders gathered early the next morning. Russian intelligence agents, entirely incorrectly, had warned military leaders that the Germans were in the advanced stages of mobilization. Those assembled concluded that immediate general mobilization was critical to the defense of the motherland. Now they had to convince the reluctant tsar to reverse his position once again. He agreed, and the orders went out. At this late stage, civil and military leaders finally worked together in an anachronistic and convoluted Russian constitutional structure to convince the hesitant tsar to prepare Russian defenses even if that risked a European war.

In the decade before the outbreak of the First World War, the Russian empire appeared to resemble its European counterparts. Yet the monarchy also had many unique characteristics. Like others, Russia felt the pressures of modernization. But Russia had in 1905 suffered a humiliating defeat at the hands of the Japanese. The convergence of domestic pressures and policy failures abroad ignited unprecedented domestic unrest against autocratic Russian rule, forcing a measure of political and social reform. At the same time, by 1914 the tsarist empire and monarchical rule had recovered somewhat and appeared to be growing stronger; this was certainly the perception held abroad, especially among foreign military experts.

In this unsettling socioeconomic context, Russia accepted war in July 1914. Did the alliance system and a calculated Russian policy of escalation prompt this war, or did it represent a government badly overreacting to the situation? What characterized the decision making process in Saint Petersburg? How important to the decisions of 1914 were memories of recent defeats and setbacks? Why did Russia assert so strong an interest in distant Serbia? How effectively did civilian and military authorities interact to allow for informed decisions and options? These questions, among others, will be addressed through the eyes of the tsar's close advisers, Foreign Minister Serge Sazonov and War Minister Vladimir Sukhomlinov.

REFORM AND REACTION IN RUSSIA

Russia had avoided the widespread European revolutions of 1848 but soon floundered with its own crisis precipitated by diplomatic and military failures in its war with the Ottoman Empire, later joined by Britain and France, from 1853 to 1856. The Crimean War exposed the relative backwardness of Russia's economy and technology. Russia's unique position of protecting its "fellow Slavs" and Orthodox Christians in the Balkans also suffered. If Russia were to regain its prestige and influence, drastic internal reforms seemed necessary.

Tsar Alexander II used his Great Reforms to modernize Russian society and to increase Russia's military strength while retaining autocratic control. Serfs were emancipated and censorship relaxed. In politics, however, the tsar retained total authority. No European ruler of the era enjoyed the same degree of absolute control.

The assassination of Alexander II in 1881 prompted a period of reaction but also witnessed the emergence of political parties demanding more rights. Most workers and peasants still accepted the tsar's traditional role of protecting and expanding Russian territory, however, and welcomed the accompanying economic growth.

For much of this period, Russia avoided conflict with Bismarck in Europe by turning east to seek territorial expansion in Asia. But as we have seen, subsequent German leaders, led by Kaiser Wilhelm II, allowed diplomatic harmony with Russia to lapse, and thus Russian officials turned to the French Republic rather than stand alone. France solidified its 1894 alliance with Russia with sizable financial loans that fueled economic expansion in Russia.

After Russian losses in the Russo-Japanese War in 1904–05, domestic revolution soon followed. A repressive governmental structure, bad harvests, and the disastrous war had encouraged workers to strike. Tsarist troops responded with lethal force. Finally, with mobs controlling the streets, the tsar reluctantly pledged a constitution with a national parliament known as the Duma and guaranteed civil liberties, though he still retained many autocratic powers.

Russia thus developed a hybrid government, one with both a powerful emperor and a parliament allowed some authority in matters of budget and legislative initiative. Although the tsar had conceded some power, he could still veto legislation, rule by emergency decree (an option exercised frequently), and summon and dismiss parliament. A budding press and public opinion stopped the tsar from ignoring parliament altogether, but in areas such as foreign and military policy, he kept complete control. He also retained the powers to declare war and to appoint and dismiss ministers of state, who still answered to him rather than to the Duma.

By 1907, the monarchy had recouped much of its previous authority while political parties fought for a more democratic form of government. In 1909, the Duma failed in its attempt to assert authority over naval appointments, thanks to the tsar's veto. Resenting parliamentary efforts to restrict his authority over military matters, Nicholas promptly appointed General Vladimir Sukhomlinov as war minister, believing that the general would maintain a strong barrier between parliament and the military.

STRATEGIC POLICY BEFORE 1914

Since the sovereign held complete authority over foreign affairs, he set the guidelines for Russian diplomatic efforts after 1905. The most important changes were a return to the Balkans, where Russia resumed its traditional role as protector of the Slavs, and a renewed effort to open the Straits of Constantinople for free passage to Russian warships. Although Russia would have to be cautious until it rebuilt its military, it could count on French support, and in 1907, these two powers joined with Great Britain to form the Triple Entente. But just as Russia's diplomatic position was improving, Austria–Hungary and Germany inflicted deep wounds and exposed Russia's weakness in the Bosnian crisis of 1908–09.

In September 1908, the foreign ministers of Russia and Austria–Hungary met at Buchlau in the Habsburg monarchy to negotiate a mutually acceptable arrangement regarding the fate of Bosnia-Herzegovina. Russia would acknowledge Vienna's formal annexation of the provinces in return for Habsburg support of free passage of Russian warships through the Straits of Constantinople. But before the Russian Foreign Minister, Alexander Isvolski, could secure French, British, and German acquiescence, the Austrians announced the annexation and proclaimed that they had Russia's support. Without the agreement of the other great powers, the Russians had been unprepared to act and necessarily felt duped by Austria–Hungary. The affair worsened when Serbia, Bosnia's nearest neighbor, mobilized to challenge Austria–Hungary and requested Russian aid. Some in Saint Petersburg wanted to resume their historic role as protector of Slavic interests. After months of tension, Germany intervened to demand that Russia back down; Tsar Nicholas and Isvolski conceded, for militarily Russia could not yet challenge the Dual Alliance. With deep embarrassment, the Russians relented, but the tsar vowed there would be no forced retreats in the future. In a letter to his mother, Nicholas wrote of the difficulty of this decision and his building resentment at the behavior of Germany and Austria–Hungary.

NICHOLAS II

Letter to His Mother

March 18, 1909

I have been very busy with a lot of rather disagreeable things. To begin with, I had to dismiss the Minister of War. . . . I have appointed Sukhomlinoff in his place; I have known him for 20 years and hope that this choice will prove a success. At the same time the Chiefs of the General Staff and the General Staff were changed too; so the whole of the higher administration of the Army has been replaced.

Last week also I held a Council of Ministers in connection with that wretched Austro-Serbian question.

This affair, which had been going on for six months, has suddenly been complicated by Germany's telling us we could help to solve the difficulty by agreeing to the famous annexation [of Bosnia and Herzegovina by Austria] while, if we refused, the consequences might be very serious and hard to foretell. Once the matter had been put as definitely and unequivocally as that, there was nothing for it but to swallow one's pride, give in and agree. The Ministers were unanimous about it. If this concession on our part can save Serbia from being crushed by Austria, it is, I firmly believe, well worth it. Our decision was the more inevitable as we were informed from all sides that Germany was absolutely ready to mobilize. Against whom? Evidently not against Austria! But our public does not realise this and it is hard to make them understand how ominous things looked a few days ago; now they will go on abusing and reviling poor Isvolsky even more than before!

19th March. I take up my letter where I left off yesterday. Nobody except the bad people want war now, and I think we have been very close to it this time. As soon as the danger is over people immediately begin shouting about humiliation, insults etc. For the word "annexation" our patriots were prepared to sacrifice Serbia, whom we could not help at all in the case of an Austrian attack.

It is quite true that the form and method of Germany's action— I mean towards us—has simply been brutal and we won't forget it. I think they were again trying to separate us from France and England— but once again they have undoubtedly failed. Such methods tend to bring about the opposite result.[1]

The Bosnian humiliation angered many Russians, who condemned Russia's betrayal of fellow Slavs. Isvolski's successor, Serge Sazonov, later commented on the grave implications of his predecessor and mentor's diplomatic blunder.

SERGE SAZONOV

Memoirs

1928

The Russian Government was called upon to choose between two weighty decisions: to sacrifice Serbia, or to renounce its openly-expressed opinion as to the illegality of the Austrian seizure. It chose the latter course, at the price of its own self-respect. Prince Bülow and Count Aehrenthal* gained a diplomatic victory over Russia and Serbia and, indirectly, over the Powers of Western Europe. Little did either of them suspect, at the time, that this victory would prove to be the first nail in the coffin of Austria–Hungary, and would contribute indirectly to the overthrow of Germany from her commanding position in Continental Europe.[2]

Prince Bülow: the German chancellor. *Count Aehrenthal:* the Austro-Hungarian foreign minister.

Although, even after this diplomatic humiliation, the Russians sought to maintain good relations with Germany, they also pledged future support to the Balkan states against Austria–Hungary.

As a first step to remedy Russia's military vulnerabilities, the army restored maneuvers in 1909, and over the next few years, military leaders would begin to gain an advantage. In 1910, the tsar secured the Duma's support for a twenty-year budget increase to improve military preparedness. Neither the tsar nor his government wanted further confrontation and humiliation because of military weakness. From the vantage point of Russia's rulers after 1905, Berlin and Vienna were always ready to exploit Russian misfortune. An impetuous Kaiser Wilhelm II pledged friendship, but the tsar remained uneasy about Germany's true intentions, especially in the Balkans. In his memoirs, Foreign Minister Sazonov recalled how, in 1910, Russia's need for peace depended upon good relations with Germany.

SERGE SAZONOV

Memoirs

1928

It goes without saying that no one in Russia ever had any thought of aggression; such a course was never taken into consideration. I found this to be the attitude of the Emperor, who was by nature a profound lover of peace; he still retained painful recollections of the unfortunate war with Japan, in the possibility of which he refused to believe even on the eve of its outbreak. But the most pronounced opponent of any sort of policy of adventure was General Sukhomlinov, the Minister for War, probably because the unsatisfactory condition of his Department was better known to him than to anyone else. Generally speaking, at the time when I joined the Russian Government [1910] there was no trace in St. Petersburg of the existence of any party which desired war; and the clanking of swords was nowhere to be heard. Although indignation with Austria–Hungary was deep and widespread, very few people took into account the fact that, without the encouragement, or at least the connivance of Germany, Aehrenthal's policy, which nearly led to war, would have been unthinkable.

It goes without saying that the peaceable current of opinion in St. Petersburg influenced the course of my negotiations in Berlin. It was essential for the Russian Government to placate German hostility for a long time to come, by means of all possible concessions in the economic sphere.[3]

After 1912, with the continual buildup of its military forces, Russia began a much more dangerous Balkan policy, encouraging the formation of the Balkan League to challenge the Turkish government and the status quo in the region. As we have seen, in the fall of 1912, the Balkan League precipitated the First Balkan War. Slavic victories prompted a delighted Sazonov to pledge his support for Serbian expansion, including access to the Adriatic. Austria–Hungary, however, as we saw in chapter 3, opposed Serbian access to the sea. Vienna and Saint Petersburg seemed to be headed for a military confrontation as both sides dramatically increased military forces along their common border. Finally, the great powers called for negotiations, and both sides backed down. Peace was preserved this time, but both Russia and Austria–Hungary concluded that their independent displays of military force had compelled the other to back away from war.

The Second Balkan War in 1913 found Russia and Austria–Hungary seeking peace, but for different reasons. Saint Petersburg wanted to maintain the Balkan League (rather than have its allies fighting one another), while Vienna hoped to stop Serbian expansion. The war was short, the League was shattered, and neither Russia nor Austria–Hungary was pleased with the results. Russian policy in the Balkans had only modest successes. Austria–Hungary fared even worse, having spent considerable financial resources to keep troops in arms without any tangible gains, and Vienna was also uncomfortable with Berlin's repeated words of caution. For both countries, the recent lessons of the Balkan Wars would significantly influence their actions as the July crisis unfolded the following year.

GOVERNMENTAL STRUCTURE AND PUBLIC EXPECTATIONS

By 1914, Nicholas had regained much of the power he had temporarily relinquished in 1905. He took his role as leader and protector of the Russian people seriously. He read dispatches and telegrams from foreign posts on a daily basis and possessed a good knowledge of international affairs, priding himself on the defense of Russian honor abroad. The public largely accepted this historic role of the tsar, but with a caveat: It also held him accountable and expected success in foreign affairs. An assessment of his career up to 1914 starkly reveals that Nicholas had little to show.

During the last decade of his reign, Nicholas tried to adjust the governmental and military structure to ensure more foreign policy success. The formation of the Council of State Defense in 1905 would, at least theoretically, unify military planning and improve military effectiveness. In practice, however, the service branches remained independent and uncooperative, perpetuating ignorance among the ministers by withholding information from other branches. The problems of uncoordinated planning and rivalry persisted, as was clearly noted by British Ambassador George Buchanan in March 1914. The envoy described the differences between Foreign Minister Sazonov and War Minister Sukhomlinov and concluded that Sazonov needed to take a more aggressive position against the Triple Alliance, given the attitude of the tsar and the vast resources being expended on Russia's military buildup.

GEORGE BUCHANAN

Letter to London

March 18, 1914

While dwelling on Russia's desire for peace, the Press has let it clearly be seen that Russia is not going to be dictated to and that, confident in the strength of her army, she is ready to face all eventualities.

In my telegram . . . of the 15th . . . I referred to the simultaneous publication . . . of two articles representing respectively the views of the Ministers of Foreign Affairs and of War. The former was couched in conciliatory language and held out a hand clothed in a velvet glove, while the latter met provocation with provocation and made an ostentatious display of a mailed fist. It is not perhaps surprising that the Ministers of War and of Foreign Affairs should advocate different methods of meeting the attack made on Russia by the German Press; but it is curious that they should both have been received in Audience by the Emperor on the 10th of this month and that two such contradictory articles should have been published two days later. According to one account which I believe to be correct, General Sukhomlinoff, who saw the Emperor after Monsieur Sazonow, expressed the opinion that it was necessary to adopt a firm attitude and to give Germany to understand that Russia was prepared and did not fear war. The Emperor apparently acquiesced and authorized the general to publish a strongly worded article to that effect. According to another account, given me by the French Minister, the question was subsequently discussed in a Council of Ministers, in which Monsieur Sazonow strongly opposed the publication of such an article but without succeeding in winning over any of his colleagues to the adoption of more conciliatory tactics. Whether this latter account is correct or not, there is strong evidence to show that the Emperor and the majority of his present advisers are in favour of giving a new course to Russian foreign policy and of adopting a firmer and more resolute attitude than that which characterized it during the recent Balkan crisis. Germany, it is argued, will go on trying to exploit Russia so long as she thinks that she can do so with impunity; and the fact that the German Press has now received the *mot d'ordre** to discontinue its anti-Russian campaign is attributed in some quarters to the outspoken language of the article. . . . Monsieur Sazonow however gave me to understand that the change which has taken place in the attitude of the German Press was due to the representations which he had made through the Russian Ambassador at Berlin; and he even attempted to deny that the article in question had really been inspired by the Minister of War. While it is but natural that His Excellency should wish to take the credit of having accomplished by diplomatic and conciliatory methods what the Minister of War proposed to achieve by rattling his saber, the fact remains that if His Excellency is to retain his position as Minister of Foreign Affairs, he will have to conform his policy to the views which now find favour both in Court and Government circles.

Russia is determined to place her house in order and to ensure it against the danger of any attacks from without by a large increase of her army. With a population, which is now estimated at about 180,000,000, she has almost unlimited resources to draw on, while her finances are on such a satisfactory footing that they will hardly feel the strain of additional expenditure which these military measures will entail. . . . A confirmed Nationalist, Monsieur Krivoscheine† advocates the adoption of a strong foreign policy, and unless Monsieur Sazonow adapts himself to the altered circumstances of the situation, it is doubtful whether he will for long retain the confidence of the Emperor.

Though Monsieur Sazonow professes to attach but little importance to the recent utterances of the German Press and though the official relations between the two Governments remain unchanged, it is difficult to forecast the future till the motives underlying this anti-Russian campaign have been more clearly established. . . . The real cause of Germany's uneasiness and nervous irritability must be sought in the steps now being taken by Russia to strengthen her military position. The temporary advantages, which Germany has secured by her Army Bill of last

---

* *Mot d'ordre:* an order, usually considered an official order.
† *Alexander Krivoscheine:* Minister of Agriculture and a rabid Russian nationalist.

year, will in a few years time be eclipsed by the counter measures which Russia has been obliged to take in self defense. By the year 1917 she will have increased by some 460,000 men the peace strength of her army, which will then amount to 1,750,000 men; while she will possess a fleet in the Baltic, which, though not very formidable in itself, will nevertheless prove a thorn in the side of Germany, should that country be at war with England. Unless therefore Germany is prepared to make still further financial sacrifices for military purposes, the days of her hegemony in Europe will be numbered; as, even without the co-operation of England, Russia and France combined will then be strong enough to confront the united forces of the Triple Alliance. There are, however, still three critical years to pass before that result is achieved. In the race for armaments Russia has more staying powers than Germany, and, as Germany is aware of that fact, there is always the danger that she may be tempted to precipitate a conflict before Russia is fully prepared to meet it. During these crucial years, therefore, Russia will stand in need of our support; and, should we fail to give it when she appeals for it, England will no longer be numbered among her friends.[4]

As we have seen, compared with the other powers, Russian rule remained highly centralized. Nicholas retained his control over foreign policy, defense, and his executive council—the Council of Ministers. Each served at his pleasure, and he often fostered competition rather than collaboration between ministers and ministries. Russia in no sense had a cabinet government, or even one organized like the Common Ministerial Council in Austria–Hungary. In practice, public opinion placed only modest restraints on Russian foreign policy and budget appropriations, and parliament could not cut off funding. In short, Russia's civil-military apparatus depended almost entirely on the tsar to make it work efficiently.

Moreover, much was expected of the Romanov leaders. Parliament had responded to the foreign policy defeats in Asia and the Balkans with increased government spending for the army and navy. After nearly a decade of buildup, the Duma wanted results. How many more times could Russia and the tsar retreat before repeated Austro-Hungarian and German threats? Although the tsar retained governmental control, his legitimacy would be tested in the realm of foreign affairs.

CIVIL-MILITARY DECISION MAKERS IN 1914

Nicholas II's ministers reflected his management style, as they operated in a governmental structure that encouraged internal rivalry rather than coordination. Ministers in turn often chose their subordinates on a similar principle, with loyalty more valued than ability. Both Sazonov, who in 1910 replaced Isvolski, and Sukhomlinov have been criticized for their choice of subordinates. Although talented in some respects, the foreign minister and the war minister each had significant weaknesses that were compounded by an awkward governmental process.

Sazonov, the most prominent civilian leader of foreign affairs after the tsar, was a modest, inexperienced, and plainspoken Muscovite who had served in Paris, Washington, London, and the Vatican before returning to Saint Petersburg in 1909. He was the brother-in-law of the reform-minded Russian premier and minister of the interior, Count Peter Stolypin (1906–11). Contemporaries and historians suggest that Sazonov was respected because of his position rather than his leadership capabilities (Figure 7).

SERGEI WITTE*

Memoirs

1912

When I asked who would replace him, [Isvolski] said that several candidates, all unsuitable, had been mentioned. . . .

I expressed amazement that there were no suitable candidates, to which he replied: "What can one do when there are none." I mentioned several possible candidates, among them Hartwig, the present minister to Serbia. He responded that under no circumstances would the Emperor appoint a man with a non-Russian surname as minister of foreign affairs.

Then I told Izvolskii that he had erred in not choosing as associates men capable of succeeding to high posts, something I had done as minister of finance. He replied that he did not see anyone in the diplomatic corps who could be appointed assistant minister, as a way of preparing that person to become minister. I suggested one such person, Sazonov, our diplomat agent to the Vatican, with whom I had become acquainted

---

* *Sergei Witte:* former prime minister and finance minister.

Figure 7.
Serge Sazonov
His banker's appearance concealed a mercurial personality eager to press Russian interests ahead in the Balkans. His responsibility for a general war is far greater than most historians concede. Popperfoto/Reuters.

when visiting Rome recently. To be sure, I said, Sazonov lacked broad experience, but if he were appointed assistant minister he could get the training necessary for him to become minister. Izvolskii was very cold to the suggestion, arguing that Sazonov's diplomatic experience was limited to minor posts in our London embassy and to service with the Vatican and that he did not have a broad enough knowledge or understanding of foreign affairs, particularly those relating to Eastern and Central Europe.

Nonetheless, he decided somewhat later to have Sazonov appointed assistant minister, as a way of winning favor with Premier Stolypin, Sazonov's brother-in-law. . . .

In my opinion Sazonov is a decent sort of person, but rather inexperienced, of modest abilities, and not in the best of health.[5]

VLADIMIR GURKO*

Features and Figures of the Past

1939

Sazonov was a man of simple thought; all issues were clear to him, but he did not understand the complexity of the international situation and the internal conditions of Russia; like most of our diplomats, he had only a hazy idea of Russia; he was Anglophile in sympathy, a trait totally unsuitable in a Russian Minister of Foreign Affairs.[6]

VLADIMIR SUKHOMLINOV†

Memoirs

1924

He [Sazonov] owed his position as Minister of Foreign Affairs above all to his family relations and the agreement of his views on Oriental politics to those of Iswolski. . . . Without having serious experience in the diplomatic arena, Sazonov was in any case a clever man with above-average education, and yet greatly dependent on those co-workers . . . who were superior to him in political experience. In the meetings of the Minister Council, he always presented the papers from his department with great energy; he did not participate in comments concerning questions of the other ministers.

I never had any kind of differences with the Minister of Foreign Affairs. Our interactions were strictly correct and solely determined by the relations arising from our official positions. The character of our official interactions was also evident outside of our official duties. We had nothing in common since I was not into diplomacy and Sazonov was not at all interested in military questions.[7]

Sazonov's chief assets included an understanding of and loyalty to the tsar's interests. Sazonov chose to focus on the Balkans, where he sought to promote Russia's role as defender of Pan-Slav unity and protector of Orthodox Christians. Having witnessed the negative results

---

Vladimir Gurko: member of the State Council.
†*Vladimir Sukhomlinov:* war minister.

of previous direct confrontations with Austria–Hungary and Germany, Sazonov initially tried to befriend the Germans. But he became deeply irritated during the Second Moroccan Crisis in 1911, when Germany rebuffed his overtures. Although he tried to keep an open mind about Germany, Sazonov, like many Russian elites, saw Berlin as a threat to Russia's modernization and status as a great power. Years later, Sazonov openly expressed his changing attitude toward Germans and their culture.

SERGE SAZONOV

Memoirs

1928

I wish to explain in a few words my attitude towards the German people and their culture. I never suffered from even the mildest form of Germanophobia, possibly because there is a strain of German blood in my veins. But I attribute my immunity to this political malady chiefly to the fact that although I was brought up under the influence of purely Russian ideas, I was accustomed nevertheless to subordinate them to the cultural principles common to all Christian peoples, which do not admit of preconceived antipathies, and still less of anything in the nature of racial hatred. Familiar since childhood with the German language, literature, and art, I learned to respect a people who had founded a science and an original culture which had not only penetrated the very center of their national life, but had also made a valuable contribution to the intellectual heritage of all thinking people. German art, in some, if not all, of its manifestations—especially in the realms of music and poetry—inspired me with genuine admiration, although this feeling referred chiefly to a remote epoch. The cultural forms of contemporary Germany appeared to me much less attractive, for I disliked the elements of coarseness and lack of taste from which they were never entirely free. These defects became more pronounced with the passage of time, even invading music, which previously bore no trace of them. It is impossible to estimate, in a cursory survey, the causes of this phenomenon, but there is no doubt that it coincided with the period which saw the foundation of the German Empire with "blood and iron" for its watchword, and marked Germany's entry upon the path of world politics—a path that finally led her and all Europe into the most appalling catastrophe ever recorded in history. As Germany moved along this path her art gradually expired, and even her science, which hitherto had never sought an end outside itself, began more and more to occupy a position subordinate to the State, until it finally assumed in many respects a character redolent of the barrack and the factory. The tree of German political and economic power grew, and threw its immense shadow over every quarter of the globe; but the source of the spiritual and moral strength of the German people began gradually to dry up. The beneficial influence which German culture had exercised on the peoples of Europe began to be lost; it' finally gave place to a feeling of antipathy, when the ultimate aims of her world policy began to emerge. At the same time, however, the old German people's national virtues, their passionate patriotism, devotion to duty, and iron discipline, were not smothered. These sentiments, combined with a rare gift for organization, enabled the German people to hold out for more than four years in an unequal struggle against a world coalition. It is impossible not to respect them for these qualities. But those who have witnessed and experienced all that has befallen our generation cannot feel love for Germany: it is enough if they do not hate her.[8]

The war minister for the five years preceding 1914, Vladimir Sukhomlinov, had numerous detractors and is often depicted as a shameless toady to the tsar. His nearly bald pate, sly looks, upturned mustache, and chubby face did little to overcome his reputation as a drawing room soldier and a vain, impulsive womanizer who had married a woman thirty-two years his junior (Figure 8). Despite his publications and lectures, many considered him a lightweight, perhaps in part because he always had a repertoire of stories, favored the pageantry of the cavalry, and liked wearing the hussar's uniform. Nicholas, however, chose Sukhomlinov for his loyalty and spoke jokingly of him as his little hussar. The perceptive Count Witte noted the tsar's attraction to Sukhomlinov's lighthearted character but also that the war minister implemented some military reforms with the tsar's support.

SERGEI WITTE

Memoirs

1912

While I was premier, I found General Sukhomlinov to be dealing with his duties as governor-general of Kiev in a calm and balanced way. He seems like an able man, but a superficial and frivolous person. He likes the ladies. He was divorced from his first two wives. His present wife is ill, perhaps fatally ill. I do not think that Sukhomlinov is capable of bringing our army up to the status required by a power such as Russia.

Figure 8.   Vladimir A. Sukhomlinov

A debonair ladies' man, the war minister *(left)* rebuilt the shattered Russian army after the Japanese defeat in 1905. He badly misled Sazonov in the July crisis about Russian mobilization options, thus helping to escalate the crisis. Imperial War Museum.

Sukhomlinov, like many a new minister, was apparently able to acquire considerable influence over the Emperor, probably because in the early stage he and the Emperor enjoyed a "honeymoon" period, such being the Emperor's nature, and partly because he likes to joke and is found amusing. Sukhomlinov set about truly subordinating the General Staff to the War Ministry and undermining Grand Duke Nicholas Nikolaevich's influence on military affairs.* In the course of the year following Sukhomlinov's appointment as war minister, the Grand Duke lost all his influence with the Emperor. . . . It seems, however, that in recent times [1912] the Grand Duke has begun to regain his influence.[9]

* Grand Duke Nikolai Nikolaevich held powerful positions within the military structure and regularly tried to influence the tsar and the military from this position. He was hated by Sukhomlinov and others for what they considered the duke's regular intrusion into the decision-making process. He was a cousin of the tsar.

Historian William Fuller helps flesh out the war minister's dubious reputation.

WILLIAM FULLER

Civil-Military Conflict in Imperial Russia

1985

Detractors of Sukhomlinov certainly have a case. The War Minister's personal life, scarred by episodes of adultery, extravagance, and peculation, does not stand up to close scrutiny. It is also true that Sukhomlinov did enjoy acquaintance with a coterie of raffish and suspicious characters . . . persons who later came to be associated in the public mind with such crimes as forgery, espionage, and treason. As for tales of Sukhomlinov's frivolity, they are legion. The favorite noun of Sukhomlinov's critics in this regard seems to have been *legkomyslennost'* (lightmindedness). To cite one typical anecdote, in 1911 Sukhomlinov saw a copy of the new journal of the Naval General Staff, assumed falsely that it was a publication of the War Ministry, and proudly displayed it to Nicholas II as such. When the Emperor corrected him, Sukhomlinov swore that he had made an honest mistake, that the Journal of the Army General Staff was similar in appearance. No such journal existed, and upon his return from Tsarskoe Selo to Petersburg, Sukhomlinov commanded that the Army General Staff start a journal—and within five days print the first number in a format identical to that of the navy's.[10]

Scholars have recently written more positively about Sukhomlinov. There is new recognition of his emphasis upon the foreign role of the military, his reforms of the reserve system, and his demands for additional money and training, all of which permitted the war minister and Russia to move to a more active policy of deterrence. In December 1912, Sukhomlinov boldly pushed for mobilization against the Habsburg and German threats, but the tsar continued with the peaceful policy advocated by Sazonov and others.

Like Sazonov, Sukhomlinov chose mediocre staffers in part because he was susceptible to conspiracy theories and felt insecure in his position. Personally averse to details, the general knew less about mobilization plans than would have been expected, and his latest chief of staff had only a few months' experience before the July crisis unfolded. His lack of knowledge, his weak character, and the competitive structure within the military, fueled by Grand Duke Nikolai Nikolaevich and Chief of Staff Nikolai Yanushkevich, created a chaotic situation. Since Sukhomlinov neither communicated with the foreign ministry about its needs nor coordinated military goals to meet foreign policy objectives, there were major policy issues that were never resolved. Russian historian D. C. Lieven has noted, "The extraordinary and dangerous ignorance of Sazonov and Sukhomlinov about each other's profession stemmed in part from the Russian governmental tradition that each ministry was an empire unto itself. The lack of control exercised by the civilian government over the armed forces contained a threat that a combination of the latter's fears and aggressive instincts would push aside the Emperor's resistance and involve Russia in war."[11]

SAINT PETERSBURG AFTER THE SARAJEVO ASSASSINATIONS

News of the assassinations in Sarajevo evoked strong reactions in Russia. Although the Orthodox Romanovs did not particularly care about the Catholic archduke, regicide repulsed them, and Austro-Hungarian accusations that a Pan-Slav plot was responsible for the murders angered many throughout Russia.

As we have seen, the tsar received the news without much alarm, being more preoccupied with his vacation, his hemophiliac son, the life-threatening assault on Rasputin, labor strikes in the capital, and an impending visit of French authorities. Sazonov also focused on the

French state visit. Initially troubled by the assassinations, by mid-July Sazonov felt at ease, having received reassurances from foreign representatives, including the German ambassador to Saint Petersburg, that this episode would pass peacefully.

Those who knew Sazonov were less comfortable. Both friend and foe considered Sazonov mercurial, given to conducting diplomacy by improvisation. Under stress, he displayed these characteristics more frequently. On July 20, just as the French officials steamed up the Neva River toward Saint Petersburg, Sazonov learned from semi-official German press accounts and from the Italian ambassador of possible war between Austria–Hungary and Serbia. Earlier, Sazonov had announced that Russia stood by the Serbs, and he felt a new confidence in the presence of French officials who had occasionally criticized the Russians for their weakness in Balkan politics. He was also influenced by Isvolski, now Russia's ambassador to France, who was in Saint Petersburg for the French visit and who served as an immediate reminder of past foreign policy blows to Russian prestige. French President Raymond Poincaré further affirmed French support and friendship; the festivities undoubtedly fed Sazonov's now-fluctuating moods. Even as he was engaged in the demanding protocol of the foreign visit, Sazonov sought reassurances from Austria–Hungary that it would not attack Serbia, emphasizing that while Russia desired peace, it would no longer be passive.

The French ambassador to Russia, Maurice Paléologue, provided a colorful account of the exchanges between the Russians and the French on this momentous occasion.

MAURICE PALÉOLOGUE

Memoirs

July 20, 1914

The weather was cloudy. Our vessel steamed at high speed between low banks towards the Gulf of Finland. Suddenly a fresh breeze from the open sea brought us a heavy shower, but as suddenly the sun burst forth in his splendour. A few pearl-grey clouds, through which the sun's rays darted, hung here and there in the sky like sashes shot with gold. As far as the eye could reach, in a limpid flood of light the estuary of the

Neva spread the immense sheet of its greenish, viscous, changing waters which always remind me of Venice.

At half-past eleven we stopped in the little harbour of Peterhof where the *Alexandria,* the Tsar's favourite yacht, was lying under steam.

Nicholas II, in the uniform of an admiral, arrived at the quay almost at once. We transferred to the *Alexandria.* Luncheon was served immediately. We had at least an hour and three-quarters before us until the arrival of the *France.* But the Tsar likes to linger over his meals. There are always long intervals between the courses in which he chats and smokes cigarettes.

I was on his right, Sazonov on his left and Count Fredericks, Minister of the Court, was opposite us.

After a few commonplaces the Tsar told me of his pleasure at receiving the President of the Republic.

"We shall have weighty matters to discuss," he said. "I'm sure we shall agree on all points . . . But there's one question which is very much in my mind—our understanding with England. We *must* get her to come into our alliance. It would be such a guarantee of peace!"

"Yes, Sire, the Triple Entente cannot be too strong if it is to keep the peace."

"I've been told that you yourself are uneasy about Germany's intentions."

"Uneasy? Yes, Sire, I am uneasy although at the moment I have no particular reason to anticipate a war in the immediate future. But the Emperor William and his Government have let Germany get into a state of mind such that if some dispute arose, in Morocco, the East—anywhere—they could neither give way nor compromise. A success is essential at any price and to obtain it they'll risk some adventure."

The Tsar reflected a moment:

"I can't believe the Emperor wants war . . . If you knew him as I do! If you knew how much theatricality there is in his posing! . . ."

"Perhaps I am doing the Emperor William too much honour in thinking him capable of willing, or simply accepting the consequences of his acts. But if war threatened would he, and could he prevent it? No, Sire, I don't think so, honestly I don't."

The Tsar sat silent and puffed at his cigarette. Then he said in a resolute voice:

"It's all the more important for us to be able to count on England in an emergency. Unless she has gone out of her mind altogether Germany will never attack Russia, France and England combined."

Coffee had just arrived when the French squadron was signalled. The Tsar made me go up on the bridge with him.

It was a magnificent spectacle. In a quivering, silvery light the *France* slowly surged forward over the turquoise and emerald waves, leaving a long white furrow behind her. Then she stopped majestically.

The mighty warship which has brought the head of the French State is well worthy of her name. She was indeed France coming to Russia. I felt my heart beating.[12]

After the visit, Sazonov became more aggressive, claiming to seek negotiations while clearly and provocatively engaging in a show of power. In part, he reflected the new Russian self-confidence. The Duma, political parties, public opinion, and of course the military favored an active Russian role in the Balkans. Now, with the reaffirmation of French support during the state visit and Sazonov's early pledge to defend Serbia, Russia was ready to take a more bellicose stance.

The Austro-Hungarian ultimatum to Serbia on July 23 further galvanized Russian policymakers, especially the increasingly pugnacious foreign minister. On the morning of July 24, he hastily summoned the chief of the Russian general staff, General Nikolai Yanushkevich, to inquire about partial mobilization against Austria–Hungary. He wanted to be prepared for his meeting later that day with the Council of Ministers. Sazonov asked the general what he thought were pertinent questions. Was Russia ready to mobilize? Could arrangements be made quickly if he called for mobilization against Austria–Hungary? Sazonov perhaps believed he could repeat the fall 1912 scenario and partially mobilize Russian forces against Austria–Hungary without triggering complications with Germany.

Rather than disappoint the minister or hint at inadequate military planning, Sukhomlinov and Yanushkevich irresponsibly ordered the hasty preparation (within the hour) of a new plan for partial mobilization. Russian military leaders had prepared only for simultaneous mobilization against Austria–Hungary and Germany. Essentially, Russia could enact a partial mobilization strategy against Austria–Hungary only by crudely splitting the general mobilization plan. If these hastily conceived ideas were followed, however, the limited Russian resources and the lack of previous planning would wreak havoc on any attempt for general mobilization later against Germany. A desperate Sukhomlinov did not want to leave Russia's border with Germany unprotected. He and Yanushkevich had egregiously misled Sazonov by not telling him that the only realistic option short of full mobilization was preparatory measures for full mobilization (against both Austria–Hungary and

Germany). Sazonov and the other ministers were led to believe, in part because they did not explicitly ask, that partial mobilization was a realistic option. Neither Yanushkevich nor Sukhomlinov notified Sazonov or the Council of Ministers on the 24th that Russia actually had no operational plan for partial mobilization.

Sazonov thus opened the Council of Ministers meeting on July 24 with a passionate appeal for limited mobilization against Austria–Hungary as a way to deter Austria from war. Advocating steps far more menacing than any other power had taken at this point, he warned that Russian honor was at stake. This time the Slavs needed to halt further German penetration into the Balkans and maintain Russian claims to the Straits. While some ministers hesitated initially, all soon supported partial mobilization. Both Sukhomlinov and Yanushkevich, who were present, said nothing about the practicality of this decision.

The most important gathering came the next day, July 25, when the Council of Ministers and the tsar debated the diplomatic crisis. Foreign Minister Sazonov had gained more de facto control over the Russian military than any other foreign minister; now he seemed determined to act. His position, given the lack of coordination between the foreign and war ministries, meant that as long as he kept the tsar's support, his initiatives would be crucial in shaping the course of the crisis.

But Sazonov acted rashly by making false assumptions and discounting unfavorable reports. In spite of increasing evidence to the contrary, Sazonov accepted the assurance given by the German undersecretary of state, Arthur von Zimmermann, that his country would not directly counter Russian mobilization if it was directed only against Austria. Sazonov also operated under the false supposition, possibly from 1912, that premobilization and partial mobilization were incremental threats that he could use to dissuade the Austrians and Germans without launching a larger war. Moreover, as we have seen, Sukhomlinov allowed everyone to believe that partial mobilization against Austria–Hungary was possible and that preparatory steps would not cross the threshold for war. By the end of the meeting, the tsar agreed in principle to partial mobilization. Stating that he hoped to deter Vienna and defend Russia's reputation in the Balkans, Sazonov determined to prepare for partial mobilization.

Journal of the Russian General Staff Committee

July 25, 1914

The Chief of the General Staff informed the members of the General Staff Committee that His Majesty the Emperor has deigned to announce that it is necessary to support Serbia, even if this entails mobilization and the beginning of hostilities, but however not before Austrian troops have crossed the Serbian border.

According to received accounts, some preparations for mobilization have been undertaken in Austria–Hungary and Italy. Therefore His Majesty the Emperor has deigned to confirm the Ministerial Council's decree that the premobilization phase will begin during the night of July 25–26.

Should it prove necessary to declare mobilization, in view of the fact that [this] one is limited merely to actions against Austria, Your Highness should mobilize military districts in Kiev, Odessa, Kasan, and Moscow. The other military districts should only be mobilized if Germany joins Austria, and not earlier, so that further diplomatic difficulties may be avoided.

In this sense the appropriate directives must be sent to the respective authorities.[13]

Tsar Nicholas, as his diary entry suggests, seemed unperturbed by the day's most consequential decision.

NICHOLAS II

Diary

July 25, 1914

Thursday night Austria declared an ultimatum to Serbia with terms, eight of which are not acceptable for an independent state. Its time expired today at 6 P.M. Obviously it's all that people are talking about. Went to the Krasnoye Selo this morning at 10 A.M. had excellent inspection of the Astrakhan regiment.

From 11 til 12 I had meeting with six ministers about the same question and precautionary measures that we should take. Had breakfast with officers of Astrakhan grenadier regiment.

At 2 went to the field aunt's Mikhen hospital.* From there went to the military hospital. Gave the prize for the best shooting in cavalry hussar regiment. Held inspection of the 9th Dragoon and 2nd Hussar Akhtir regiments. All the chiefs attended. At 6 there was a promotion of military cadets.

There was a dinner with officers from both regiments at 7. After talking, went to the theater with three older daughters. It was long jubilee show on the occasion of its 50th anniversary.

Returned to Peterhof at 1:15 A.M. and went to sleep after 3 A.M. because of a lot of paperwork.[14]

* Mikhen was Mariya Pavlovna, widow of Great Duke Vladimir Aleskandrovich.

At the meeting on July 25, neither Sukhomlinov nor Yanushkevich explained the logistical impracticalities of partial mobilization nor suggested that Berlin and Vienna would undoubtedly interpret any military steps, even premobilization measures, as the equivalent of war. Whereas Russian mobilization was a lengthy process with numerous opportunities for delay, disruption, or cessation, the German plan, the major outlines of which were known to Sukhomlinov, depended upon a tight, almost irrevocable timetable to be enacted as soon as war appeared imminent. In his interwar memoirs, Sukhomlinov tried to exonerate himself from responsibility, claiming that he had made clear his opposition to partial mobilization and placing the blame squarely on Sazonov.

VLADIMIR SUKHOMLINOV

Memoirs

1924

I exercised a kind of caution on that day [July 25] that must have seemed strange to my subordinates since I otherwise usually tended to fulfill my duties with great emphasis. On that disastrous day Yanushkevich was in fact the army's leading figure in the spotlight. . . . I was even less allowed to partake in this role since after the extent of the reform work of the army, I wanted to keep peace — naturally not at the cost of a renewed humiliation to Russia. Not being a diplomat and therefore only being able to view the political situation on the surface, I did not have the ability to specify in what way this humiliation was to be avoided. For this reason I held back and did not join in the celebrations of my younger comrades when the iron dice were cast.

The Tsar saw the military minister [Sukhomlinov] as just a technician who must build the instrument for war, and the Tsar was the one who would decide the time for implementation and use of it. At the same time, between July 24 and 30, the conclusive word belonged to high nobility [the tsar]. It was clear from the decision that was made at the meeting on July 25th. Sazonov—a diplomat but not the military minister— was given authority to choose the form of mobilization (global or partial) depending on circumstances, although with a report to the Tsar. . . .

Whoever someday may want to find out the behind-the-scenes tales for the outbreak of the war will have to pay particular attention to the days of Poincaré's visit, as well as the days immediately following, sometime around July 24–28. I am totally convinced that the decision on war and peace was made in this time, in the sense that Grand Duke Nikolai Nikolaevich, Sazonov, and Poincaré had made a conspiracy to make war, in any case, should all attempts to find peaceful solutions fail.

During and after President Poincaré's visit, I was cut off from the Tsar until August 2, at which time the war machine had already been set into action through the diplomats, and a stop would only have been possible by breaking the word that the Tsar had given to the confederate ally. In all these days, I was systematically prevented from being alone with the Tsar and I was also systematically prevented from getting an inside view of the current political situation. Sazonov and the grand duke negotiated behind the scenes up till the departure of the President of France, completely without any contact with the Ministry of War but supported by the resolutions of the Royal Council of July 25 and the mandate given to the minister of foreign affairs. Above all, the grand duke took over the role of enticing the Tsar for war and keeping him in this mood.

. . . Yanushkevich, the willing confidant of the grand duke, only acted according to his direct instructions. At the time I had no way of keeping an eye on to what extent that occurred. I therefore know nothing of the fact that the general under me was at the Tsar's daily and held presentations behind my back, although I believe I had convinced the Tsar that the chief of the general staff was only to be allowed to make presentations in the presence of the minister of war. It seems, however, that as of July 25, the Tsar already felt he was in the role of the commander in chief and, . . . he therefore believed he could go above the head of the minister of war and negotiate directly with the person he had in mind for the chief of general staff of the army field forces without upsetting the minister of war.[15]

While the documentary record does not entirely support Sukhomlinov's postwar account, his description of the confusion and petty politics appears valid. Whatever the tsar thought, Sazonov clung to his illusions of Russian military deterrence. On July 26, he spoke directly with the Austro-Hungarian ambassador to assess the attitude in Vienna. To avoid unwanted surprises, he also tried to assure an anxious German ambassador that Russia had only initiated preparatory measures for mobilization.

Sazonov's initial optimism about his deterrence strategy dissipated, however, when he learned that Austria–Hungary had declared war against Serbia on July 28. Dismayed that diplomacy through deterrence had not protected Russian honor or its Serbian client, Sazonov hastily reached the extreme conclusion that Berlin and Vienna had wanted war all along and that further negotiations were useless.

More dangerously still, Yanushkevich's staff had finally explained to Sazonov on July 27 the logistical implications should Russia begin an improvised partial mobilization and then decide to escalate to full mobilization. Russian war plans called for a double offensive, one against the Germans in East Prussia and another from Russia's Polish territory against Austria–Hungary. The operational distances between the two theaters were enormous, and there were few north-south railways to move troops back and forth between the two areas. To deploy along the south and then decide on full mobilization would force some troops deployed in the south to retrain and move eastward before being sent north. (See Map 4 in chapter 3.) In any event, the change in plans risked chaos along the Russian railway system. Nor apparently had Sazonov appreciated earlier that Russia's precautionary measures already under way involved some actions along the extensive German frontier, actions that the German intelligence service readily interpreted as mobilization steps. Sazonov ignored or failed to grasp these risks, even as he sought to convince Berlin that Russia's partial mobilization against the Habsburgs was not a threat to Germany.

In all of this, the general staff still sought to meet the foreign minister's wishes. Yanushkevich prepared two mobilization orders—partial and full—with the idea that troops would be called up on July 30. On Wednesday, July 29, the tsar reluctantly yielded to Sazonov's plea for mobilization (whether partial or full is a matter of some dispute). A gloomy Sukhomlinov now faced the prospect of war. Yanushkevich prepared to cable the military districts and the Baltic Fleet to begin mobilizing. Again, French ambassador Maurice Paléologue sheds light on these decisions.

MAURICE PALÉOLOGUE

Memoirs

July 29, 1914

At eleven o'clock tonight, Nicholas-Alexandrovitch Basily, Deputy-Directory of the chancellery of the Foreign Office, appeared at my embassy. He came to tell me that the imperious language used by the German Ambassador this afternoon has decided the Russian Government (1) to order this very night the mobilization of the thirteen corps earmarked for operations against Austria–Hungary; (2) secretly to commence general mobilization.

These last words made me jump:

"Isn't it possible for them to confine themselves—provisionally at any rate—to a partial mobilization?"

"No. The question has just been gone into thoroughly by a council of our highest military officers. They have come to the conclusion that in existing circumstances the Russian Government has no choice between partial and general mobilization as from the technical point of view a partial mobilization could be carried out only at the price of dislocating the entire machinery of general mobilization. So if today we stopped at mobilizing the thirteen corps destined for operations against Austria and tomorrow Germany decided to give her ally military support, we should be powerless to defend ourselves on the frontiers of Poland and East Prussia. Besides, isn't it as much to France's interest as our own that we should be able to intervene promptly against Germany?"

"Those are strong arguments but I still think that your General Staff should take no step without previous discussion with the French General Staff. Please tell M. Sazonov from me that I should like his most serious consideration of this matter and a reply in the course of the night."[16]

But even as Paléologue was advising that no steps be taken until the French and Russian general staffs conferred, Tsar Nicholas suddenly rescinded the order for mobilization. Not convinced of the necessity of a European war, Nicholas had just received an encouraging telegram from his cousin and fellow monarch, Kaiser Wilhelm of Germany. The cousins exchanged telegrams—the so-called Willy-Nicky correspondence—in which they called on one another to take decisive steps to avoid war. The letters that follow are in order of their dispatch. Some of them crossed each other, and that is noted.

NICHOLAS II

Telegram to Wilhelm II

July 29, 1914, 1:00 A.M.

Am glad you are back. In this most serious moment, I appeal to you to help me. An ignoble war has been declared upon a weak country. The indignation in Russia, shared fully by me, is enormous. I foresee that very soon I shall be overwhelmed by the pressure upon me, and be forced to take extreme measures which will lead to war. To try and avoid such a calamity as a European war, I beg you in the name of our old friendship to do what you can to stop your allies from going too far.

Nicky

The following telegram crossed with the one above.

WILHELM II

Telegram to Nicholas II

July 28, 1914, Sent July 29, 1:45 A.M.

It is with the gravest concern that I hear of the impression which the action of Austria against Serbia is creating in your country. The unscrupulous agitation that has been going on in Serbia for years has resulted in the outrageous crime to which Archduke Francis Ferdinand fell a victim. The spirit that led Serbians to murder their own king and his wife still dominates the country. You will doubtless agree with me that we both, you and me, have a common interest, as well as all Sovereigns, to insist that all the persons morally responsible for the dastardly murder should receive their deserved punishment. In this politics play no part at all.

On the other hand I fully understand how difficult it is for you and your Government to face the drift of your public opinion. Therefore, with regard to the hearty and tender friendship which binds us both from long ago with firm ties, I am exerting my utmost influence to induce the Austrians to deal straightly to arrive to a satisfactory understanding with you. I confidently hope you will help me in my efforts to smooth over difficulties that may still arise.

Your very sincere and devoted friend and cousin

Willy

WILHELM II

Telegram to Nicholas II

July 29, 1914, 6:30 P.M.

I received your telegram and share your wish that peace should be maintained. But as I told you in my first telegram, I cannot consider Austria's action against Serbia an "ignoble" war. Austria knows by experience that Serbian promises on paper are wholly unreliable. I understand its action must be judged as trending to get full guarantee that the Serbian promises shall become real facts. This my reasoning is borne out by the statement of the Austrian Cabinet that Austria does not want to make any territorial conquests at the expense of Serbia. I therefore suggest that it would be quite possible for Russia to remain a spectator of the Austro-Serbian conflict without involving Europe in the most horrible war she ever witnessed. I think a direct understanding between your Government and Vienna possible and desirable and as I already telegraphed to you, my Government is continuing its exertions to promote it. Of course military measures on the part of Russia which would be looked upon by Austria as threatening would precipitate a calamity we both wish to avoid and jeopardize my position as a mediator which I readily accepted on your appeal to my friendship and my help.

Willy

NICHOLAS II

Telegram to Wilhelm II

July 29, 1914, 8:20 P.M.

Thanks for your telegram conciliatory and friendly. Whereas official message presented today by your Ambassador to my Minister was conveyed in a very different tone. Beg you to explain this divergency. It would be right to give over the Austro-Serbian problem to the Hague conference. Trust in your wisdom and friendship.

Your loving Nicky

NICHOLAS II

Telegram to Wilhelm II

July 30, 1914, 1:20 A.M.

Thank you heartily for your quick answer [refers to telegram of July 29]. Am sending Tatistcheff* this evening with instructions. The military measures which have now come into force were decided five days ago for reasons of defense on account of Austria's preparations. I hope from all my heart that these measures won't in any way interfere with your part as mediator which I greatly value. We need your strong pressure on Austria to come to an understanding with us.

Nicky

Ilya Leonidovich Tatischeff: an aide to Tsar Nicholas.

WILHELM II

Telegram to Nicholas II

July 30, 1914, 1:20 A.M.

Best thanks for telegram [July 29]. It is quite out of the question that my Ambassador's language could have been in contradiction with the tenor of my telegram. Count Pourtalès was instructed to draw the attention of your government to the danger and grave consequences involved by a mobilization; I said the same in my telegram to you. Austria has only mobilized against SERBIA and only a PART of her army. If, as it is now the case, according to the communication by you and your Government, Russia mobilizes against Austria, my rôle as mediator you kindly instructed [entrusted] me with, and which I accepted at you[r] express prayer, will be endangered if not ruined. The whole weight of the decision lies solely on you[r] shoulders now, who have to bear the responsibility for peace or war.

Willy[17]

These exchanges over two days deeply shook Sazonov and the military leaders. As noted earlier, the generals had implored Sazonov to secure the tsar's consent to general mobilization, warning that undue delay would render Russia defenseless. Sazonov now pressured the tsar for immediate general mobilization. The Germans would not force Vienna to stop its mobilization against Serbia; Russia must act to prevent a Habsburg defeat of Serbia. Around 4 P.M. on July 30, Nicholas succumbed to Sazonov's pleas, and the foreign minister immediately telephoned Yanushkevich to order general mobilization.

RUSSIAN MINISTRY FOR FOREIGN AFFAIRS

Diary

July 30, 1914

The Chief of Staff implored S. D. Sazonov to convince the emperor at all costs that he should give his consent to ordering general mobilization, as we would be in extreme danger if faced with a war with Germany unprepared, if circumstances forced us to take more energetic measures after all, after the success of a general mobilization had been compromised by the previous implementation of a partial mobilization. General Yanushkevich asked the minister to inform him immediately from the Peterhof by telephone if he could convince the emperor, so that he could make the necessary preparations without delay, because it was necessary to convert the already initiated partial mobilization to a general one and to replace previously sent orders with new ones. "Afterwards," stated Yanushkevich, "I will go away. I will destroy my telephone and otherwise do everything necessary to ensure that I cannot be found, in case there is an opposing order, such as a renewed revocation of general mobilization. . . .

At two o'clock the foreign minister drove with General Major Tatischtschew* to the Peterhof, where they both were received by His Majesty in the Alexander Palace. The minister attempted for over an hour to prove that war had become unavoidable, that it could be seen from all that had transpired that Germany was determined to let things lead to a conflict; otherwise Germany would not have rejected all the peaceful overtures made to it and would have easily brought its allies to their senses. In this situation nothing remained to be done but to carry out everything that was necessary to enter war fully armed and in the most favorable position. Without recoiling from the knowledge that we are provoking war by our preparations, it would be better to make these preparations carefully rather than be surprised by a war we were afraid to give a pretext for starting.

The burning wish of the emperor to avoid war at all costs, the horrors of which had filled him with deep disgust, as well as the knowledge of the great responsibility resting on his shoulders in these difficult hours, forced His Majesty to search for all necessary means to stave off the encroaching danger. Therefore he was long unwilling to approve of measures that were absolutely necessary from a military standpoint, but which were, as he clearly saw, liable to accelerate the decision in an undesirable fashion.

The inner tension that the emperor experienced in these moments was expressed among other things by the unusual irritability with which His Majesty interrupted General Tatischtschew. The latter, who had not partaken in the conversation during its entire course, said in a moment of silence, "Yes, it is difficult to decide." The emperor replied sharply and angrily, "The decision will be made by me," thus putting an end to any further interference in the conversation by the general.

Finally the emperor conceded that under the present circumstances it would be the most dangerous course not to make timely preparations for what seemed to be an inevitable war, and therefore gave his permission to initiate general mobilization. . . .

He [Sazonov] conveyed His Highness's order to General Yanuschkevich, who was waiting for the same with impatience, adding, in reference to their conversation held earlier that morning, "Now you may destroy your telephone." The emperor, however, was still hopeful that a way could be found to prevent the order for general mobilization from becoming an irrevocable cause for war. Therefore the emperor promised Kaiser Wilhelm in a telegram sent out the very same day that he, despite the order for mobilization . . . [Document breaks off here.][18]

---

*Also spelled Tatischeff.

While still hopeful for peace, the tsar, on the basis of Austro-Hungarian military actions, refused Germany's demand on July 31 that Russia cease mobilization.

NICHOLAS II

Telegram to Wilhelm II

July 31, 1914

I thank you heartily for your mediation which begins to give one hope that all may yet end peacefully. It is technically impossible to stop our military preparations which were obligatory owing to Austria's mobilization. We are far from wishing war. So long as the negotiations with Austria on Serbia's account are continuing, my troops shall not take any provocative action. I give you my solemn word for this. I put all my trust in God's mercy and hope in your successful mediation in Vienna for the welfare of our countries and for the peace of Europe.

Nicky

The following telegram crossed with the one above.

WILHELM II

Telegram to Nicholas II

July 31, 1914, Berlin

On your appeal to my friendship and your call for assistance began to mediate between your and the Austro-Hungarian Government. While this action was proceeding your troops were mobilized against Austria–Hungary, my ally. Thereby, as I have already pointed out to you, my mediation has been made almost illusory.

I have nevertheless continued my action. I now receive authentic news of serious preparations for war on my eastern frontier. Responsibility for the safety of my Empire forces preventive measures of defense upon me. In my endeavors to maintain the peace of the world I have gone to the utmost limit possible. The responsibility for the disaster which is now threatening the whole civilized world will not be laid at my door. In this moment it still lies in your power to avert it. Nobody is threatening the honor or power of Russia, who can well afford to await the result of my mediation. My friendship for you and your Empire, transmitted to me by my grandfather on his deathbed, has always been sacred to me and I have honestly often backed up Russia when she was in serious trouble, especially in her last war.

The peace of Europe may still be maintained by you, if Russia will agree to stop the military measures which must threaten Germany and Austria–Hungary.

Willy[19]

That same day, Austria–Hungary ordered general mobilization. Later that day, Germany declared war on Russia. On August 6, Austria–Hungary declared war on Russia as well. Although the tsar did not want war, he chose to defend Serbia and Russian promises in the Balkans, all for Russian honor.

A few months later, in talking to French ambassador Paléologue, the tsar recalled the exchanges with Wilhelm and the tension of that fateful week.

MAURICE PALÉOLOGUE

Memoirs

November 21, 1914

The Emperor rose, offered me another cigarette and remarked in the most casual and friendly way:

"What glorious memories we shall share, my dear Ambassador! Do you remember? . . ."

And he reminded me of the days immediately preceding the war, that harassing week from July 25 to August 2; he recounted even the most trivial details and laid particular emphasis on the personal telegrams which had passed between the Emperor William and himself:

"He was never sincere; not for a moment! In the end he was hopelessly entangled in the net of his own perfidy and lies. . . . Have you ever been able to account for the telegram he sent me six hours after giving me his declaration of war? It's utterly impossible to explain what happened. I don't remember if I've ever told you. It was half-past one in the morning of August 2. I had just received your English colleague who had brought me a telegram from King George begging me to do everything possible to save peace. I had drafted, with Sir George Buchanan's help, the telegram with which you are familiar, which ended with an appeal for England's help in arms as the war was forced on us by Germany. The moment Buchanan had left I went to the Empress's room, as she was already in bed, to show her King George's telegram and have a cup of tea with her before retiring myself. I stayed with her until two in the morning. Then I wanted to have a bath, as I was very tired. I was just getting in when my servant knocked at the door saying he had a telegram for me. 'A very important telegram, very important indeed . . . a telegram from His Majesty the Emperor William!' I read the telegram, read it again and then repeated it aloud . . . but I couldn't understand a word. What on earth does William mean, I thought, pretending that it still depends on me whether war is averted or not! He implores me not to let my troops cross the frontier! Have I suddenly gone mad? Didn't the Minister of the Court, my trusted Fredericks, at least six hours ago bring me the declaration of war the German Ambassador had just handed to Sazonov? I returned to the Empress's room and read her William's telegram. She had to read it herself to bring herself to believe it. She said to me immediately: 'You're not going to answer it, are you?' 'Certainly not.'

"There's no doubt that the object of this strange and farcical telegram was to shake my resolution, disconcert me and inspire me to some absurd and dishonourable step. It produced the opposite effect. As I left the Empress's room I felt that all was over for ever between me and William. I slept extremely well. When I woke, at my usual hour, I felt as if a weight had fallen from mind. My responsibility to God and my people was still enormous, but at least I knew what I had to do."

"I think, Sire, I could give a somewhat different explanation of the Emperor William's telegram."

"Really! Let me have it!"

"The Emperor William is not a man of courage . . ."

"He is not."

"He's a comedian and a braggart. He never dares to go right through with what he undertakes. He has often reminded me of an actor playing the murderer in melodrama who suddenly finds that his weapon is loaded and that he's really going to kill his victim. How often have we not seen him frightened by his own pantomime? . . . I am inclined to think that the moment he had issued his declaration of war he got frightened. He realized the formidable results of his action and wanted to throw all the responsibility on you. Perhaps, too, he clung to some fantastic hope of producing by his telegram some unexpected, inconceivable, miraculous event which would enable him to escape the consequences of his crime. . . ."

"Well, your explanation is quite in keeping with William's character."
The clock struck six.

"My word, it's late!" the Emperor said. "I'm afraid I've wearied you, but I'm glad to have had an opportunity of talking freely to you."[20]

By 1914, the autocratic Tsar Nicholas II had regained his authority by excluding the Duma, his ministers, and his Council of Ministers from foreign policy and military decision making. Although in previous conflicts he had advocated peace, the tsar alone decided for war. In 1914, he had a reconstructed army with a standing force that outnumbered all others in Europe. Russia's economy was strong and growing, having recovered from the Russo-Japanese War and the Revolution of 1905. With ongoing heavy spending on military personnel and matériel and the third largest economy in Europe (behind Germany and Britain), Tsar Nicholas could confidently risk war in July 1914.

Sazonov has often been criticized for not knowing enough about military operations. But as we have seen, the tsarist governmental structure did not encourage such knowledge. Sazonov had worked closely with the tsar to avert international crises over Morocco in 1911 and the First Balkan War in 1912. But in 1914, Sazonov's mercurial character came to the fore as he wavered between feelings of assertiveness and despair. He clearly looked to 1912 and the Russian show of strength as a guide for his responses in 1914. But Sazonov understood neither the problems of partial mobilization nor what preparatory steps were even required for partial mobilization—with dire consequences.

General Sukhomlinov, for all his foibles, had significantly rebuilt and improved Russian military forces in accordance with the tsar's wishes, providing Nicholas with the tools to remain a player in European politics. At the same time, Sukhomlinov fought off the demands of parliament and the challenges presented by his critics. Yet the war minister failed in his communications with the tsar and the Council of Ministers, especially Sazonov. Like the foreign minister, the general saw no need for close civil-military cooperation.

Perhaps no European nation symbolizes the folly and futility of war better than Romanov Russia. Military blunders and defeats eventually undermined the tsar's legitimacy and led to two more Russian revolutions and a civil war.

For nearly a decade, Russian planners had put all their energy into rebuilding Russia as a great power, largely ignoring public opinion and the parliament. As we have seen, neither the system nor the individuals encouraged effective interaction among ministries. The singular emphasis upon status and departmental isolation created a tunnel vision that would destroy the monarchy and the country. Ironically, we can turn to the warnings of Rasputin who, had he been in Saint Petersburg, might just have made a difference.

RASPUTIN

A Warning

1914

In 1914, still lying in bed in Siberia recovering from his stab wounds, he [Rasputin] telegraphed, "Let Papa not plan war, for with the war will come the end of Russia and yourselves and you will lose to the last man." Anna Vyrubova, who delivered the telegram to the Tsar, reported that he angrily tore it to pieces before her eyes. Rasputin was undeterred. Taking a large piece of paper, writing in almost illegible letters, he scrawled this ominous prophecy:

> Dear friend, I will say again a menacing cloud is over Russia lots of sorrow and grief it is dark and there is no lightening to be seen. A sea of tears immeasurable and as to blood? What can I say? There are no words the horror of it is indescribable. I know they keep wanting war from you evidently not knowing that this is destruction. Heavy is God's punishment when he takes away reason that is the beginning of the end. Thou art the Tsar Father of the People don't allow the madmen to triumph and destroy themselves and the People. Well, they will conquer Germany and what about Russia? If one thinks then verily there has not been a greater sufferer since the beginning of time she is all drowned in blood. Terrible is the destruction and without end the grief.
>
> Gregory[21]

NOTES

[1]Nicholas II, *The Secret Letters of the Last Tsar: Being the Confidential Correspondence between Nicholas II and His Mother, Dowager Empress Maria Feodorovna,* ed. Edward J. Bing (New York: Longmans, Green, 1938), 238–40.

[2]Serge Sazonov, *Fateful Years, 1909–1916* (London: Jonathan Cape, 1928; reprint, New York: Kraus, 1971), 19.

[3]Ibid., 32–33.

[4]G. P. Gooch and Harold Temperley, eds., *British Documents on the Origins of the War, 1898–1914,* vol. 10, part 2 (London: His Majesty's Stationery Office, 1938), no. 528.

[5]Sergei Witte, *The Memoirs of Count Witte,* trans. and ed. Sidney Harcave (Armonk, N.Y.: M. E. Sharpe, 1990), 702–3.

[6]Vladimir I. Gurko, *Features and Figures of the Past: Government and Opinion in the Reign of Nicholas II,* trans. Laura Matveev, ed. J. E. Wallace Sterling, Xenia Joukoff Eudin, and H. H. Fisher, The Hoover Library on War, Revolution, and Peace, no. 14 (Stanford, Calif.: Stanford University Press, 1939), 562.

[7]Vladimir Sukhomlinov, *Erinnerungen* (Berlin: Reimar Hobbing, 1924), 375.

[8]Sazonov, *Fateful Years,* 36–38.

[9]Witte, *Memoirs,* 729.

[10]William C. Fuller Jr., *Civil-Military Conflict in Imperial Russia, 1881–1914* (Princeton, N.J.: Princeton University Press, 1985), 237–38.

[11]Dominic C. B. Lieven, *Russia and the Origins of the First World War* (New York: St. Martin's Press, 1983), 63.

[12]Maurice Paléologue, *An Ambassador's Memoirs,* trans. F. A. Holt, 3 vols. (London: Hutchinson, 1923), 1:11–13.

[13]M. N. Pokrowski and Otto Hoetzsch, eds., *Die Internationalen Beziehungen im Zeitalter des Imperialismus: Dokumente aus den Archiven der Zarischen und der Provisorischen Regierung,* series 1, vol. 5 (Berlin: Reimar Hobbing, 1934), no. 79.

[14]In his diary, the tsar was remarkably vague. Diary of Nicholas II, 12(25) July 1914, Krasnyi Archiv, 1934, no. 3(64), p. 136, in State Archives of the Russian Federation (GARF).

[15]Sukhomlinov, *Erinnerungen,* 373–76.

[16]Paléologue, *An Ambassador's Memoirs,* 1:42–43.

[17]*Kautsky Documents.* nos. 332, 335, 359, 366, 390, and 420.

[18]Pokrowski and Hoetzsch, *Internationalen Beziehungen,* series 1, vol. 5, no. 184.

[19]*Kautsky Documents,* nos. 487, 480.

[20]Paléologue, *An Ambassador's Memoirs,* 1:196–98.

[21]Robert K. Massie, *Nicholas and Alexandra* (New York: Atheneum, 1967), 268.

6

San Giuliano, Cadorna, and Italian Neutrality

On August 2, 1914, the Italian government informed its allies—Germany and Austria–Hungary—that it planned to remain neutral in the unfolding European war. That decision resulted from intensive debate among senior Italian political leaders throughout July. Antonino di San Giuliano, the Italian foreign minister, thoroughly dominated these discussions because Lieutenant General Alberto Pollio, chief of the Italian general staff, had died on July 1 following a heart attack. With Pollio's death vanished the one chance that Italy might fulfill its alliance commitments, since Pollio, unlike San Giuliano, strongly supported Italy's participation in the Triple Alliance. Pollio was not replaced until July 27 by Major General Luigi Cadorna, who held the post until 1917. Ironically, the new chief's first impulse was to support the Triple Alliance commitments, a stance that illustrates the habitual disarray of the strategic policy process in Italy, the so-called least of the great powers.

The Italian decision to remain neutral, following Rome's inability to persuade Austria–Hungary to offer a major territorial concession from Habsburg lands, is best understood in the context of Italian civil-military relations. Those relations, which had fluctuated dramatically over the decades, were rooted in the history of Italian unification and of Italy's participation in the Triple Alliance. Taken together, these perspectives help explain Rome's decision to abandon the alliance in August 1914 and, in May 1915, to enter the war on the side of the Triple Entente.

THE TRIPLE ALLIANCE AND ITALIAN POLITICS

Italy had joined the Triple Alliance in 1882. Strongly backed by the king, Umberto I, the alliance became the public bedrock of Italian foreign policy, though its secret terms were hidden from successive chiefs of staff and most cabinet ministers. Renewed periodically, its last affirmation came in December 1912, during the height of the Balkan Wars. During the 1880s and 1890s, military planners discussed the possibility of Italy's dispatching troops to help Germany in the event of a war with France. These plans were revised from time to time, including in the months before July 1914.

Italy's strategic position shifted significantly, however, after 1900. The Anglo-German naval race was disconcerting, for if Britain took the naval war against Germany (and the Triple Alliance) into the Mediterranean Sea, the long Italian coast and the Italian navy might suffer British attacks. That its alliance obligations might place Italy in conflict with Britain was a most unappealing prospect. At the same time, French foreign policy achieved success in Rome with a secret agreement that virtually nullified Italy's obligation to fight against France. And the accession of thirty-year-old Vittorio Emmanuel III to the Italian throne in June 1900, following his father's assassination, brought a new monarch far less committed to the Triple Alliance. Kaiser Wilhelm II's personal contempt for the young king did not help either, as the German monarch had allegedly called the Italian king's consort, Queen Elena, daughter of King Nikita of Montenegro, "a peasant girl" and "the daughter of a Montenegrin cattle thief."

The real tensions in the Triple Alliance were, however, between Italy and Austria–Hungary. Italy's defeat of the Habsburgs in the wars of Italian unification still rankled Vienna, while Vienna's retention of Italian-populated areas in the Trentino and the Tirol only inflamed Italian irredentism.* These frictions were further aggravated by strong Habsburg support of the Papacy in its continuing quarrels with the secular Italian state. Nor were strategic relations helped by General Franz Conrad von Hötzendorf, whose principal desire was to attack Italy. Indeed, as we saw in chapter 3, his repeated demands that Austria–Hungary attack Italy got him removed from office. In naval matters,

---

* *Irredentism:* the term describes the particular Italian longing for territories populated by Italians but under the rule of another government.

tensions increased after the Archduke Franz Ferdinand pressed the expansion of the Habsburg navy, precipitating an Austro-Italian naval race after 1900 that neither country could afford. Yet despite these tensions, the two allied enemies continued to develop elaborate plans for naval cooperation against a future French enemy.

A final source of tension was the archduke himself, whose contempt for the Italians was well-known. He was not a popular figure in Italy, where his family had disputed property rights; many Italians believed he wanted to regain Venice and thwart Italy's ambitions in the Adriatic. The Italian public's attitude was starkly revealed in the days after Sarajevo, when there was open jubilation over the archduke's death. The diplomats immediately took note, as correspondence between the Russian ambassador and foreign minister and between the British ambassador and foreign secretary makes clear.

ANATOL KUPENSKY

Letter to Saint Petersburg

June 30, 1914

I have covered in my reports the political questions about present-day Rome. But I could not in the reports communicate the full truth about the impression that the despicable murder of the Archduke Franz Ferdinand and his wife have called forth. In the indignation about the deed is mixed a feeling of relief from an unknown danger. The less-than-friendly feelings that the archduke had for the Italians and his warlike inclinations are taken as a given fact, and with his passing the chances for peace have increased. Thus the rise of the stock market after the arrival of the full reports from Sarajevo. Even in Austria itself—in Trieste— the Hungarian bonds rose the day after the murder of the archduke from 72 crowns to 100. San Giuliano told me, "The crime is awful, but it will not disturb world peace." Worse and more heartless, however, was the demonstration in the crowded cinemas, which are very full on Sundays, where the public, after learning of the news of Sarajevo, demanded the royal march. "Marcia reale, marcia reale," they began to cry, and the orchestra played it for the spectators. So the public here loves the Habsburgs, and of such tactlessness is it capable in these tragic circumstances.[1]

RENNELL RODD

Letter to London

July 7, 1914

It has been curious to study here the effect of that abominable assassination at Sarajevo. While ostensibly the authorities and the press have been loud in their denunciations of the crime and full of sympathy with the Emperor [Franz Joseph], it is obvious that people have generally regarded the elimination of the late Archduke as almost providential. I heard from two bankers here that at Trieste when the news was received Hungarian stock rose from 72 to 80. He was almost as disliked it seems in Hungary as in Italy.[2]

Luigi Albertini, a prominent Italian politician at the time and also editor of *Corriere della Sera,* an Italian daily newspaper in Milan, later wrote in his magisterial history of July 1914 of the Italian reaction to the news.

LUIGI ALBERTINI

The Origins of the War of 1914

1953

A Sicilian nationalist society went so far as to publish a manifesto expressing satisfaction over the crime and even the Foreign Minister San Giuliano's commemorative speech in the Senate spoke so unfeelingly of the victims as to rouse a protest from the Socialist *Avanti.*

Still more callous was San Giuliano in telephoning the news of the outrage to Prime Minister [Antonio] Salandra:

Is that you, Salandra? Do you know, we shall have no more bother about the Villa d'Este affair.*—How do you mean?—This morning they've murdered the Archduke Francis Ferdinand at Sarajevo.[3]

Villa d'Este affair: a property dispute involving Franz Ferdinand.

Given these strong reactions, Italian leaders had to consider the degree to which the public would support intervention on the side of its erstwhile allies. In fact, options for the Italian statesmen were far more limited than foreign observers believed—most of all the Austrian leaders, who fully expected Italy to help.

CONSTITUTIONAL ARRANGEMENTS AND CIVIL-MILITARY RELATIONS

The Triple Alliance, with its obligations and sharp Austro-Italian contradictions, formed the external framework for Italian foreign policy after the 1880s. The internal framework was equally contradictory and often self-defeating, owing to the history of Italian unification, the country's poverty, and the lack of an efficient central government. To complicate matters further, Italy, like Serbia, remained a fragile constitutional monarchy. Strong forces on the right wanted more monarchy and less parliament; emergent forces on the left wanted more parliament and less monarchy; and some wanted no monarchy at all. Forced to navigate among these positions was the monarch Vittorio Emmanuel III, who unlike his father attempted to address some of the country's social problems. Attentive to work but often unimaginative, Vittorio Emmanuel was inclined to let his ministers take the lead.

The monarch's constitutional position necessarily dictated the shape of civil-military relations in Italy. Under the constitution, the king retained complete control over the army, navy, and foreign policy, with parliament essentially serving as a consultative body. Italian parliaments were not informed about and had little say in foreign policy decisions and had less control over the military budget than almost any of their European counterparts. A pattern of royal decrees, press censorship, and outright bribery of the press helped to keep the king's power intact, and it ensured government ministers extensive freedom of activity.

The chief of the general staff was another key player in the policy process. He reported directly to the king, and he alone had authority to formulate the war plans and to prepare the army for war. But the generals who served in this position had almost no contact with civilian ministers or with diplomats. Rather, their principal contacts were with the war ministers, who rotated through office with bewildering rapidity before 1914. Moreover, in the years before 1914, only a single war minister had been a civilian, creating a situation whereby the military controlled the military. Blurring the civil-military distinction still more, military and naval officers were allowed to serve in parliament while on active duty. But appearances were misleading about the true power of the army in Italian politics on the eve of the Great War.

A few observations help explain the gap between the apparent political position of the army and the actual power that politicians had over it. First, the army budget usually took nearly half of disposable state revenues. Yet debates about military spending were infrequent and often ill informed; more often than not, the parliament simply ratified earlier royal decrees, which meant ratifying what the politicians had decided. Second, although military conscription meant that Italian men were expected to serve, in practice there were many exceptions. Life with the forces was extremely unpleasant, with shoddy quarters, poor food, and inept leadership. Nor was the soldiers' morale helped by their frequent use in quelling labor disputes. The army was not immune to increasing antimilitarism from a growing urban socialist movement, especially in northern Italy. Even Italian officers, though given great adulation on occasion, were treated poorly and underpaid.

Most important, the government ministers treated the Italian army as a political pawn, an instrument for glorifying the state and the monarchy and for advancing their own political careers. Paradoxically, in a state where the parliament as an institution had almost no effective control over the military, its civilian ministers—acting as the king's agents—had virtually unfettered control.

At the time of General Pollio's death on July 1, extensive staff talks were being conducted, planning for Italy's military cooperation with its Triple Alliance partners. This included the possible movement of up to three army corps through Austria to fight with Germany against France, as well as naval preparations. Yet these arrangements were dependent upon the personality and presence of General Pollio, whose Germanophile sentiments (he had an Austrian wife) had been carefully nourished by General Helmuth von Moltke and even General Conrad. His sudden death changed all of the calculations and left a void that Foreign Minister San Giuliano quickly filled, since Luigi

Figure 9.
Luigi Cadorna
Appointed at the end of July 1914, his first impulse was to support Berlin and Vienna even as his civilian superiors were planning to desert them. He gave mediocre leadership to Italian troops during the war, though he was never in doubt about his judgments.
Gianna Rocca, *Cardona* (Milan: A. Mondadori, 1985).

Cadorna was not appointed as the new chief of staff until the very last week of July 1914.

Cadorna's appointment as chief did not wholly come as a surprise. The son of an aristocratic Piedmontese military family, Cadorna had, like Conrad, spent his entire life in the military, serving in the infantry, the general staff, and as a corps commander. Small and not especially attractive, the sixty-three-year-old Cadorna was a harsh disciplinarian who trusted no one and often imagined conspiracies where there were none (Figure 9). As we shall see later, his ignorance about the actual condition of the Italian army and of the alliance arrangements with Germany and the Habsburgs further complicated Italian strategic policy as the war approached.

FOREIGN AND DOMESTIC POLICY
ON THE EVE OF WAR

Antonino di San Giuliano became Italian foreign minister in 1910, having served briefly in the position in 1905–06. This able foreign minister was a Sicilian, and a direct descendant of the medieval Norman conquerors; like Leopold Berchtold, San Giuliano was an aristocrat's aristocrat (see Figure 4 in chapter 3). His first political efforts at the local level were not successful. But once elected senator, his rhetorical skills won him wide public notice. During stints as undersecretary in the department of agriculture, in the foreign ministry, and then as postmaster general, San Giuliano had traveled widely, in the Balkans, Africa, and even to the United States. He had significant literary talent, becoming a recognized authority on drama and art, and at one time owned a leading Italian journal. Polished and urbane, his smooth manner masked a cynical attitude and an occasionally ruthless approach to politics worthy of Machiavelli.

After his first brief stint as foreign minister, he served as Italian ambassador, first to London and then to Paris. He returned to Rome in March 1910 as foreign minister in the first of three successive governments. San Giuliano played a leading role in the Italian decision to invade Libya, strongly supporting efforts of Italian Prime Minister Giovanni Giolitti to expand the Italian colonial empire. But by 1914 his health, always marginal (he had suffered from gout since his youth), had worsened, forcing him to leave Rome periodically for stays at various spas. For most of July 1914, he was at Fiuggi Fonte, a splendid resort outside Rome. His death in October 1914 deprived Italy of an able and successful political leader.

Since 1910, San Giuliano had presided over one of the most tumultuous periods of Italian foreign policy. Rome was worried about French efforts to control Morocco, and indeed, by early 1911, Paris appeared ready to take over the North African country, an action that led to the Second Moroccan Crisis. This alarmed San Giuliano, who feared that Paris might try to block Italy's long quest for Libya. In September, with European attention fixed on the Moroccan issue and a possible Franco-German war, San Giuliano and Giolitti pushed General Pollio and the Italian army into attacking the Turks in Libya, an operation that started in early October 1911.

Then the trauma began. The Turkish resistance stiffened, as did that of the native Arab population. On October 23, the Italian forces were defeated at Sciara Sciat. Nonetheless, San Giuliano declared victory, announcing the annexation of Libya on November 5, even ,as fighting continued. While the government-subsidized Italian press might boast of great colonial victories, the reality was far different.

During 1912, the continuing friction with the French government drew Italy more closely toward its supportive alliance partners. With the onset of the Balkan Wars in October 1912, San Giuliano hastily concluded peace with the Turkish government over Libya so he could face the consequences of the rapid collapse of Turkish power in the Balkans.

When the Balkan fighting resumed in early 1913, San Giuliano had to reckon with a far stronger Serbia and the ambitions of his own monarch's father-in-law, King Nikita of Montenegro, who seriously threatened the peace of Europe in May 1913. He also had to face the prospect of Austro-Hungarian intervention in the fighting. Nevertheless, for diverse and not altogether differing reasons, Austria–Hungary and Italy worked together to salvage their Balkan position. Moreover, in December 1912, Italy agreed to a five-year renewal of the Triple Alliance. Among the terms of the alliance were two clauses that prominently shaped San Giuliano's decisions, or his purported rationale for those decisions, in July 1914.

Fifth Treaty of the Triple Alliance between Austria–Hungary, the German Empire, and Italy
December 5, 1912, Vienna

Article III. If one, or two, of the High Contracting Parties, without direct provocation on their part, should chance to be attacked and to be engaged in a war with two or more Great Powers nonsignatory to the present Treaty, the *casus foederis* will arise simultaneously for all the High Contracting Parties. . . .

Article VII. Austria–Hungary and Italy, having in mind only the maintenance, so far as possible, of the territorial status quo in the Orient, engage to use their influence to forestall any territorial modification which might be injurious to one or the other of the Powers signatory to the present Treaty. To this end, they shall communicate to one another all information of a nature to enlighten each other mutually concerning their own dispositions, as well as those of other Powers. However, if, in the course of events, the maintenance of the status quo in the regions of the Balkans or of the Ottoman coasts and islands in the Adriatic and in the Aegean Sea should become impossible, and if, whether in consequence of the action of a third Power or otherwise, Austria–Hungary or Italy should find themselves under the necessity of modifying it by a temporary or permanent occupation on their part, this occupation shall take place only after a previous agreement between the two Powers, based upon the principle of a reciprocal compensation for every advantage, territorial or other, which each of them might obtain beyond the present status quo, and giving satisfaction to the interests and well founded claims of the two Parties.[4]

These clauses represent a careful attempt to anticipate change; they also suggest that neither Rome nor Vienna believed the status quo in the Balkans or the Ottoman Empire could long endure. Their actions, as we shall see, soon guaranteed that outcome.

While Austro-Italian relations were often rocky, Rome's connection with Berlin remained strong. The German government took every opportunity to flatter San Giuliano, including the conferral of the Order of the Black Eagle in 1912. Nor could the Italian politicians ignore the predominance of German capital and technology in the life of the Italian economy. Rome, moreover, could reasonably believe that Berlin might restrain Vienna from pressing any issue to the breaking point.

The reasonably cordial relations of 1912–13 with Vienna did not long endure. The outcome of the Balkan Wars helped to ensure that. Almost immediately, Rome and Vienna began to contend for control of the newly created Albanian government. The modest détente between Rome and Vienna had largely eroded by early summer 1914, as the jubilant reaction of the Italian public after Sarajevo suggested.

As San Giuliano sought to expand Italian influence in Albania and while General Pollio continued the staff talks mentioned earlier with Austria–Hungary and Germany, the domestic political situation in Italy veered dangerously out of control. Prime Minister Giolitti had resigned in the spring of 1914. His inexperienced successor, Antonio Salandra, within weeks of his appointment, had to face major domestic unrest, culminating in the so-called Red Week in June, when police fired on striking workers in the north. This action prompted still larger strikes. Cities proclaimed their independence from the monarchy, rail transport ended, newspapers shut down, and the country careened toward total chaos. The government called thousands of troops to duty in an effort to defuse the tense political situation. When the Sarajevo assassinations occurred, Salandra was totally preoccupied with Italian domestic politics. These demands, coupled with Pollio's death on July 1, assured Foreign Minister San Giuliano virtually complete control of Italian foreign policy during the July tensions.

SAN GIULIANO BEFORE THE ULTIMATUM
TO SERBIA

The Sarajevo deaths did not immediately alarm the Italian political leadership. While suitable regrets were expressed, the politicians were notably relieved to have the archduke and his vehement anti-Italian views off the scene. Although reports from Belgrade expressed concern over possible Habsburg action, the dispatches from Vienna and Berlin remained calm, even as the two northern allies agreed on July 5–6 that forceful action against Serbia ought to be considered.

Berlin, moreover, agreed with Count Berchtold's demand that Italy and Rumania be excluded from any prior knowledge of Vienna's true intentions. The Austrian foreign minister feared, correctly, that any possible Habsburg action would trigger either Italian opposition or a demand for territorial compensation. His stance also reflected Vienna's assessment that San Giuliano was fundamentally pro-Slav and thus almost certain to inform Serbia about Vienna's intentions. Whether logical or not, the decision to exclude Rome betrayed a carelessness about diplomacy that suggested that Germany did not consider Italy even the least of the great powers.

Almost immediately, however, Berlin began to fret about leaving Rome in the dark and soon decided that it really had to alert its envoy in Rome about Vienna's plans. Thus on July 11, the German Foreign Office informed its ambassador to Italy, Hans von Flotow, that the Habsburgs planned to confront Serbia with a set of demands that were likely to be unacceptable. This meant that war with Serbia was a strong probability. Flotow received the message at the Italian spa, Fiuggi Fonte, where coincidentally San Giuliano was taking the waters as well, at the same hotel. In a moment of unauthorized candor, Flotow revealed the gist of the dispatch to the Italian foreign minister. San Giuliano wasted no time in alerting his key ambassadors and ministers, including the Italian ambassador to Russia, Andrea Carlotti, and chargé d'affaires in Belgrade, Giuliano Cora; those alerts would have far-reaching consequences.

ANTONINO DI SAN GIULIANO

Telegrams to Saint Petersburg and Belgrade

July 14, 1914, 2:30 P.M.

From a very genuine source I have learned that the Austro-Hungarian government will ask the Serbian government for the dissolution of the Pan-Serbian associations and will not concede on this point. Perhaps it would be advisable for the Serbian government to anticipate such a demand by dissolving [the associations] on its own initiative. There is no lack of support for doing this in the legislatures of each country, and no means are lacking for the gradual reconstitution in less dangerous moments and under different names those associations which have been dissolved. Naturally, this suggestion cannot be the focus of official conversations between Your Excellency and the [Serbian] government, but perhaps you can find a way for it to come indirectly to the Serbian government so it can be prepared for it. It is necessary and urgent, in order for Serbia to avoid grave danger, that it cease the Pan-Serbian propaganda in Bosnia-Herzegovina which the Austro-Hungarian government believes is fomented by Serbian agitators resident in Belgrade.[5]

A further conversation with Flotow only deepened San Giuliano's fears and prompted still new warnings, again to Saint Petersburg and Belgrade, but also to Ambassadors Riccardo Bollati in Berlin and Giuseppe Avarna in Vienna.

ANTONINO DI SAN GIULIANO

Telegrams to Vienna, Berlin, Saint Petersburg, and Belgrade

July 16, 1914, 3:15 P.M.

I have recently had several conversations with the German ambassador [Flotow] about the probable Austro-Serbian conflict. He believes that Austria will ask Serbia for serious measures against Pan-Serbian propaganda, and if Serbia resists, [Austria] will use force. He does not believe that Austria has a goal of territorial expansion, and he has begged me to influence our press to advocate localization of the future conflict.

I have answered him that I will continue to influence the press in the friendliest possible way toward Austria, but I will certainly not succeed if Austrian demands are not just and [if they] do not conform to the liberal principles of our public law. I have repeated to him that we consider as contrary to our interests Austrian territorial aggrandizement and that we will do everything possible to prevent it. I have added that if the Austrian demands are excessive and of a reactionary nature, our press and our public opinion will be unanimous against Austria, and if the press allows itself to uphold localization of the conflict, that will certainly not convince Russia to allow Serbia to be crushed. I communicate to Your Excellency the preceding

[For Vienna and Berlin] for the use you consider advisable.

[For the others] for your exclusive personal information.[6]

There were further consequences to Flotow's indiscretions. The Austrian code breakers made quick work of the Italian cipher when the second telegram reached Vienna. Berchtold thus knew that the Germans had revealed the main lines of Habsburg policy and that Italy, Russia, and probably Serbia would also know what Vienna planned. He therefore became even more secretive in his dealings with his allies. And he now knew what he had already suspected: that San Giuliano was not ready to support the Dual Monarchy against Serbia. The Italian action reinforced his determination to leave Rome in the dark and to ignore Germany's hints about the need to compensate Italy with Italian-speaking territory from the Habsburg monarchy.

While Vienna studiously pursued its unilateral policy and continued to ignore Rome, San Giuliano for his part began to reconsider the fundamental basis of Italian foreign policy. A thoughtful dispatch from his Berlin ambassador, Riccardo Bollati, had prompted much of his new thinking.

RICCARDO BOLLATI

Letter to Antonino di San Giuliano

July 8, 1914

It is impossible to imagine a stranger or more dangerous situation, as you are a hundred times correct, Your Excellency, and it is urgent to rush to the situation. But which problem? If there were nothing more than the Albanian question dividing us! But there are so many other causes of dissension, so many other areas of friction: the Lovčen question,* the possible conflict between Austria and Serbia, the frightening problem of a possible union between Serbia and Montenegro . . . the possession by Austria of provinces of Italian race and tongue which in the Kingdom belong to Italy *by right* and must one day or another belong to her also *by fact;* the treatment by Austria of the population of those provinces; the clerical question; the failure to return our Sovereign's visit. . . . I touch very briefly; but one knows that in such conditions the slightest incident is sufficient to cause complications and jeopardize the stability of the alliance.

In reality, there is not a single question in which the interests of Italy are not, or are not thought to be, in conflict with those of Austria, in which the policy of each of the two governments is not intent on jealously watching and often opposing that of the other, on setting up safeguards against it, and is not inspired by the conviction that what helps the one must necessarily hinder the other.

And furthermore there are those differences, those antagonisms between the basic mentality of the ruling classes and of public opinion in the two states. It has been often said — and I believe it — that the principal reasons for the disagreement and misunderstanding between Italy and Austria–Hungary have been the fact that the two countries do not know each other. For some time now, I have begun to believe that if they knew one another better, an agreement would be even more difficult. It would be enough — on the occasion of the hereditary archduke's

---

* *Lovčen question:* Mount Lovčen, a part of Montenegro, dominated the Habsburg harbor at Cattaro (today Kotor) along the Adriatic coast; Habsburg naval leaders wanted control of the mount to ensure the safety of their ships.

funeral in Vienna where the ancient considerations of etiquette are superimposed upon every political and human judgment—to understand the profound abyss that exists among the dominant forces. It is true that the same differences exist between France and Russia, but that alliance has an extremely powerful cement that unites the two allies: communal hatred against the German enemy. In our case, this is lacking. In Italy, there is not even antagonism toward France. If in Italy hatred exists in the popular culture, it is against the ally; in Austria, in essence there is not even this, and you could say that Austria–Hungary even hates herself, given the dynamic and reciprocal hostilities among the diverse nationalities of which the Dual Monarchy is composed.

All these things, fundamentally, are banal truths that Your Excellency knows better than I but which bear repeating and confirm the difficulty of maintaining intact and legitimate the Triple Alliance. In the four years that you have directed Italian foreign policy, all of your collaborators have seen what prodigious activity and ability you have exerted in bringing harmony to our international situation in the popular Italian conscience. And, if you will allow me to say it, you have done a marvelous job characterized by a series of partial successes. . . . And yet there is no hope, in my opinion, that even after the disappearance of he [Franz Ferdinand] who posed as the most fearsome adversary of Italy, that the situation [in the alliance] will get better.

For this there is another axiom almost universally admitted in which I no longer have faith—that pronounced by Count Nigra*—Italy and Austria must necessarily be allies or enemies. And I ask myself with greater urgency and insistence whether the dissolving of our ties with Austria would lead fatally to war. Rather, would not it make for a more loyal and better rapport between the two states if they did not have the difficulty of maintaining the special obligations of the alliance?

But I understand, on the other hand, that "a jump in the dark" would represent a break with the system formed so long ago as the basis of all foreign policy and that, after all, has had the undeniable advantage of assuring us of peace for thirty years. And thus I remain frightened. And after thinking, also too long on all of the inconveniences and dangers of the present situation, I see no way of remedying our position with effective and enduring results.

In all of this I have taken the liberty of discussing extensively with Your Excellency the relations between Austria and Italy and have not considered—in the area of my special competence as the royal ambassador to Berlin—the position that takes and will take us to the framework of our relations with the third ally [Germany]. On this point, I believe I can express, quickly enough, that the German government,

---

* *Count Nigra:* The Italian ambassador to The Hague Peace Conference in 1899.

before and indeed very much before, holds a very high value in maintaining the participation of Italy in the Triple Alliance. . . . Berlin sees that the cordiality between Italy and Austria must be maintained and will do everything possible to remove issues of discontent between the two allies or to neutralize their consequences. But if the day should fatally arrive and if the differences became insurmountable and led to a break between Austria–Hungary and Italy, Germany would opt for Vienna and not Rome.[7]

The ambassador's assessment was jarring. In his opinion, the contradictions of the Triple Alliance were detrimental to Italy, but he could see no other policy. And to make things worse, he feared the reaction of the German government if it had to choose between its two allies. What he did not know was that Berlin had in fact just made that choice by giving Vienna the "blank check" and allowing Berchtold to ignore Rome.

The Italian foreign minister responded immediately to the disturbing missive from his Berlin ambassador.

ANTONINO DI SAN GIULIANO

Letter to Berlin

July 14, 1914

I thank you greatly for your most interesting letter of the 8th, which I received today.

Your Excellency confirms my fears that relations between Italy and Austria could be threatened in the very near future by the serious questions that we must confront and resolve, involving important interests that are not easily reconciled by the two Adriatic powers. I believe it is not in our best interests to be caught unaware of these events; rather, we should hasten to stipulate—if possible—which accords between Italy and Austria might be mutually satisfactory. . . . I do not underestimate the difficulty of reaching such agreements, and while it is dangerous to leave unresolved doubts regarding the attitudes that the two powers should maintain, it could possibly be even more dangerous at this moment when things might be avoided or retarded. Between these opposite dangers the wisest path seems to me for now that of avoiding direct negotiations between Italy and Austria and of letting Germany sound the terrain in Vienna in order to see on which bases a possible Italian-Austrian accord for Albania and in general the Balkan peninsula could be reached. While Your Excellency goes ahead with the above-mentioned steps in Berlin and the government will do so in Vienna, I will have time to confer with the President of the Cabinet [Salandra] and to take orders from his Majesty the King, since Your Excellency will understand that on these serious matters I alone cannot take binding resolutions for the Royal government. I will wait therefore, with impatience, to learn the results of [your] conversations with Jagow [German foreign minister], and, where necessary, with the chancellor [Bethmann Hollweg].

Your Excellency has confirmed for me what, more than once, Flotow has said to me, that the German government sees the dangers which threaten Italian-Austrian relations and in turn the Triple Alliance, and he urges that Your Excellency take advantage of this in order to get definite results. Until positive actions take place, it is necessary that this government and that of Austria–Hungary explore more deeply the profound differences which exist between their countries and the absolute impossibility for the Italian government to follow a policy unwanted by the public and the majority in the Chamber of Deputies. Agreements between Italy and Austria must therefore be acceptable to the will and thought and sentiment of the public and of parliamentary opinion. The German and Austrian leaders must understand this. . . .

The same considerations apply to the possible Austrian-Serb conflict resulting from the assassination of the hereditary archduke.

All of our policies should be geared to impeding also in this case an increase of Austrian territorial expansion which does not bring to us corresponding adequate territorial compensation. And in this case the difficulty is aggravated for us, as I explained to Flotow, by the impossibility of supporting Austria in whatever she presents to Serbia incompatible with the liberal principles of our public law and inspired by the ideas of the Holy Alliance* about legitimacy and the divine right of kings, which is not yet dead in Berlin or Vienna.

I leave it to Your Excellency to make the German government understand all of this.

I come now to the serious problem of whether it is suitable for Italy to remain in the Triple Alliance.

To me it seems possible, even probable, that in the near future it will be feasible for us to exit the Triple Alliance. But for the moment it is better to remain in it. For the moment, in fact, the Triple Alliance is

---

Holy Alliance: a diplomatic alignment supporting peace after the end of the Napoleonic Wars. It has often meant, and does in this case mean, the reactionary policies associated with Russia, Austria, and Prussia after those wars.

stronger on land than is the Triple Entente (and the outcome of a war will be decided on land). Beyond this, above all France would dictate unacceptable conditions which would be incompatible with our interests, our dignity, and our future if they knew we were isolated and no longer supported by our allies.

Before even discussing the practicalities of coming to the final decision of whether or not to stay in the Triple Alliance, Italy must strengthen itself economically and militarily and demonstrate to the world that the fears caused by the recent disorders about the solidity of the monarchy and of the nation are not valid. And we need . . . to create . . . an atmosphere of greater reciprocal sympathy between us and the Triple Entente. But above all, before making a decision this serious it is necessary that we be assured of the true strength of forces of the two [alliance] groupings.

It is probable but not certain that in four or five years Russia will be even stronger than today. . . .

I believe as well that Austria is tending toward weakness and to disintegration, but for now it is militarily very strong and certainly able to damage us greatly, nor is it possible to see how long—possibly very long—it will take for the process of disintegration, which seems unavoidable. . . .

The prognosis is therefore reserved for the future, and I do not exclude the probability of leaving the Triple Alliance within the next few years in order to align with another group or to remain neutral. But . . . I do not believe leaving would improve our relations with Austria because the very causes which place our relations in danger (Albania, Lovčen, etc.) would not be lessened, while it would diminish those which reduce our dangers, which is the conciliatory work of Germany in maintaining Austria and Italy in the Triple Alliance.

Nor do I believe that it is in our best interest, as Your Excellency seems to conclude, to limit ourselves and risk the damage or danger of doing nothing to stop or to mitigate the situation. The situation is difficult, but that does not mean we should not attempt to reach an agreement, and I believe that the moment is propitious because there are in the governments in Vienna, Berlin, and Rome faithful men convinced of the necessity and efficiency of the Triple Alliance, and there are ambassadors to Vienna and Berlin who are highly appreciated by the countries to which they are posted, such as Your Excellency and the Duke of Avarna.[8]

San Giuliano's reply to Bollati, the Italian ambassador to Berlin, reflects both concern for the future of the Triple Alliance and for the role played by Italian public opinion. He agreed with the ambassador's assessment of the difficulties of maintaining the alliance but had determined that, for the time being, it was best to maintain the status quo. And he had sent a clear signal to Berlin about the limits of Italian support for Austria–Hungary in its struggle with Serbia.

The Italian army, meanwhile, remained leaderless. There are no indications that either the army or the navy leadership had any advance notice from San Giuliano of Vienna's intention. The Italian defense establishment remained out of the information loop.

Vienna's delivery of the ultimatum profoundly challenged the Italian foreign minister, who felt he had been betrayed, ignored, and even ridiculed by Vienna. These feelings governed his strategy during the next two weeks.

THE ROAD TO NEUTRALITY

Because the ultimatum apparently violated Section VII of the Triple Alliance, which called for consultation about possible territorial gains in the Balkans, the foreign minister asserted early—but with adequate ambiguity—that Italy had no obligation to help Austria–Hungary. From the start, he and Prime Minister Salandra were in full accord on the Italian position. He moved to inform his key diplomats—Bolatti in Berlin and Avarna in Vienna—and the king of his thinking, but he made absolutely no effort to inform the army or the navy.

ANTONINO DI SAN GIULIANO

Telegrams to Vienna and Berlin

July 24, 1914

To-day we have had a long conversation between the Prime Minister, Flotow and myself, which I summarize for the personal information of Your Excellency and for your guidance in further conversations.

We, Salandra and I, first of all drew the Ambassador's attention to the fact that Austria had no right, according to the spirit of the treaty of the Triple Alliance, to undertake a *démarche** such as she has made to Belgrade without previous agreement with her allies.

Démarche: a diplomatic term for "step" or "action" or "overture."

By the style in which the note [the ultimatum] is couched and the demands it contains, which, while ineffective against the Pan-Serb danger, are deeply offensive to Serbia and indirectly to Russia, Austria has plainly shown that she means to provoke a war. We therefore told Flotow that, in view of this behaviour on the part of Austria and of the defensive and conservative character of the treaty of the Triple Alliance, Italy is under no obligation to go to the help of Austria in case that, as a result of this *démarche* of hers, she finds herself at war with Russia, since any European war in this case is the consequence of an act of provocation and aggression by Austria.[9]

ANTONINO DI SAN GIULIANO

Letter to King Vittorio Emmanuel

July 24, 1914

Sire,
    As Your Majesty will have seen from the telegrams going off, both I in my instructions to Your Majesty's representatives and in conversations with foreign representatives, and Salandra and I in . . . to-day's conversation with Flotow, have up to the present said and done nothing that might limit Italy's freedom of action in the events which may derive from the Austrian *démarche* at Belgrade.

    It was, indeed, our duty to await and we do await Your Majesty's orders; and to Your Majesty's high wisdom I submit the line of conduct proposed by me to the President of the Council and approved by him, subject to Your Majesty's approval.

    We are both convinced that it is most difficult, perhaps impossible, and certainly extremely dangerous to drag Italy into taking part in an eventual war provoked by Austria and waged in the interest of Austria.

    It is also necessary before committing ourselves to a definite line of conduct to assure ourselves that it will be the one most corresponding to our interests. It seems to me, then, that what is expedient for us is:

1. To maintain to our allies that for reasons adduced in the telegram now being dispatched we are under no obligation to take part in the eventual war;
2. To assure ourselves, before supporting our allies even diplomatically, that they accept our interpretation of Article VII of the treaty of the Triple Alliance;

3. To assure ourselves of eventual compensation for any increase of territory whatsoever on the part of Austria;

4. To assure ourselves of eventual compensations for our eventual, but not probable participation in the war, a participation to be decided pro or contra freely when the time comes;

5. Possibly also to secure for ourselves doubtless very minor compensation, or at least guarantees that our interests shall not be damaged, in return for any diplomatic support given to our allies.

This attitude on our part is for the moment facilitated by the fact that Austria–Hungary has not up to the present asked us for any support or even for any opinion whatever regarding her note to Serbia.[10]

While San Giuliano prepared to shift Italian policy, his ambassador in Vienna, Avarna, continued to suggest to Berchtold that Italy would support Habsburg actions. Part of this was deception; part reflected the groping nature of Italian thought about what would most benefit Italy. But by July 27, the foreign minister's position was clear as he twice cabled Berlin and Vienna, each time with increasing urgency.

ANTONINO DI SAN GIULIANO

Telegrams to Vienna and Berlin

July 27, 1914, 3:35 A.M.

I beg you to speak immediately with [German Foreign Minister Gottlieb von] Jagow because the urgency is extreme. Direct negotiations are not possible between Italy and Austria. They would lead to almost certain breakdown. It is very urgent that such discussions be initiated by Germany. The only territorial compensation possible for Italy is to gain a part of Austria's Italian provinces that correspond to her territorial expansion elsewhere.... Without adequate territorial compensation, it would cause an irreparable split in the Triple Alliance and would also provoke Italian public opinion to such excitement as to force the government to go to war with Austria. It is extremely necessary to rush to the barricades, and only Germany can do it. Your Excellency may, as if it were a personal indiscretion, also show this telegram to Jagow.

It is of utmost urgency that Germany open discussions at Vienna because until such doubt is cleared up, our entire position must necessarily be in substance anti-Austrian or at least inspired by suspicion toward Austria, and for that reason it must be aimed at creating obstacles to her action and away from proceeding toward an agreement with Russia. Today I expressed myself more or less in the following terms to Flotow, who however seems to me less convinced than he was the other day of the urgency of German action in Vienna; he manifested his faith in Austria's intention not to desire territorial expansion.

July 27, 1914, 12:10 P.M.

The Treaty of the Triple Alliance has for its goal the maintenance of the territorial status quo, especially in the Balkan peninsula. For this reason, if Austria modifies it even in a small way to her advantage, she violates it, and since we have an interest that this does not occur, it is clear that in such a case we would be released from all the obligations, even moral ones, of the alliance, and our politics would be completely identical to and coordinated with Russia's and with all those powers averse to the territorial aggrandizement of Austria.

[For Berlin only] It seems to me that, in a private, friendly, and non-threatening manner, unofficially but as a debt of loyalty, Your Excellency could find a way to have Jagow know about what has gone before.

[For Vienna only] I have said to Bollati that he should find a way to let Jagow know the preceding information naturally in a private, non-threatening, unofficial and friendly manner, and I rely on the tact of Your Excellency to leave an impression of loyalty and a desire for friendship to the extent that Berchtold is completely convinced of it.[11]

What do these telegrams suggest about the true goals of Italian foreign policy? Was San Giuliano being a clever opportunist, a realistic diplomat, or a traitor to his allies? Does his position seem a principled one, and how would it appear to Vienna? What does it say in terms of overall Italian strategic policy, and why did he exclude the military in his formulation?

Gradually, as the crisis unfolded, San Giuliano's position hardened. Supported by Prime Minister Salandra, the foreign minister left no doubt in Berlin and Vienna that Italy must receive assurances of compensation or it would stand aside. Later critics, including his contemporary and political opponent, Luigi Albertini, accused San Giuliano of behaving irresponsibly, seeking territorial gains for Italy when he should have focused his efforts on thwarting Vienna's drive to war.

San Giuliano steadfastly held to compensation as the price of Italian intervention. And he had reason to believe it might be forthcoming, for Berlin had urged Berchtold on a number of occasions to make territorial concessions. But Berchtold believed that Italian neutrality was arguably the best he could expect from any alliance arrangement, hence his unwillingness to offer firm assurance about the bestowal of territory. And Italian neutrality was precisely what Austria–Hungary got. On August 2, the civilian government adopted a policy of neutrality, which it announced on August 3.

In reaching this decision, the Salandra government had strong support from the Italian public. Among the many displays of support, one of the most ironic came from the future Italian dictator, Benito Mussolini, who in July 1914 edited a socialist paper, the *Avanti*. George Seldes, an early biographer of Mussolini, made these observations.

GEORGE SELDES

Mussolini and the War

July 1914

The Socialist Party on July 29, 1914, issued its proclamation:

"It is to the interest of the proletariat of all nations to impede, circumscribe, and limit as much as possible the armed conflict, useful only for the triumph of militarism and parasitical business affairs of the bourgeoisie.

"You, the proletariat of Italy, who, in the painful period of crisis and unemployment of the recent general strike have given proof of your class consciousness, of your spirit of sacrifice, must now be ready and not let Italy go down into the abyss of this terrible adventure."

The phrasing of the proclamation was Mussolini's; his name was signed with that of other leaders. One day earlier, he had written in *Avanti*, "The proletariat must no longer temporize, it must express immediately its desire for peace. If the government does not heed unanimous public opinion but enters into the new adventure, the 'truce of arms' declared by us at the close of the Red Week [the June upheavals] will be ended."

And another day: "In the case of a European conflagration Italy does not want to precipitate itself into the ultimate ruin, but has one attitude to take—neutrality."[12]

Within weeks, Mussolini would abandon the Socialist Party and would soon become one of the leading proponents of Italian intervention into the war. He later described his feelings at this time.

BENITO MUSSOLINI

My Autobiography

1928

It is interesting to-day [1928] when democracy is challenged to recall that the Liberal Democratic pacifist group, headed by Giovanni Giolitti, a man of great influence in parliament and also a shrewd organizer of political schemes, was busy in an attempt to find a formula which would solve the problem of righting the borders of Italy, but which would save our country from the burden, the sacrifice and the loss of life that every war imposes. Giolitti promised that, even without war, Italy could obtain a great deal. This "great deal" awakened a feeling of sarcasm in the generous hearts of Italians. Naturally they are realists and the enemies of all forms of political bargaining.

Italians were looking beyond those peaceful concessions and those petty betterings of the borders. They did not believe in the sincerity of this scheming. I considered it weak statesmanship—the statesmanship of compromise. There were seers who saw in the European conflict not only national advantages but the possibility of a supremacy of race. In the cycle of time, again a dramatic period had come which was making it possible for Italy by the weight of its army to deal as an equal with the leading nations of the world.

That was our chance. I wanted to seize it. It became my thought of intensity.

The World War began on July 28, 1914. Within sixty days I severed my official connection with the Socialist party. I had already ceased to be editor of the *Avanti*.

I felt lighter, fresher. I was free![13]

While Mussolini made his switch, Giolitti, as the future dictator suggested, supported the more cautious approach of San Giuliano and Salandra. An exchange of letters between Giolitti and San Giuliano at the very time of the neutrality proclamation reveals much about the uniformity of Italian opinion at this point, a uniformity that Mussolini would later do much to undo.

ANTONINO DI SAN GIULIANO
Letter to Giovanni Giolitti
August 3, 1914

Ruspoldi* has telegraphed me your opinion on the policy we should adopt, which is, in fact, the same I proposed at once to Salandra and to His Majesty and which has been approved. Once more you and I have had the same idea without having been able to communicate previously. Salandra has been looking for you in order to know your opinion and he will now be very happy to learn that it coincides with the attitude he has adopted. I sincerely trust you are in good heath.

*Prince Mario Ruspoldi, first secretary of the Italian embassy in Paris.

GIOVANNI GIOLITTI
Letter to Antonino di San Giuliano
August 5, 1914

Dearest Friend,
    I have been in Vichy, Paris, and London, and I must confess that I did not think it possible that a European war could be provoked so light-heartedly. I was only convinced on July 31st and the day after I hurried back to Italy.
    The manner in which Austria has precipitated the conflict is nothing less than brutal, and proves either a total lack of conscience on her part, or a direct intention to bringing on a European war. I may be mistaken, but my impression is that she will pay the penalty more than anyone else.

Happily matters were so ordered as fully to justify our neutrality. I make no concealment of the danger that we may also suffer thereby, but the government now has no other alternative. A conflict between Italy and England is out of the question, and the way in which the war was brought about would have made it very difficult for our country to enter into it with enthusiasm. I may add that the ends Austria has in view are evidently not in keeping with our interests.

In my opinion, now more than ever, we should keep on good terms with England and should do our utmost to limit the duration and consequences of the conflict.[14]

While San Giuliano and Salandra moved to the decision for Italian neutrality, they belatedly also began to deal with the military aspects of the unfolding European crisis.

GENERAL CADORNA'S CONFUSED REACTION TO THE CRISIS

Since July 25, Rome had been receiving reports of Habsburg military preparations. This initial information went to the general staff, which had no chief until Major General Cadorna's appointment on July 27. This appointment came not a moment too soon, since there were continuing reports and rumors of mobilizations across Europe.

On July 29, for example, Cadorna received the following intelligence assessment from the Italian ambassador in Vienna about Habsburg preparations.

GIUSEPPE AVARNA

Telegram to Antonino di San Giuliano

July 28, 1914, Arrived July 29, 7:15 A.M.

For the Chief of the General Staff.*

The military attaché provides me news of a general nature, which I believe important to communicate.†

*The question marks reflect missing code groups from the original telegram.

†Military attachés frequently routed their reports through foreign ministries for security purposes.

The first day of mobilization is under way. Until now the mobilization of six army corps plus some Landwehr [reserve] divisions had been discussed. Now information indicates that eight army corps in addition to Landwehr divisions along with the Landsturm [third-line troops] of respective geographical areas will be mobilized. This would bring the number to more than 450,000 soldiers. I still cannot specify the army corps that will be mobilized, but based on what many have said and given the railway arrangements involved, I believe we are almost certainly talking about the army corps from Budapest, Temsevar, Sarajevo and Ragusa; those from Prague, Leimeritz, Kaschau, and Agram are doubtful, as are those corps at Graz and Vienna (?) . . . around the initial day of operations. About two weeks will be needed to mobilize and assemble this great mass, but one does not know whether the Imperial and Royal Government may have secretly taken prior measures to accelerate mobilization and concentration operations, and thus from what moment the above-mentioned period of mobilization must be calculated.

Along the Sava and Danube [rivers dividing the adversaries] many Serb forces have apparently (?) vacated large areas of land, it seems. Serious fights there are thus unlikely. It is not so on the Bosnia-Herzegovina frontier, where fighting could break out soon if the Serbians and even the Montenegrins maintain themselves in the adjacent mountains along the border. The initial operations depend in great part on the campaign plan; it seems, however, certain that preparatory or partial operations could (?) still take place in a few days. The major advance will not take place until the concentration of forces is completed, that is, as soon as possible within the above-indicated period, or around two weeks. If, however, the Austro-Hungarian command want to wait to have all forces in place—even second and third line—it will take (?) even more time. Some cavalry will be sent to Galicia [on the Russian frontier], and other precautionary measures will be taken on the Russian border. Numerous Dalmatian troops are concentrated in Cattaro and surrounding areas.[15]

This report, along with others, confirmed the broad outlines of Habsburg mobilization. At this point, of course, the plans focused on operations against Serbia and limited precautionary measures against Russia. Italy's northern neighbor clearly intended to settle accounts with Belgrade.

Far more surprising, General Cadorna's initial reaction was to support the ally's intentions. In fact, on his first day in office, he told the German military attaché that he affirmed all of the alliance arrangements, and he put this in writing to General Moltke the same day. The general's inclination was thus to follow the plans developed by his predecessor, General Pollio, and approved by both the king and the government and to affirm support of the Triple Alliance. Conrad was overjoyed, if surprised, at the prospect of Italian assistance—so much so that he wrote the following to Cadorna on August 1, a letter that arrived in Rome after Italy had proclaimed neutrality.

FRANZ CONRAD VON HÖTZENDORF

Letter to Luigi Cadorna

August 1, 1914

The serious situation which has suddenly arisen compels me to request Your Excellency to proceed with those negotiations, begun verbally, which I personally carried on in strict secrecy with his late Excellency, Pollio. The substance of them was that, over and above the forces which, in pursuance of already existing agreements, Italy is to send in direct support of Germany, further forces are to be rendered available . . . for the direct support of Austria–Hungary.

I beg Your Excellency kindly to furnish information about what these would be and where they are available and further ask you to allow the requisite agreements to be made between the two General Staffs for the taking over and transport of these forces as was already the case for the forces put at the disposal of Germany. I beg you to send Your Excellency's delegate to Vienna and provide him with the requisite plenary powers.[16]

Cadorna, even before Conrad's letter, had already started to honor Pollio's arrangements. In fact, on August 2, the same day neutrality was decided, he got King Vittorio Emmanuel's approval to send all Italian troops not involved in Libya northward to help Germany against France. General Cadorna's confused reaction illustrates the compartmentalization of Italian military planning, where a very senior military commander could make a transnational agreement without the knowledge of the civilian leadership. His apparent total ignorance of the evolving diplomatic situation revealed far less about his abilities than about senior Italian politicians' lack of regard for their military associates. In this instance, there was an apparent problem in civil-military relations, but only because the civilian leadership had paid scant attention to the military issues during July and had asked few if any questions about the nature of the Triple Alliance's military and naval arrangements.[17] One might also ask why the king, who was privy to all of the diplomatic maneuvers, did not clarify the situation.

In any event San Giuliano soon discovered that as he was moving Italy toward neutrality, the new chief of the general staff was pushing ahead with preparations to support the Triple Alliance. This remarkable divergence speaks worlds about the problem of governmental coordination, even at moments of the greatest crisis. The following detailed and nuanced account was given by Luigi Albertini, an astute and well-placed observer.

LUIGI ALBERTINI

The Origins of the War of 1914

1957

Pollio's successor, General Luigi Cadorna, who took over the command on 27 July 1914, found a spiritual heritage and tradition of studies which from the outset swept him along in the wake of his predecessor. He never doubted that Italy would range herself with her allies and therefore on 29 July ordered "the emergency military measures necessitated by the international situation." The first four army corps for concentration on the French frontier were to recall their effectives.* Storehouses and shelters in the Alps were to be reprovisioned. The V, VII and XI Corps of the Rhine Army and the first two cavalry divisions were to be brought up to strength. Fortress artillery was dispatched to the fortifications barring the Alps. Authorization was sought for the immediate transfer of artillery from the eastern to the western frontier, leaving the Austrian frontier undefended in order to strengthen the French frontier. Moreover, on 31 July Cadorna laid before the King a *Short Memorandum on the north-western concentration and on the transport to Germany of the largest possible force.* After summarizing the previous agreements and referring to the promise lately made to Germany to dispatch three army corps and two cavalry divisions to the Rhine, Cadorna continued:

* *Effectives:* soldiers equipped for duty.

It is my firm conviction that the proposed solution will not fully meet the needs of the Triple Alliance until it reaches the limits of its capacity. In other words, I think we ought not only to reassign five army corps (in addition to the cavalry divisions) to the army destined for Germany (this, moreover, was one of the wishes and proposals of the late General Pollio); but we must also aim at sending to what will be the chief scene of operations in the war all surplus forces in excess of our needs on the north-west frontier and at home. . . . Our interests cannot but coincide with the general interest of the alliance group to which we belong. The balance of power between the hostile group of States is tilting against the Triple Alliance; failure on our part to exert full strength in order to restore stability would be disastrous for the general interest and for ours in particular.

Two days later, on 2 August, General Brusati, the King's first aide-de-camp, replied to Cadorna that "H.M. the King, to whom I submitted the *Short Memorandum on the north-western concentration and on the transport to Germany of the largest possible force,* approves of the basic conceptions developed by Your Excellency." This, however, does not mean that on 1 August the King was persuaded to enter the war on the side of Germany and Austria–Hungary. . . . [Albertini notes the confusion in the Italian government.]:

The fact is that between the political and the military leadership the necessary close understanding was lacking. . . . Hence while the Government was preparing to deny the occurrence of a *casus foederis* Cadorna sent word to [the Austrians] that he was making every effort to collaborate with the allies.[18]

When the politicians finally notified Cadorna of their neutrality decision, he stopped the anti-French movements. More surprisingly, he did an immediate about-face, calling for total mobilization and preparations for an attack on Austria–Hungary. This adventurous idea San Giuliano also thwarted, preferring instead to prepare the army more carefully and to await the best territorial offer, whether from London or Vienna, before committing Italy to war. San Giuliano and Premier Salandra judged the opposing military forces too balanced and an Italian decision to intervene too dangerous until the war revealed some results. Eight months later, in May 1915, Italy joined the Triple Entente and went to war. By 1918, more Italians had died in the conflict than lived in the coveted area of Trentino for which they fought.

The July crisis saw Italian civil-military relations continue their earlier dysfunctional pattern. There was no coordination, no disclosure, no shared estimates of the dangers. As in 1911, San Giuliano and Salandra controlled the policy and made the key decisions. Even the monarch played a very secondary role. Thus in one sense, the civilian leadership had firm control of the situation. San Giuliano carefully determined the risks and opted for neutrality. Whether Italy might have gained had Rome supported Berlin and Vienna can only be speculated. Italian help would probably not have made much difference in the west, nor would Italian naval help have much altered the flow of the Mediterranean naval action.

But Italian civilian ambitions had their limits, most of them harmful. The civilians wanted to see Italy treated as a great power, and this meant territorial gains even if the Italian military might not be able to fulfill that desire. To be sure, the months after August 1914 saw hurried efforts to improve Italy's fighting forces, but they remained inadequate. The earlier weaknesses could not easily be overcome. Only in the naval sphere could Italy hope to match and possibly overcome Austria–Hungary. Thus when war came in 1915, the Italian army failed. Paradoxically, as the army failed, its power to run its own operations increased enormously. By late 1915, Cadorna exercised virtual dictatorial powers in northeastern Italy.

After 1915, the civilian leadership, as well as the monarch, had almost become spectators. The military leadership was determined to guarantee that Italy remained a great power. The question after 1915 became whether the military could endure long enough to let military developments elsewhere on the Continent ensure them a measure of success. These developments finally came in late 1918. Italy then saw itself as a victorious power and thus a great power, rather than more realistically as the beneficiary of others' victories instead of its own. Those illusions of success would persist, helping not least in bringing fascist dictator Benito Mussolini to power in 1922. Militarism, not civilian values, would ultimately triumph and continued to do so in Italy until 1944.

NOTES

[1] M. N. Pokrowski and Otto Hoetzsch, eds., *Die Internationalen Beziehungen im Zeitalter des Imperialismus: Dokumente aus den Archiven der Zarischen und der Provisorischen Regierung,* series 1, vol. 4 (Berlin: Reimar Hobbing, 1934), no. 29.

[2] *British Documents on the Origins of the War, 1898–1914,* vol. 11 (London: His Majesty's Stationery Office, 1926), no. 37.

[3] Albertini, *Origins,* 2:216–17.

[4] Sidney B. Fay, *The Origins of the World War,* 2d ed., 2 vols. (New York: Macmillan, 1930), 1:548–49.

[5] *I Documenti Diplomatici Italiani,* 4th ser., 1908–1914, vol. 12 (Rome: Libreria della stato, 1964), no. 201. (Hereafter cited as *DDI.*)

[6] Ibid., no. 272.

[7] Ibid., no. 120.

[8] Ibid., no. 250.

[9] Albertini, *Origins,* 2:315; the original is in *DDI,* no. 488.

[10] Albertini, *Origins,* 2:318–19; the original is in *DDI,* no. 470.

[11] *DDI,* nos. 575, 584.

[12] George Seldes, *Sawdust Caesar: The Untold Story of Mussolini and Fascism* (New York: Harper Brothers, 1935), 50.

[13] Benito Mussolini, *My Autobiography* (New York: Charles Scribner's Sons, 1928), 37–38.

[14] Giovanni Giolitti, *Memoirs of My Life,* trans. Edward Storer (London: Chapman and Dodd, 1922), 380–81.

[15] *DDI,* no. 633.

[16] Albertini, *Origins,* 3:308.

[17] On this issue, John Gooch, *Army, State and Society in Italy, 1870–1915* (London: Macmillan, 1989), is very helpful.

[18] Albertini, *Origins,* 3:307–8.

7

Poincaré, Joffre, and the Effort to Protect France

During the July crisis, the French government exerted more effective control over its military than any other great power. This control continued the pattern begun after the celebrated Dreyfus affair and affected both the development of French strategic plans and their actual implementation in 1914. To be sure, throughout the crisis, the French government found itself reacting to developments more than any other power except Great Britain; thus France's military choices were always limited. But the degree of civilian supervision remains impressive.

By July 1914, the two key French leaders—President Raymond Poincaré and Chief of the General Staff General Joseph C. Joffre— had been interacting with each other since early 1912. Each understood the assumptions of French military strategy and the limitations imposed by the Triple Entente and by the persistent current of French antimilitarism. Each perceived the dangers posed by formidable Germany and the strategic risks created by the alliance with Russia. The interplay of these two men offers yet another perspective on civil-military relations on the eve of the Great War.

FRANCE AFTER THE SECOND MOROCCAN CRISIS

The French Third Republic, created in the 1870s following France's defeat by Prussia in 1870–71, had to overcome France's strong monarchical tradition. Despite the French Revolution, after the fall of Napoleon Bonaparte in 1815, two short-lived monarchies were succeeded by the reign of Louis-Napoleon, nephew of the great Napoleon, but that regime lay defeated by Bismarck and the Prussian armies after 1870. The republic's early existence had in fact been highly provisional, as many believed a monarchical restoration would take place.

Instead, what had emerged was a republic formally headed by a president elected for a seven-year term by the French senate and with a parliament composed of a senate and a chamber of deputies. The senate and the chamber, especially the latter, were considered the true repository of national power. The president's major responsibilities were representational, as the head of the French state. The most significant presidential duty was to select the head of the government, the prime minister, based on his estimate of who would form a working and durable cabinet from among the deputies and the senators.

This presidential task was not an easy one since in France political parties existed in only the most informal sense. Instead, there were political blocs and factions, often shifting on every significant issue. With the exception of the socialists, the absence of strong party discipline (unlike in England, where the lines were very distinct) meant that parliamentary coalitions were constantly shifting. In practical terms, this made for a rapid turnover of parliamentary regimes, with premierships often measured in months and not years.

The full impact of this instability was partially offset by the frequency with which the same ministers returned to power. At the same time, the ministerial turnover meant that the bureaucratic staffs, especially those of the French Foreign Office and the Army General Staff, were exceptionally powerful players in the development of diplomatic and strategic initiatives.

Paradoxically, after the Second Moroccan Crisis of 1911, an unusual degree of stability ensued. Poincaré became premier in January 1912 and stayed in power a year. Then he won election to a seven-year term as president of France. This first-ever elevation of a premier conferred an element of continuity. So also did the presence of Joffre, who had been appointed chief of the general staff in July 1911 at the height of the Moroccan crisis. He would serve until 1916. Before July 1914, the two men had thus worked together closely for nearly thirty months on a series of interlocking problems, some of long duration, others dictated by Germany's response to the Moroccan crisis, and still others by the shifting attitudes of the French public.

For more than four decades, following the defeat by Germany and the loss of the provinces of Alsace and Lorraine to Berlin, French national self-esteem had suffered. Berlin or London always seemed to hold the upper hand. The successful extension of the French colonial empire in 1911 with control of Morocco, followed by the German retreat over the issue, stirred emotions and prompted a revival of French nationalism.

On the domestic front, this resurgent pride had to confront some troubling military legacies. First, in the prolonged Dreyfus affair, the French general staff had persistently refused (from 1897 to 1906) to exonerate the unjustly convicted Jewish captain, Alfred Dreyfus, of spying for Germany, even after Dreyfus received a presidential pardon in 1899.[1] This failure damaged the army's standing among leading republican politicians and writers, such as Émile Zola. The obvious anti-Semitism of the affair troubled many republicans, who blamed the aristocratic and Catholic officer corps, thus creating tensions on the civil-military front. Later, the Dreyfus affair came to represent the latent but potent anti-Semitism not only in France, but across all of Europe. Second, and perhaps more damaging, the political use of the army to quell strikes in 1906 and after eroded the army's position with the French public. In this atmosphere, not surprisingly, the French socialists and trade unions trumpeted the virtues of a "nation in arms" militia and derided the professional military establishment. These political attacks in turn contributed to a lack of army discipline and caused additional problems for the army leadership.

Then came the Second Moroccan Crisis. While the French public probably did not fully appreciate the risk of war, it did appreciate the diplomatic success. Further, the public was more prepared, as later passage of a three-year military service law revealed, to accept some additional burden to strengthen France against Germany. Above all, as their reaction in August 1914 showed, the French people were less antimilitary than simply opposed to army involvement in domestic labor issues. It was in this more positive environment that Joffre and Poincaré operated after early 1912.

THE IMPACT OF POINCARÉ ON FRENCH POLICY

Raymond Poincaré reached his long-sought premiership in January 1912 at the age of fifty-two. Born in the French province of Lorraine in 1860, he had seen his homeland overrun by the Germans in the Franco-Prussian War in 1870 and his family forced to flee. Eventually, they returned to Bar-le-Duc, which remained French, and endured three years of German occupation that ended when France paid off the financial penalty imposed by the Germans as part of the peace settlement in 1871. After local schooling, Poincaré was sent to Paris and the famous lycée Louis-le-Grand. He then went on to study law. In 1880, he embarked on a successful legal career, at the same time becoming a reserve sublieutenant in the *chasseurs à pied* (light infantry).

Slowly, Poincaré established himself as a rising national politician. In 1886, he won a local election and a year later gained victory in the parliamentary elections to become the youngest member of the Chamber of Deputies in Paris. Working on parliamentary committees and avoiding the limelight, he committed himself to the "service de la France." His first ministerial post came in 1893 as minister of public instruction, the fine arts, and religion. Energetic, and scrupulous in his work and political dealings, Poincaré epitomized the pragmatic, republican deputy firmly committed to secular values yet also tolerant of the place of the Catholic Church in France. Contemporaries expected great things from Poincaré, as he did himself (Figure 10).

Poincaré came to office without a publicly defined foreign policy. Nevertheless, his quiet ability and good political judgment served him well. First, he worked to revive and strengthen France's alliance with Russia. Damaged by the efforts of German diplomacy and Russia's basic disinterest in any Moroccan war, the alliance with Russia gave France that added margin of protection against an aggressive Germany. Poincaré sought to encourage closer military collaboration with Saint Petersburg and secured French funds for crucial Russian railroad construction. He visited Russia in August 1912 and engaged in frank and cordial talks with Tsar Nicholas II and senior Russian officials. By late 1912, Poincaré had done much to strengthen the Franco-Russian alliance.

Poincaré also sought to buttress the Anglo-French relationship. His arrival in office coincided with Anglo-German talks that rattled Paris. Throughout 1912, the premier tried assiduously to convert the ambiguous but tenacious entente with Britain into a written agreement. The entente, first signed in 1904 as a colonial agreement between London and Paris, had evolved into a strategic partnership with secret military arrangements. Nevertheless, the British government always insisted that it was an entente—or "understanding"—not a written alliance,

Figure 10. Raymond Poincaré

Ardently nationalist and deeply anti-German, as premier and president Poincaré kept French military planners closely controlled while working hard to
assure France of British and Russian support. His absence from Paris on a
state visit to Russia in July 1914 probably hurt the cause of peace.

Getty Images.

thus leaving British policymakers' options open. This cross-Channel relationship was reinforced by the Anglo-Russian entente, as well as the formal Franco-Russian alliance dating from the 1890s. Taken together, these three agreements came to be known as the Triple Entente. Not surprisingly, Poincaré wished to put these crucial strategic relationships into writing, especially the ties with London. But Sir Edward Grey showed little willingness to accede to French pressures. Still Poincaré persisted, never wavering from his conviction in 1912 (or in the July crisis) that British support was imperative for French survival.

Finally, in the fall of 1912, the British foreign secretary agreed to exchange letters with the French ambassador, Paul Cambon, and thereby make the nature of the Anglo-French relationship more precise. As the final, written articulation of Anglo-French relations before July 1914, the Grey-Cambon letters pledged the two governments to discuss any threatening attack by a third power and to consider what measures they might take. The joint military and naval staff conversations would form the basis for consultation, but those talks committed neither government to a definite course of action. Approved by the British cabinet in November 1912, the Grey-Cambon letters were not revealed to the Parliament or to the public.

Over the next two years, as premier and then president, Poincaré continued his efforts to stay close to London. In the spring of 1914, King George V and Sir Edward Grey received a tumultuous welcome in Paris. On that occasion, in his toast to the king, the French president made his feelings about the entente quite clear.

RAYMOND POINCARÉ

Toast to George V

April 21, 1914

The visit of Your Majesty and Her Majesty the Queen today to France is a striking confirmation of the friendship that has heretofore endured through time and experience and which has demonstrated its permanent effectiveness and which matches the thoughtful will of two powerful nations, equally attached to peace, equally passionate for progress, equally accustomed to the habits of liberty. During the brief hours that

Your Majesty will spend among us, it will only be possible to see a few aspects of France's physical and moral life.

The artistic, athletic, and military events will help France to show, if in summary form, some elements of our national character. You will easily find in the honorable virtues of our democracy some of the traditional forces that have made, for a long time, the grandeur and glory of England: the sense of moderation, order, and social discipline, the presence of patriotic duty, the joyful acceptance of necessary sacrifices, the fervent cult of an ideal which is never eclipsed and which fills with light the life of the entire nation.

After a long rivalry which has left these immortal lessons and mutual respect, France and Great Britain have opted for friendship, to coordinate their thoughts and unite their efforts. Ten years ago, the two governments settled peacefully the questions which divided them. The agreements settled that day, so happily prepared by the perceptiveness of His Majesty King Edward VII and his ministers, have given birth to a more general entente, which has henceforth become one of the sure guarantees of the European equilibrium. I do not doubt that under the auspices of Your Majesty and His government, these intimate ties will be strengthened daily, to the great profit of civilization and universal peace. It is this wish that I very sincerely give in the name of France.[2]

Poincaré, at the same time, never relaxed his vigilance toward the Triple Alliance. If he did not encourage anti-German sentiment in the national revival that he came to symbolize, he did not discourage it either. There were no efforts to seek a détente with Berlin. He wanted to keep the Germans defined as the key French defense problem, not as a possible partner in an international agreement. Nor did he move to improve relations with the least reliable member of the Triple Alliance, the fickle Italians. For Poincaré, the Triple Alliance represented a solid, cohesive block.

By the end of 1912, Poincaré's year as premier and foreign secretary had been productive. He had enhanced the standing of the Triple Entente and had avoided France's being dragged too deeply into the Balkan Wars. He had refused to follow any path that relaxed tension with the Triple Alliance, a policy that Germany's increasing military manpower only helped to ratify. And in all of this, Poincaré supported and encouraged the chief of the French general staff, General Joffre, whose own efforts to improve French security against Germany had also prospered during 1912.

JOFFRE MOVES TO REVAMP FRENCH STRATEGY

Joffre had been appointed at the height of the Second Moroccan Crisis. His military career to this point did not suggest that he would become one of the most important generals in French history. The son of a Pyrenean barrel maker, Joffre, like his Italian and Austro-Hungarian counterparts, had spent his entire adult life in the military. After serving during the Franco-Prussian War while a student at the École Polytechnique, Joffre had spent his early military career largely in France's expanding colonial empire. In 1905, he had returned to France as director of engineers, having thus avoided the political intrigue of the Dreyfus case. In his new position, he performed so well that he became a divisional and later corps commander. Then, in 1910, Joffre was appointed director of support services, a key logistical assignment that he again handled very well. Yet despite his lengthy career, Joffre had never attended the École Supérieure de Guerre, the staff college, nor had he commanded an army-size unit in any of the summer maneuvers (Figure 11).

Instead of that background, he brought to his new assignment proper political and religious credentials and an almost peasantlike intuitiveness for good decisions once the fighting started. This background did not, of course, necessarily ensure that his overall approach to strategic planning would be especially creative. On the other hand, when the war actually came, his calm demeanor served France well, as did his insistence on good meals and a good night's sleep, even at the time of the greatest German threat to Paris in early September 1914. Joffre's skills at the Battle of the Marne saved France, even as his strategic plans nearly brought disaster before then.

Thanks to Adolphe Messimy, the war minister in 1911, Joffre consolidated his power quickly, for Messimy gave the new chief of the general staff unprecedented authority over both preparations for war and war planning. The new, unified position allowed Joffre to impose his strategic views, and those of his key associates, upon the army far more effectively than any of his predecessors.

If the general brought no preconceived views on strategy to his new position, he soon subscribed to the concept of the "ardent offensive" as the only strategy worthy of the French soldier. While Joffre never entirely forgot the requirements of defense, he had an exaggerated faith in an offensive strategy against Germany, believing that it

Figure 11. Joseph Joffre

Regarded as imperturbable, the general *(left)* wanted France to attack Germany through Belgium, but Poincaré blocked it. Only Joffre's calm leadership at the Battle of the Marne saved France from the mistakes of the war plan that he had prepared.
Imperial War Museum.

would ensure quick victory. His command position guaranteed, moreover, that his views became the prevailing orthodoxy and the credo soon affected development of a new French war plan.

Joffre faced a number of major problems in revising Plan XVI, his predecessor's war plan, which called for an initial defensive posture against Germany and an "army of maneuver" to attack offensively at a selected point later. From the start, Joffre thought Plan XVI did not guard enough against an attack through Belgium, since he believed, as did his fellow generals, that Germany would violate Belgian territory. He also believed—like his German counterparts, who would actually do so—that an offensive thrust through neutral Belgium offered France the surest way to victory over Germany. He reached this conclusion early, and he never abandoned his efforts to implement Plan XVII. (See Map 5 in chapter 4.)

One of his first attempts came on February 21, 1912, as Joffre tried to persuade the newly installed Poincaré to sanction a Belgian invasion. His account of the strategy session reveals the arguments for and against the plan.

JOSEPH JOFFRE

Memoirs

1932

The problem for us, therefore, was extremely difficult. I felt it my duty to inform the Government as to the possible consequences of its decision concerning the attitude we must reserve in regard to Belgium. An occasion presented itself on February 21, 1912, at the secret conference held at the Ministry of Foreign Affairs, which lasted from 9 P.M. until midnight. . . . Its object was to discuss the last measures concerted between the Russian and French General Staffs for the application, in case of necessity, of the terms of the Alliance, and to set forth the nature of the secret pourparlers* between the British and French General Staffs.

The Minister of Marine explained the nature of the naval arrangements arrived at between the British Admiralty and the French Naval Staff. . . .

On my side, I informed the meeting that our conversations with the British Staff touching the land forces had taken as a basis six infantry divisions, one cavalry division and two mounted brigades, a total of one hundred and twenty-five thousand combatants. . . .

Taking the strictly military point of view, which my duty obliged me to make clear to the Government, I then explained to the Conference that if we could conduct our offensive across Belgium—*assuming that no other considerations prevented such a course and that we could come to an understanding with the Belgian Government beforehand*—the problem presented to us would be simplified and our chances of victory would be singularly increased. Asked to elaborate this idea, I expressed myself as follows:

* *Pourparlers:* talks.

In case of war with Germany, the plan which would be most fruitful in decisive results consists in taking from the very start a vigorous offensive in order to crush by a single blow the organized forces of the enemy.

The existence close to the Franco-German frontier of natural obstacles and fortified barriers, restricts our offensive to narrowly limited regions. . . . Therefore neither in Alsace nor in Lorraine do we find ground favourable for an offensive having in view immediate decisive results. . . .

From this statement of the case I deduced the conclusion that we had a major interest in feeling free to push our armies into Belgian territory, and do it without waiting until such time as the Germans had themselves violated Belgium, as it was probable they would do. I added that it might perhaps be possible to suggest through diplomatic channels to the British Government the solution that appeared to us the most advantageous. . . .

But the Prime Minister, M. Poincaré, pointed out that an invasion of Belgium by France would run the risk of setting against us not only Europe but the Belgians themselves, by reason of the difficulty of coming to an understanding with them beforehand; under these conditions it seemed essential that our entrance upon Belgian territory be justified at least by a positive menace of German invasion. Indeed, it was this fear of an invasion of Belgium by the Germans which, in the first place, had led to the military agreements with Great Britain. We, therefore, had to be sure that a plan based upon a march by us through Belgium would not have for its effect the withdrawal of British support from our side.[3]

Poincaré thus flatly refused to consider the Belgian option. Not only did he think the Belgians would not agree (and later soundings proved him correct), he intensely disliked the risk of offending London. Subsequent negotiations with London during 1912 confirmed that the British would never accept a French violation of Belgium before a German move. Even General Henry Wilson, the strongest advocate of British intervention, warned Joffre in November 1912 not to consider a Belgian move as a strategic option.

Poincaré's intervention represents — quite simply — the most significant civilian intervention in all of pre-1914 strategic planning. In no other country, including Britain, did a civilian exert such formative influence as the French premier and foreign minister in 1912. His determination to secure British aid eventually succeeded. At the same time, this diplomatic consideration set French strategy on a course that almost proved disastrous in 1914. Still, it can be argued, in fairness to Poincaré, that he correctly assessed the diplomatic situation. The failure to gauge the extent of the German offensive, the failure to consider possible German use of reserve troops, and a total commitment to an "offensive attack" were Joffre's own contributions to the near disaster of August 1914.

The general's failures, aside from his commitment to the offensive, centered upon the fundamental problem of manpower. Since 1904, the French general staff had various intelligence reports that indicated that Germany planned to violate Belgian neutrality and to use reserve units in the process. Most senior French generals dismissed the possibility of a German offensive dependent on reserve troops. Then Berlin's decision in 1912 to increase sharply the size of its standing army, from 646,000 to 782,000, convinced the French generals anew of their views about reservists. Why would the Germans increase their standing force unless they wanted to reduce dependence on reservists and thus be ready to launch an immediate attack on France?

The German decisions had domestic political ramifications in France. Given the population differences (Germany had 65 million citizens, France 40 million), the French responded in the only way possible: a three-year service obligation for all conscripts. Poincaré and Joffre strongly supported this increase in service time. Passed by a solid parliamentary majority in 1913 over vehement socialist protest, the law became a central issue in the general election of 1914. Indeed, opposition was so strong that Poincaré and Joffre feared that the law might be repealed in late 1914. Not surprisingly, the law became the rallying cry for all who disliked the French army, and once more, antimilitarism reared its head. Still, the law was in effect when the assassinations in Sarajevo occurred, and France had the benefit of 90,000 extra troops.

After the May 1914 general election had seen substantial gains by the socialists and the opponents of the three-year law, René Viviani formed the new government. Elected originally as a socialist deputy from Paris in 1893, Viviani had actually voted against the three-year law. His appointment by Poincaré represented a concession to the surge of public opinion against the law and to the leftward shift seen in the elections. On the other hand, Viviani, no longer a socialist, had pledged to the president not to seek the repeal of the law, and thus it remained on the books as the July crisis began to unfold. Still, the leadership of the government was in the hands of a former socialist who was serving as both premier and foreign minister and whose previous ministerial experience was limited. Not surprisingly, Poincaré would intrude into government operations during the July crisis far more than his constitutional responsibilities should have allowed.

During 1913, Joffre had also worked to complete what became known as Plan XVII. While Poincaré watched from the Élysée presidential palace, Joffre and his colleagues crafted an offensive strategy that went into effect in February 1914. Joffre planned to position French forces so they could resist a German offensive through the Belgian Ardennes below the Meuse-Sambre or defend against a German thrust from Lorraine. But the plan's central intention was to launch an immediate attack between Metz and Thionville, a bold step unlike the cautious approach of Plan XVI. In addition, British forces would extend his left flank in the area of Le Cateau. Despite the British location in 1914, two German armies (the first and second) would completely outflank both the British and the French forces.

In his determination to seize the offensive, Joffre had severely underestimated the German use of reserve troops and had endangered France's fundamental security. But these realities would only become apparent in August 1914. In the meantime, Joffre and Poincaré could believe that, with Plan XVII, they had secured France's strategic position. The ties with Russia and Britain were stronger than ever. National morale had improved, and new, more comprehensive war plans had been prepared. All of their efforts would be tested far sooner than they expected.

SARAJEVO, FRANCE, AND POINCARÉ'S TRIP TO RUSSIA

On Sunday, June 28, President Poincaré and his wife were at Longchamps, the famous French racecourse, for one of the major racing events of the season, when word came of the assassinations in Sarajevo. In his memoirs, Poincaré recounts the arrival of this news.

RAYMOND POINCARÉ

Memoirs

1927

I had presided at the hotel, Palais d'Orsay, over a corporate lunch with the departmental republican press, and I had been received by the group with fraternal good spirits. That afternoon, it was the Grand Prix de Longchamp.* Madame Poincaré and I, following the custom, had to attend the race. We traveled in splendid weather, in a carriage and four, and in the streets of the Bois, a happy and carefree crowd pressed around us. One can never say enough about the services rendered by the sun to the popularity of heads of state. We found in the presidential box the presidents of the chambers [of the senate and the deputies] and the diplomatic corps. Our hosts had prepared a buffet. The purity of the sky, the affluence of the spectators, the elegance of the dress, the beauty of the racecourse with its great field of green—all made for a charming afternoon. I followed with little distraction the galloping of the horses, when a telegram from the Havas agency† was brought to us and threw us into consternation. It reported that in a visit to Sarajevo, the archduke Franz Ferdinand, heir to the Austrian throne, and his morganatic wife,‡ the duchess of Hohenberg, had been mortally wounded. Two successive attacks had been committed: the first, they said, by a printer of Serbian race but an Austrian subject, with the name Kabrinovitch, who had thrown a grenade, but only wounded some passersby; the second by a student, named [Gavrilo] Princip, also an Austrian subject, who had fired several shots from a Browning pistol, nearly point-blank, at the archduke and the duchess of Hohenberg, wounding the former in the head, the latter in the abdomen. Both were transported to the Konak,§ where they died some minutes later.

Although this news was not official, I felt obliged to show the telegram to Count Szécsen, the ambassador of Austria–Hungary, who was not far from me in the box. He turned pale and asked my permission to leave to return to his embassy in order to await information from his government. The other ambassadors were informed but did not

* *Grand Prix de Longchamp:* one of the most important French horse races.
† *Havas agency:* a news group.
‡ Emperor Franz Joseph, who had not wanted Franz Ferdinand to marry Sophie because her aristocratic standing was not high enough, had insisted that the couple agree to a morganatic marriage, which meant that none of their children could succeed to the throne. Whether Franz Ferdinand would have honored that arrangement, had he lived, is another matter.
§ *Konak:* city hall.

retire, and I found myself forced to stay until the end of the races. But all we could speak of was the murder and the political complications that might ensue. Some asked themselves what would be the future of the Habsburg monarchy, the children of the archduke and his morganatic marriage having been excluded from succession to the throne by Franz Joseph. Others worried about the new problems being posed in the Balkans. M. Lahovary, the Rumanian minister, was very somber. He feared that the crime would give Austria the pretext to declare war.

Returning to the Élysée, I immediately telegraphed the old emperor: "I have learned with indignant sadness of the attack which inflicts upon Your Majesty a new pain and which puts a new sorrow on the imperial family and on Austria–Hungary."[4]

During the next two weeks, the French government carefully followed dispatches from Vienna on the Habsburg reaction to the assassinations. Some reported talk of Austro-Hungarian demands on Belgrade; others suggested that Franz Joseph would keep the military party under control. On July 6, from Saint Petersburg, where Maurice Paléologue now served as ambassador, came Russian Foreign Minister Serge Sazonov's warning that it would be dangerous for Vienna to pressure Belgrade too much. Yet French officialdom did not believe that a major international crisis was at hand.

Members of the French press devoted far more attention to the aftermath of Sarajevo than their British counterparts did. While there was ample coverage of the Franco-Russian alliance and the impending French state visit to Russia, the Parisian papers followed the Balkan tangle closely and left few doubts that French sympathies were with the Slavs.

LE TEMPS

Austria–Hungary and the Slavs

July 2, 1914

No one should be astonished at the profound and sad sensation that the Sarajevo assassination has provoked in Austria–Hungary. Everyone understands that the authorities, which did so poorly in protecting the lives of the archduke and the duchess of Hohenberg, are putting particular ardor into finding the criminals and their possible accomplices. But it would be deplorable if innocent people are charged and if the Sunday tragedy further deepens the abyss that separates Austria–Hungary and Serbia.

Reports from Sarajevo and Agram* indicate that damage to Serbian property runs to two million crowns and that some Serbs have fled, while others remain hidden in their houses. The Serbian minister in Austria has received death threats. Viennese students have run through the streets, crying, "Down with Serbia! Down with Peter! Down with Alexander! Down with assassins." This is unacceptable violence, and it is, we hasten to add, condemned by the majority of Austro-Hungarian opinion.

*Agram: the capital of Croatia, known today as Zagreb.

LE FIGARO

Austrian Nervousness

July 3, 1914

The anti-Serb manifestations that had taken place at various points in the Austro-Hungarian monarchy have reached such a point that the government has to do something about them. In Sarajevo, the Muslim population has attacked Serbian shops, and even the police, who did so poorly in protecting the archduke, have not intervened during the attacks. In Agram, the Croats, one of the most turbulent races, have broken windows of Serbian shops and vandalized some cafés. This is not the first time that this has occurred in the Croatian capital; it happened ten years ago when I was visiting Austria–Hungary; I arrived the day after such attacks had taken place in Agram.

This does not mean that the Viennese authorities are intentionally closing their eyes to the violence. But the situation does allow that conclusion to be drawn by public opinion.

Legally and diplomatically, Serbia is in an unassailable situation. No country in the world could be held responsible for the acts of isolated individuals, even if the crime is outside the bounds of humanity. That is so evident that it does not require a minute of discussion. If the Austrian police believe that they have traces of a true plot that might have certain ramifications in Serbia, then it would be sufficient to tell the Serbian authorities. The latter, without waiting to be asked, would at once do whatever is needed to assist the legal actions as the authorities would all do in civilized countries.

Before the Sarajevo Investigation

July 10, 1914

Le Temps said, on the day after the death of the archduke, what it thought of his ideas and his projects. We persist in believing that he was a great deal more a man of his country than a man of a clan. That does not make less true that certain parties who attached themselves to him have not changed their method and attempt to graft to his tragic death various enterprises suggested by their passions: This is true for the military party and the Catholic party whose actual violence expresses itself in something other than disinterested sadness. . . .

We do not deceive ourselves: The future of eastern peace and perhaps of Europe depends on the direction taken by the Sarajevo investigation. If it holds to the facts, nothing is risked. There are victims, assassins, weapons of murder: the guilty arrested, the criminals confessed, the weapons seized, all elements for a serious trial and a fair judgment.

But there is another eventuality that could happen, following a poor tradition, of making of the investigation of the two fanatics a monstrous process against Serbia and Serbism, that is to say, against the South Slavs—retracing all of the consecutive events of the annexation, of grouping a collection of tendentious accusations that represent Serbia as a people of conspirators and murderers whose existence is an obstacle to European peace, in order to reject finally everything Slavic and to project on the Russians, champions of the Slav ideal, a part of the responsibility attributed to the Serbs.

The second eventuality could put into question the peace of Europe.[5]

On July 16, Poincaré and Viviani confidently embarked at Dunkirk for a long-scheduled state visit to Russia. They arrived at the Russian capital on July 20 for a three-day visit. The two leaders were not scheduled to return to France until the very end of July, since state visits to Scandinavia were also planned. Thus, in the critical days of July 1914, the two most senior French leaders were away from Paris, and day-to-day government operations rested in the hands of second-rank officials.

The Russian trip gave new evidence of the strength of Franco-Russian relations. During the visit, Poincaré pointedly warned the

Austro-Hungarian ambassador in Saint Petersburg that Vienna should not press Serbia too far. He also discussed the details of a Franco-Russian naval convention. Whether talks with Sazonov and others went into extensive detail about the possible Balkan crisis remains uncertain.

Still, two facts seem clear. First, Poincaré and his close associate, Ambassador Maurice Paléologue, were thoroughly committed to the Russian alliance, and the Russians knew this. Second, the French military expected the Russians to launch an offensive by the fifteenth day after the start of Russian mobilization, thus putting deterrent pressure on Germany. Poincaré, though a civilian, fully grasped that the Russian strategy was to intimidate both Berlin and Vienna, not just the latter. His civilian counterparts in Britain never fully understood how Russia's aggressive policy might send the crisis out of control, since it meant that the Germans would implement the Schlieffen-Moltke plan rather than conduct further negotiation. But that grim reality was days away. When Poincaré and Viviani left Saint Petersburg on the afternoon of July 23, they were confident about the strength of the alliance. Many hours later, the two leaders learned of Vienna's ultimatum to Belgrade.

While Poincaré and Viviani visited Russia, French domestic attention focused not on Sarajevo, but on the murder trial of Henrietta Caillaux, wife of former prime minister, Joseph Caillaux. In March 1914, Madame Caillaux had confronted Gaston Calmette, editor of *Le Figaro,* over a series of scandalous articles about her husband's previous mistress and later first wife. She ended the conversation with a revolver, killing the editor immediately. Arrested and charged, she came to trial on July 20. All of France followed the proceedings; indeed, not until July 25 would the emerging Balkan crisis get any notable press coverage at all. On July 28, Madame Caillaux was acquitted, a stunning reversal of expectations.

The acquittal tarnished Joseph Caillaux's political career, making him the target of attacks during the war from those who charged him with being pro-German. For her part, Madame Caillaux would be seen by some as the symbol of a new feminism that the war would help to strengthen.

While the trial unfolded, Poincaré and Viviani began their trip home. The president's memoirs tell much about his changing mood as the days passed.

RAYMOND POINCARÉ
Memoirs
1927

JULY 23–24:

With a speed of 15 knots, the *France* made its way during the night into the Gulf of Finland. Softly rocked by a nearly imperceptible roll, I slept in complete ignorance of the Austrian ultimatum. We were still far from the Baltic when I awoke. From my cabin, I went to the bridge. The Russian torpedo boats had continued to escort us, as on our arrival. All morning and a greater part of the afternoon they stayed with us. They did not leave until about five o'clock. . . .

In order to occupy ourselves, I read extracts of the Parisian press, which had arrived at Saint Petersburg and which had come to us before departing. . . .

Little by little, incomplete radiograms arrived, but scarcely reassuring given their disorder and obscurity. We learned that Austria had sent a harsh note to Serbia and that she had demanded, in a delay of twenty-four hours, satisfaction of which we did not know the details. . . . It was only in bits and pieces by the radiograms that we learned the contents of the Austrian note.

. . . M. Viviani, M. de Margerie,* and I discussed this grave Austrian initiative, so long delayed and so brusquely executed. It seemed to us that the conditions posed by Austria would be very difficult for Serbia to accept and that they constituted a violation of the rights of the people. But we did not want to push Serbia into a resistance that could lead to grave complications. M. Viviani telegraphed to Saint Petersburg and, by Saint Petersburg, to Paris and London the following opinion: (1) that Serbia immediately offer every satisfaction compatible with its honor and its independence; (2) that Serbia demand a delay of twenty-four hours; (3) that we support this demand in Vienna; (4) that the Triple Entente seek to substitute an international inquiry for an Austro-Serb one that risked humiliating Serbia. . . .

JULY 25:

The order is given at dawn to hoist the grand set of flags. A Swedish fleet came to meet us. We entered into the passes of the archipelago that forms, before Stockholm, a multitude of green islands. . . . We are far from Vienna and Sarajevo! . . .

---

* *Pierre de Margerie:* a senior foreign ministry official.

JULY 26:

We are ignorant even of a great deal of what is happening in Paris. The radio often brings us only broken and incomplete phrases. Our communications with land seem to be systematically troubled; and they are, in effect, as we will later learn. During our trip, the German government had given an order to disrupt the communications. . . .

Thus not only had they [the Austrians] waited until we left Russia to send the ultimatum, they did not want the French government to work with its allies to approach Austria and Serbia. But they sought, after the event, to make it impossible for the president of the Republic and the president of the council to communicate with their own country.

Meanwhile, on a pale sea, nearly deserted, indifferent to the human conflicts, our ships, separated from the world, follow in a line a monotonous route that seems interminable. M. Bienvenu-Martin* [from Paris] sought, on the 26th, to send by wireless to the *France* a comprehensive summary of the Austria actions. Fearing we would not get it, he cabled it to Copenhagen, where he thought we would stop and his message would not be interfered with: "Although the Serbian government has, it is said, ceded on all but two small points, the Austro-Hungarian ministry has broken relations, proving thus that it intends to act against Serbia." . . .

JULY 27TH:

The telegrams from Paris that arrived tonight, so informed as they are, express clearly the uncertainty and impatience. They want us to return home. M. Bienvenu-Martin tells us that this is the unanimous view of the ministers. M. Abel Ferry† telegraphs, for his part, that the public and the press have begun to reproach us for continuing the trip at this critical moment.

. . . We could not remain deaf to the appeals of our countrymen. With a common accord, M. Viviani and I decide to return directly to France. This decision taken, we immediately inform by wireless the Quai d'Orsay, as well as the ministers of France in Denmark and Norway. To the kings of those countries, I telegraph that the grave events make it an imperative duty to return promptly to Paris. . . .

. . . We sail, for our part, in a southwestern direction with a speed of sixteen or seventeen knots. . . .

[On board, Viviani (and thus Poincaré) sent the following telegram to Saint Petersburg:]

Jean-Baptiste Bienvenu-Martin: minister of justice in the Viviani government and nominally in charge of the French government in the absence of Viviani.

†*Abel Ferry:* the undersecretary for foreign affairs and in charge of the French Foreign Ministry during the absence of Viviani.

On board the *France,* July 27, 1914: M. le President of the Republic, having judged, as I, that the situation does not permit us to stay away from Paris, have abandoned our stops in Copenhagen and Christiana. We are returning as quickly as possible and will be in France in the afternoon the day after tomorrow. Please tell M. Sazonov that France, appreciating as Russia the great importance which the two countries in their affirmation of a perfect understanding toward other powers and neglecting no effort to resolve the conflict, is ready, in the interests of general peace, to support the efforts of the imperial government.

[Poincaré continues:] The day of July 27th passed lamentably slowly. We sailed north and went through the Belts* with the usual precautions. Only later, after we had turned southwest, did we go to 19 knots, the maximum speed of the ship. With the ship contractors on board, and as they were still within the limits of their responsibility, they did not want to go faster.... Since we could not be exactly informed of events, and having only the essentials in mind, M. Viviani suffered in his spirit and his coloring. He walked with great agitation on the deck of the *France,* resting with long silences, then resuming, and at intervals, telling me of his anguish.

TUESDAY, JULY 28TH:
We are on our last day of the voyage. We have entered into the North Sea, and we have contacted Dunkirk.... We have telegraphed for a train to be ready to depart, from early morning, in order to take us directly to Paris....

The radiograms are clearer. The British proposal is better understood. It concerns the four disinterested powers intervening not only at Vienna and Saint Petersburg, but also in Belgrade to prevent any action.... After having conferred with M. de Margerie, M. Viviani telegraphs Paris to accept the proposal....

WEDNESDAY, JULY 29TH:
At eight o'clock, we arrive at the harbor of Dunkirk. The ship stops, the anchor is lowered, the baggage is unloaded, and we disembark. An innumerable crowd from the city and its environs—bourgeois, merchants, workers, dockers, men, women, and children—are on the jetties and docks.... It is truly France that awaits, and we go before her. I feel pale with emotion and make every effort to contain my concern.

---

*The *Belts:* the shallow water around the Danish coast that links the North Sea with the Baltic Sea; careful navigation is required.

The disquiets, which have assailed me the last four days, are multiplied by the crowd. [He noted that the crowd seemed to say:] "We have every confidence that you will try to avoid war. But if it comes, you can count on us."[6]

Many questions spring from these diary entries: Would it have made a difference if Poincaré had been in Paris during the crisis? Would he have cautioned Russia to delay its move toward mobilization? How would Britain have responded if London had had to deal directly with an insistent Poincaré? How influential was Prime Minister Viviani during these critical days, and what extraconstitutional role had the president already assumed while at sea? These and other questions might well reflect just how firmly the civilians controlled the decision process in Paris; as it was, Poincaré dominated the situation on the ship and back in Paris.

PARIS WITHOUT POINCARÉ: THE CIVILIANS RETAIN CONTROL

With Poincaré absent, the Parisian officials had to deal with the unfolding drama. On July 25, the Quai d'Orsay, the French Foreign Ministry, learned from Paléologue that Russia planned some "clandestine military preparations" that very day. The next day, French Ambassador Jules Cambon cabled from Berlin that any Russian military measures would almost certainly trigger a German response. Further, Cambon warned that France should avoid giving Germany any pretext for action.

General Joffre, for his part, had already begun to worry about the situation. Late on Friday, July 24, War Minister Messimy told Joffre that he feared Germany would support Vienna and that war might come. During the next few days, the two men reviewed the various mobilization arrangements. Messimy, once again thrust into a major international crisis, as in 1911, kept careful control, awaiting the return of Poincaré and Viviani. The following diary entries illustrate his calm demeanor.

ADOLPHE MESSIMY

Memoirs

1937

SUNDAY, 26 JULY.

From Vienna and Berlin we learn that the announcement of the rupture of relations between Austria–Hungary and Serbia has been welcomed in both capitals with delirious manifestations of bellicose enthusiasm.

At nine o'clock Joffre is in my office. . . .

He brought a memorandum from April 1914 that indicates the series of measures to be taken during a period of extreme political tension. They are very numerous and very diverse and touch not only on military concerns, but also on civilian areas (Interior, police, the railways, the postal and telegraph authorities, the prefect of police . . .).

It is my duty to institute these measures or to invoke them if the situation becomes more aggravated.

The memorandum classes them by order of urgency:

Precautionary measures,
Surveillance measures,
Protective measures,
Preliminary organizational measures,
Preparation measures for operations.

A similar list had been presented to me at the beginning of the political tension over Agadir, in the summer of 1911. But on 26 July, from the first glance, I could tell that since that time very detailed, minute plans had been prepared. I saw in this instance the remarkable results realized in the preparation of the mobilization under the methodical style of General Joffre. I did not hide my satisfaction.

He [Joffre] pressed me at this point to recall all of the officers and soldiers on leave.

"Are you certain, my general, that all those on leave in Germany have been recalled?"

"I have reason to believe that my intelligence on this is correct; but I have not verified it in a formal fashion. Anyhow, what does it matter? You are free to recall those on leave."

"Certainly, from the national and international point of view, I am free to do so. But the step is too grave not to have explicit agreement about it. I want to take no measure that might stir opinion without first consulting the cabinet. I will support the ideas that you and I have agreed upon; you can count on that. But I express the condition that I will make no decision about any preparatory mobilization steps unless we are absolutely certain the Germans have already done so."

"I would be completely in accord with you if we were not, on this issue, in a state of obvious legal inferiority compared to the Germans. I want to show you the Ludendorff document."

"I do not know it."

... [A staff officer], who was present, then gave me the report known by that name.* It showed the dispositions that the Germans would take to mobilize secretly the entire nation, disguising the recall of the reservists under the form of convocations, hiding measures of strategic concentration, and attacking suddenly, by surprise and violence, at previously unsuspected places.

I did not conceal from Joffre my surprise at having this document presented at just the moment when it might be necessary to draw grave conclusions that might unleash dramatic consequences: on the one hand, that we would hasten too much and thus give our adversaries the ability to call us aggressors; on the other, that we would lose valuable time and allow the Germans to advance on us.

We agreed, Joffre and I, to take no first steps, but at least to execute all of the preparatory steps that corresponded to those taken by our adversaries. . . .

In the course of the day of 26 July, I gave the order to recall officers on leave and to have them rejoin their troops by road, rather than by rail transport, since that might be interpreted as an indicator of mobilization measures.

But against the opinion of Joffre, the cabinet joined me in refusing to recall the soldiers on leave who were very numerous, given the large numbers who were at this time doing agriculture work—6,000 in the 2nd corps, 8,500 in the 6th corps, 6,600 in the 20th corps etc. . . . nearly 100,000 altogether. . . .

The memory of this splendid Sunday remains. Late in the afternoon, I walked back to my house by the quay. From the Gare d'Orsay were streaming joyous groups, arms full of flowers and greenery.

I felt a horrible agony in thinking of the prideful folly that the kaiser was going to loose on the world, which no one doubted would constitute a bloody cataclysm.

For the next five years, this summer Sunday would be the last to reflect happy feelings.[7]

---

*This was an operational part of the German war plan; it did not reveal the overall strategic arrangements.

As these French precautionary steps got under way, new reports arrived about Russian and German military moves. Meanwhile, the Anglo-French naval staffs had already initiated contacts in accord with their earlier naval arrangements. It was at this point that the frantic Paris group radioed Poincaré to return at once, though he did not actually reach Paris until the afternoon of July 29.

During this awkward interval of seventy-two hours, Joffre secured Messimy's consent to recall all troops to their units, with the order going out on July 27. By this point, Joffre was convinced that France was headed for war. Thus he found the civilian government's attitude overly cautious, reacting to German actions and not anticipating them. Not surprisingly, Joffre and Messimy disagreed on July 28 about whether the Germans had already taken secret measures. (Actually, they had taken no more than the French.) The general desperately wanted to put his "cover" troops into place along the borders. The war minister refused, saying that Poincaré would have to make that decision the next day. In his memoirs, Messimy described the preparations he did set in motion.

ADOLPHE MESSIMY

Memoirs

1937

In the course of the evening and early morning, the intelligence from Germany became more disturbing.

Not only those on leave but also those traveling have been recalled to their garrisons. A certain number of reservists have also been recalled. On the borders, surveillance positions have been taken. In the afternoon, I learned that rail equipment for the transport of troops had been recalled to the interior and that the military railheads along the frontier region had been cleared in view of debarkations.

Here are the measures taken by me during the 28th at the demand of General Joffre to meet the menacing preparations.

During the night, the recall of all troops on leave. The return by rail of all of these troops as well those traveling or at instructional camps. The organization of the frontier but without calling troops or the reserve elements to status of permanent surveillance, leaving that to the customs officials. Public establishments (central telegraph offices, gas stations etc.) will be watched by the civilian police. The telegraph, telephone bureaus in the frontier regions will be put on full service in order to transmit dispatches, day and night.[8]

POINCARÉ TAKES CHARGE

When Poincaré reached Paris on the 29th, he found that the civilian officials still retained full control over the pace of French military measures. He also found that his own position (and that of the inexperienced Viviani) had not been eroded by Joffre's increasingly insistent demands. Henceforth, Poincaré became the dominant civilian figure in the decision process, exploiting to the full his powers as president.[9]

At his first cabinet meeting late on the 29th, Poincaré was briefed about a situation that had grown far more serious than he had imagined. Still, only limited further military measures were authorized, chiefly precautionary ones. Then, in the early hours of July 30, Paris learned that the Germans had warned Russia to stop its military preparations against Austria–Hungary or face German countermeasures. Equally discomforting were new reports that the Germans were putting their own cover troops into place. Joffre and Poincaré now faced fundamental decisions about the implementation of Plan XVII.

But if Poincaré had to worry about France's situation, he also faced a second major issue: Russian overreaction to the crisis. In his absence, Quai d'Orsay officials had already cautioned Sazonov to avoid provoking a German reaction. Early on July 30, Poincaré and Viviani repeated these injunctions in a special telegram to Saint Petersburg. Imprecisely informed about the extent of the military measures already taken by Russia, Poincaré wanted Russia to appear the victim, not the aggressor. But this did not happen, for Saint Petersburg ordered full mobilization late that same day. Paris did not learn of this measure for another twenty-four hours, thanks to errant cable traffic. The Russian action guaranteed a German response; it also exposed France to the full risks of its longtime alliance with Russia. Soon French soldiers would die because of Russia's decision to support the Serbs, not because of any Franco-German quarrel.

On Thursday, July 30, the French cabinet and Poincaré continued to consider the policy options, completely ignorant of the Russian escalation of the crisis. Despite Joffre's urgent requests, civilian leaders still insisted on controlling the pace of the mobilization. He could order covering troops into place, but the troops had to march to position and were not allowed to use the railways. Nor could any reservists be recalled. Most important, and directly contradicting an assumption of Plan XVII, all covering troops had to be at least 10 kilometers away from the German border. This last stipulation was to prevent any preliminary clashes between the two forces that might allow Germany to claim that France had provoked a German attack.

At 5:00 P.M. on July 30, orders with these restrictions were sent for the deployment of the covering forces. However phrased, this civilian modification of a war plan was unprecedented among the other great powers in 1914, and it clearly troubled Joffre greatly.

JOSEPH JOFFRE

Memoirs

1932

The night of July 29th/30th, brought information clearly confirming my anticipations touching preparations for war by the Germans. . . .

In short, all the measures of protection were being executed exactly in their anticipated order as laid down in a report* that had previously come to my knowledge. As far as I was concerned, therefore, there existed in my mind no doubt as to the fatal outcome of these preparations: and this absolute certainty that the Germans were taking each step of their programme in the methodical way which characterized them, gave me the conviction that war was inevitable and proved to me the necessity of ourselves getting ready for it without a moment's delay.

Faced by this menacing situation, we had taken practically not a single measure for our defense, and I had not even received from the Government permission to establish our covering forces in place. When I saw M. Messimy on the morning of the 30th, I once more urged the absolute necessity of the Government's taking this decision. He shortly afterwards went to a Cabinet meeting and there informed his colleagues of my insistence. . . . After several hours of deliberation, the Minister of War sent to inform me that the Cabinet agreed that the covering troops should be put in place, but with the following reservations:

The only units to be moved up would be those which could reach their stations by march route, no movement by railway being authorized. No reservists were to be called up for the moment, and no requisitions made. Horses immediately needed to complete those on hand

* Presumably the Ludendorff document mentioned by Messimy.

with the troops were to be bought in the open market. Lastly, no covering troops were to approach closer than 10 kilometers (6 miles) from the frontier, in order that contact between French and German patrols might be avoided.

When the Minister communicated this decision to me, I strongly protested against the refusal to call up reservists and against the restriction imposed by limiting all movements to march route; I also represented to him that these half-way measures would in no fashion protect us from a sudden irruption across our frontier. . . .

But my protest remained without effect. The decision had been taken at a Cabinet meeting and M. Messimy could not alter it on his own authority. . . .

FRIDAY, JULY 31ST: . . . About 2 o'clock I learned the news of the ultimatum addressed on the afternoon of the 29th by Germany to Russia. These events led me to feel that it was my duty to place the Government squarely in face of its responsibilities. I, therefore, drew up a note which recited the last information received; I handed it to the Minister of War at 3:30 P.M., just as he was leaving for a Cabinet meeting, and I urged him to present it to his colleagues. It was couched as follows:

> The measures we have taken up to the present fall far behind those effected by the Germans. This is especially the case in respect of the last forty-eight hours. . . .
>
> In the present condition of affairs it is no longer possible for us to execute further measures of detail, other than those already ordered, without running the risk of gravely disturbing arrangements prescribed for covering troops and for mobilization; this especially applies to the railway service. If the present tension continues and if the Germans, under cover of diplomatic conversations, continue to take the various steps comprised in their plan of mobilization—though without pronouncing that word—it is absolutely necessary for the Government to understand that, starting with this evening, any delay of twenty-four hours in calling up our reservists and issuing orders prescribing covering operations, will have as a result the withdrawal of our concentration point by from ten to twelve miles for each day of delay; in other words, the initial abandonment of just that much of our territory.
>
> *The Commander-in Chief must decline to accept this responsibility.*

In handing this note to M. Messimy I made the strongest representations to him. . . .

The Cabinet assembled at 5 P.M. and my note was read. This time M. Viviani gave his approval. It was now 5:15 P.M. However, the Cabinet

decided to satisfy my demands only in part, for while I was at last authorized to send the telegram which would put our covering troops into
position, I was not allowed to call up the reservists. It was only at 5:40 P.M.
that the telegram went out saying: "Despatch covering troops. The initial hour is fixed at 9 P.M." I must confess that I drew a great sigh of
relief that this had been done. For it was high time.

A little while after this telegram was sent, the German Ambassador,
Baron von Schoen, went to the Quai d'Orsay and announced to M. Viviani
that the Kaiser had decided that day to take the step known in Germany
by the term "Declaration of Danger of War." He also stated that Russia
had ordered a general mobilization, and he was instructed to inquire
what would be the attitude of France in the case of a conflict between
Germany and Russia.

On learning this serious news, I immediately urged the Minister of
War to give orders for our general mobilization without an instant's
delay, for I considered it imperative. M. Messimy promised me to insist
upon this step when the Cabinet assembled in the evening.

At 9 P.M. the third Cabinet meeting of the day was held. While it was
in session, news came of the assassination of Jaurès.* This horrible
crime caused considerable anxiety lest troubles should break out. . . .
The next morning, thanks to the calmness of the Paris population, it
became evident that order would not be disturbed; for the approach of
danger had united all parties and classes in France. . . . As for the question which so much preoccupied me, that of ordering a general mobilization, it was now too late for the first day to be fixed sooner than
August 2nd at midnight. The cabinet, therefore, decided to wait a few
hours more, though at the same time giving me the assurance that if no
improvement took place in the situation, the order would be sent out
before 4 o'clock, the last limit possible which would permit it to reach
the most distant villages and ensure its execution the following morning. But I obtained permission from the Minister to send all army corps
a preparatory warning, stating that "most likely, orders for mobilization
will be issued today, August 1st, during the evening. Proceed at once to
make all preparations which would facilitate mobilization."[10]

* *Jean Jaurès:* the most influential French socialist of his time, an international figure,
and a political leader suspicious of the French officer corps.

While Joffre and the cabinet wrestled with what military measures
were needed, the French diplomats sought to learn British intentions.
And predictably, the French injected the 10-kilometer self-restriction
into the Anglo-French diplomatic discussions. While this self-denial
may not have brought British intervention (the invasion of Belgium

did that), Poincaré had correctly understood the delicacy of Grey's position and the need for France to avoid any suspicion that it had provoked a German attack. The degree to which Paris sought to assure London about France's prudence can be seen in the instructions sent to Ambassador Paul Cambon in London.

RENÉ VIVIANI
Telegram to London
July 31, 1914

PARIS, JULY 31, 1914. 12:30 P.M.

The German army has taken positions along our frontier. Yesterday, Friday [*sic*], German patrols twice crossed into French territory. Our advanced posts have retreated 10 kilometers away from the frontier. The populations thus abandoned have protested this action. But the government wants to show the French public and the English government that France will in no case be the aggressor. . . .

We have called up *no* reservists, although Germany has done so. I also add that all of our information shows that the German preparations began last Saturday, the same day as the Austrian note [*sic*].

This information, added to that of yesterday, you can show to the English government to demonstrate our peaceful intentions and the aggressive intent of the Germans.[11]

Despite these French moves and the rapidly deteriorating situation, Paul Cambon could report no success from his discussions with Sir Edward Grey. But Poincaré continued to insist that the 10-kilometer restriction remain in effect. Not even the decision on August 1 to mobilize French troops would see the president yield on this point. And to Joffre's dismay, Poincaré continued to block plans for a French incursion into Belgium until German troops had actually violated the neutral state. In this crisis, the French political leadership showed complete mastery of the linkages between and among diplomacy, strategy, and national policy. The general could execute his military strategy, but that execution would not be allowed to overcome larger considerations of grand strategy. In his memoirs, Poincaré notes how he and the cabinet reasoned on these key issues, even as the Germans were moving ahead.

RAYMOND POINCARÉ

Memoirs

1927

JULY 31, 1914:
... In the presence of the confirming information, could we close our eyes and fold our arms? M. Messimy, minister of war, does not think so. At the Cabinet that morning, I had already noted the desire expressed strongly by General Joffre that the cover dispositions are taken without delay. That led to the mobilization of the 2nd, 6th, 7th, 20th, 21st regions and all of the cavalry divisions. Units were ordered to the frontier from Reims, Châlons-sur-Marne, Besançon, Paris, and even some garrisons in the west. Grave decisions to take. The Cabinet is unanimous in not wanting to fail to take any necessary precautions. But it feared that our initiatives could be exploited against us by Germany in England and Italy and that Germany would seek to make us the aggressor despite all of the evidence.[12]

While Poincaré and Joffre worried about the German actions, the president also had to consider the domestic situation. His 10-kilometer restriction had a domestic audience as well, as he wanted to be sure that he and the government could not be accused of provoking Germany. Then came the assassination of Jean Jaurès, the leading socialist politician, by a student on the evening of July 31. As Joffre's memoirs have already shown, there was concern that public demonstrations might erupt, but Paris remained calm, and senior French officials were diligent in seeking to assure the public (and hence the socialists) of their esteem for Jaurès. The tone can be seen from comments in the French press.

The Assassination of M. Jaurès

August 2, 1914

Immediately after learning of the assassination of M. Jaurès, the president of the republic sent Madame Jaurès the following letter:

> Madame:
> I have learned of the abominable attack of which your husband has been the victim. Jaurès was often my adversary. But I had great admiration for his talent and his character, and at this hour where national union is more necessary than ever, I want to express to you the sentiments that I have for him.
> I ask you, madam, to believe, in this loss which strikes you, that you have my profound and respectful sympathy.
>
> R. Poincaré

LE TEMPS

The Assassination of M. Jaurès

August 2, 1914

Paris was a place of calmness and gravity the day of the attack. It was the eve of the first day of vacations. Even the thought of imminent war—a thought present in all minds—did not change the habits of the public. One could see families crowded at the stations, having decided long ago to go to the country or the ocean. In the streets, mainly toward the approach of night, people bought the special editions of the newspapers, reacting to the latest news without gestures, without noise, without affectation, without apparent nervousness. It was an admirable attitude of a people attached to the cause of peace. . . .

Then suddenly the word spread that M. Jaurès had been assassinated. Nothing was more capable of damaging the sense of patriotic solidarity, which we had proclaimed and fortified. It is the turn of *L'Humanité** to surround itself in mourning. We do not need this coinci-

---

* *L'Humanité:* Jaurès's newspaper.

dence† to share the sadness of our colleagues and to salute the man who on almost all questions, domestic and international, was our most determined adversary.[13]

†One of *Le Temp's* own editors had recently died.

Paris was still assimilating the news of Jaurès's death when foreign news once again intruded. On that Saturday, August 1, Germany declared war on Russia. Then came German moves into Luxembourg early the next day.

Poincaré was now able to point to these moves as examples of aggressive German behavior. He could also cite reports of numerous German violations of the French border—violations that finally led Poincaré to end the 10-kilometer restriction, effective late on Sunday, August 2. Yet even now, the orders said that French units were to take no offensive action into Germany.

JOSEPH JOFFRE

Orders to the Commanding Generals of the 2nd, 6th, 20th, 21st, 7th Corps and the Cavalry Corps

August 2, 1914, 5:30 P.M.

Secret General Order for Cover

1. Intelligence reports indicate that the Germans have violated the French frontier this morning at these places: a, between Delle and Belfort; b, before Cirey-sur-Vezouze; c, north and south of Longwy. Given these conditions, the prohibition of moving eastward beyond the line indicated by telegram No. 129-3/11 of 30 July and the distance of 10 kilometers is lifted.

However, for reasons of national morale and imperative demands of a diplomatic nature, it is indispensable to let the Germans bear the entire responsibility for the hostilities.

Consequently, and until a new order, the cover troops will restrict themselves to repelling any troop attack, but without pursuing them and entering into enemy territory.[14]

By late on Sunday, August 2, Poincaré's grand strategy was beginning to succeed. The disparate political groups in French society were rallying to the defense of France. *L'Union sacrée* of French politics—that is, the unity across the political spectrum that France enjoyed in the first years of the war—provided Poincaré with assurances that the country supported the army and the government. His proclamation of a state of emergency evoked strong nationalist fervor.

Across the Channel, the British cabinet late on that same Sunday agreed to make the violation of Belgium a *casus belli,* or cause for war. Already the British cabinet had agreed to defend France's northern coasts against any German naval attacks. These steps moved London much closer to intervention. Then the next day, August 3, Sir Edward Grey publicly warned Germany not to violate Belgium. The French press, not surprisingly, rejoiced at this news.

LE FIGARO

England Is for Us

August 4, 1914

Declaration of Sir Edward Grey

MOBILIZATION OF THE FLEET AND THE ARMY

It is done. England has declared itself. With declarations made yesterday to the applause of the entire House [of Commons], Sir Edward Grey has stated the following:

1. The English fleet will guarantee France against the German fleet.
2. England will appeal to the Belgian king to defend the neutrality of Belgium.

On the other important points, Sir Edward Grey announces the mobilization of the fleet and the army, which starts at midnight.

Ireland will leave the English with free hands.

As you can see, it is not M. [Herbert Henry] Asquith, the prime minister, but Edward Grey, minister of foreign affairs, who makes known the English decisions.

The Revolt of Europe

August 4, 1914

Germany, throwing a new defiance at Europe, demands that Belgium allow it to violate her neutrality. The Belgians have replied to this insolent demand by preparing to defend their frontiers with all means at their disposal.

Great Britain, even before learning of the violation of Belgian neutrality, had given the order to its fleet to block the pas-de-Calais, that is to say, to cover the French coasts against German aggression.

Italy . . . has notified the French government of its neutrality, saying that the aggression of Austria and Germany violates the terms of the Triple Alliance.[15]

The German moves against Belgium created a new situation for the French. Suddenly, all restrictions on possible French activity into Belgium eased, and late on the afternoon of August 4, the Belgian government gave permission for the French troops to make any necessary moves. This gave Joffre a chance to initiate offensive action in Belgium, putting a variant of Plan XVII into effect. But his moves came too late and were far too conservative compared to the broad scope of the Schlieffen-Moltke plans. Almost immediately, Joffre discovered that the Germans valued reserved troops and had employed them in a sweeping attack far into Belgium.

This onslaught soon came, for Germany had already declared war on France late on August 3. A day later, Poincaré's written speech to the joint chamber-senate session proclaimed France's determination to defend itself and to honor its alliance. After the Great War, the French left blamed Poincaré for maneuvering France into the war to help Russia. Rather, the reverse had been true. Poincaré had simply ensured that France would make the best of a very bad situation in August 1914.

Other critics blamed him for his timidity over the 10-kilometer issue, arguing that he had given up French territory unnecessarily. His replies to these charges were always simple: British help provided the margin of victory in the critical days of 1914 and throughout the war, and that help might not have been forthcoming had France been perceived to have provoked the German action.

The interaction between diplomatic/political considerations and the formation of French military strategy was nearly continuous from January 1912 through July 1914. From his first moments as premier, Poincaré and successive ministers appointed by him placed definitive geographic restrictions on Joffre and his staff. Those limitations were as unambiguous as were the reasons for them. France would not violate Belgian neutrality. France would not take any action that might provoke German retaliation. This defense-minded, conservative approach had two major goals: keep the French public supportive and assure France of Britain's crucial assistance.

Poincaré, though neither a strategist nor even a foreign policy expert by training, exploited the essence of the *entente cordiale.* A careful, clever politician, Poincaré understood Grey's dilemma probably better than anyone else. Both men realized the essential fact of the Anglo-French relationship: Britain and France must assist each other in resisting Germany. Both men would succeed in their policy objectives.

As the discussion of British policy will reveal, Britain's own military leadership would prove far more difficult to restrain than Joffre and the French military leadership. The general and his colleagues completely accepted, if they did not like, the thrust of Poincaré's views and did nothing to complicate Poincaré's position. In return, the generals were rewarded with strong government support from 1911 to the end of the July crisis and beyond. That unity would soon be severely tested as the clash of battle proceeded.

There is a further consideration: Did the fact that France, alone of the European governments, had a republican and not a monarchical system make any difference to civil-military relations? Scholars continue to debate the question of whether democracies will fight other democracies. But what if there is only one republic amid a sea of other systems? Will it prove able to control its military? Had one answered the question for France in the decade of the 1890s, the answer might well have been unflattering to the civilians. But after the Dreyfus affair, the balance shifted toward the civilians. In 1914, French political leadership, with greater success than any other government, controlled their military colleagues.

NOTES

[1]Michael Burns, *France and the Dreyfus Affair: A Documentary History* (Boston: Bedford/St. Martin's, 1999).

[2]Raymond Poincaré, *Au Service de la France: Neuf Années des Souvenirs,* vol. 4, *L'Union Sacrée, 1914* (Paris: Librairie Plon, 1927), 107–8.

[3]Joseph C. Joffre, *The Memoirs of Marshal Joffre,* trans. T. Bentley Mott, 2 vols. (London: Geoffrey Bles, 1932), 1:49–51.

[4]Poincaré, *Au Service de la France,* 172–74.

[5]*Le Temps,* July 2 and 10, 1914; *Le Figaro,* July 3, 1914.

[6]Poincaré, *Au Service de la France,* 286–88, 297, 327–29, 333–37, 346–47, 360–61.

[7]Adophe Messimy, *Mes Souvenirs* (Paris: Librairie Plon, 1937), 131–35.

[8]Ibid., 136–37.

[9]J. F. V. Keiger, *Raymond Poincaré* (Cambridge: Cambridge University Press, 1997), is especially helpful on this.

[10]Joffre, *Memoirs,* 1:123–27.

[11]*Documents diplomatiques français, 1871–1914,* 3d ser., vol. 11 (Paris: Imprimerie Nationale, 1936), no. 390. (Hereafter cited as *DDF.*)

[12]Poincaré, *Au Service de la France,* 423–24.

[13]*Le Figaro,* Aug. 2, 1914; *Le Temps,* Aug. 2, 1914.

[14]*DDF,*, no. 594.

[15]*Le Figaro,* Aug. 4, 1914; *Le Temps,* Aug. 4, 1914, afternoon ed.

8

Grey, Wilson, and the Struggle to Commit Britain to War

Britain in July 1914 faced the most serious domestic tensions of any European country. The government headed by Prime Minister Herbert Henry Asquith was embroiled in a major constitutional crisis over the question of home rule for Ireland. Like the Caillaux trial in France, the Irish question temporarily obscured for the British public and decision makers the dangers posed by the Sarajevo murders. It also severely limited British Foreign Secretary Sir Edward Grey's options when he (and then the Asquith government) finally and fully confronted the threat of a European war.

The turmoil within the British army in 1914 has often been overlooked in assessing the British decision for war. But Britain in the summer of 1914 had in Major General Henry Wilson its own version of Austria–Hungary's General Franz Conrad von Hötzendorf and Serbia's Dragutin Dimitrijević (Apis); all three men sought a military confrontation. Not only would civil-military issues influence British diplomacy and intrude into the decision-making process, but the legacy of bitterness between the Liberal government and its senior military figures would greatly influence British policies during the war itself. When viewed from the perspective of civil-military relations, the British move to war in the summer of 1914 illustrates still other aspects of how a government may (or may not) control its military subordinates.

BRITAIN ON THE EVE OF WAR

In 1914, Great Britain was the most formidable world power. Headed by a constitutional monarch with carefully circumscribed powers, the British government consisted of the Parliament—the House of Commons and the House of Lords—and the cabinet, which exercised executive power. The prime minister came from the party (or a coalition of the parties) that controlled the most seats in the House of Commons. Although the Commons was the focal point of political power and its members (called members of parliament, or MPs) were the major ministers in the cabinet, the House of Lords had until 1911 considerable veto power over all legislation. Within the Parliament, two political parties dominated: the Conservatives (often called Unionists because they wanted Ireland to remain united to Britain) and the Liberals. The Conservatives, who strongly supported the minority Protestant faction in Ireland, opposed concessions for home rule, which would have turned local government over to an Irish parliament dominated by majority Irish Catholics. On other issues, the Conservatives supported defense and imperial matters, while opposing social legislation. Moreover, given the aristocratic composition of the House of Lords, the Conservatives dominated that body. Their opponents, the Liberals, favored some form of home rule for Ireland and had pressed for unemployment insurance and social security. On defense questions, the Liberals opposed excessive expenditures, and the radical wing of the party distrusted any formal connection or alliance with France or Russia.

A Liberal government had been in office since December 1905. Its ministers had thus experienced every major event of pre-1914 European diplomacy: the two Moroccan crises, the Bosnian affair, and the Balkan Wars. Prime Minister Asquith, War Minister (and later Lord Chancellor) Richard Haldane, and Sir Edward Grey, joined later by Chancellor of the Exchequer David Lloyd George and First Lord of the Admiralty Winston Churchill, had responded to the progressive deterioration of Anglo-German relations by embarking on a costly naval buildup, strengthening the entente with France, and negotiating an agreement with Russia. Not surprisingly, by 1914 these ministers, in power for nearly nine years, were exhausted as they grappled with the vexatious question of Irish home rule.

After 1910, Ireland had increasingly dominated the domestic agenda, along with the movement for women's suffrage and mounting labor unrest. The Liberal government could not escape the Irish problem because its political fortunes depended upon success on the issue since Irish MP support had contributed significantly to its winning the second general election of 1910.

In 1914, it became apparent that the House of Commons would soon pass the Home Rule Bill for the final time. The law would give political control to an Irish Catholic parliament in Dublin. This prospect alarmed the six Ulster counties in Northern Ireland with their substantial Protestant majorities, galvanized the Conservative Party leadership, and sharply divided the senior British military officers who might be called on to enforce the new law.

In March 1914, nearly sixty Anglo-Irish officers at Curragh, a military post thirty miles from Dublin, threatened to resign rather than implement future government policy in Ireland. This mutiny, encouraged by Wilson, the director of military operations, provoked a major civil-military confrontation and led to the fall of War Minister John Seely and the resignations of the chief of the imperial general staff, Sir John French, and the adjutant general, Sir Spencer Ewart. To weather the crisis, Asquith took over the War Office as well as the prime ministership, thus making his position even more sensitive for the unhappy military officers.

No one appreciated this more clearly than the prime minister himself, whose leadership was under severe attack. Asquith, like Conrad, was having an affair with a beautiful young woman more than thirty years his junior, Venetia Stanley. His letters to her provide insights into the Irish question and the events of July 1914. In March 1914, Asquith gave her a running account of the Curragh mutiny.

HENRY ASQUITH

Letter to Venetia Stanley

March 30, 1914

Dearly beloved, your letter which I found here this morning was the greatest solace & joy, as the thought of you & our delicious drive has been all thro' the wet dreary Sunday at the Wharf. I drove away from you in solitude & missing you so much, but the memory of things you had said "flashed upon the inward eye."

I started the idea of the two offices at once, & I need not tell you that Winston [Churchill]'s eyes blazed, and his polysyllables rolled, and his gestures were those of a man possessed. . . .

... When I got back this morning I heard (as I expected) that the Generals (i.e., French & Ewart) had come back to the position that as a matter of personal honour they must go. Poor Seely, who was there, of course was bound to follow suit. French behaved admirably, & when I told him privately that I thought of going to the W.O.,* he was delighted and promised all his help. So then I proceeded to the King & put my scheme before him. He remarked—naively, as Bonar Law† would say—that the idea had never occurred to him! but he was quite taken with it and gave it emphatic approval. So after questions—as you will see by the papers—I threw the bombshell on the floor of the House [of Commons], and I think the effect was all that one cd. have hoped.[1]

* *W.O.:* War Office.
† *Andrew Bonar Law:* leader of the Conservative Party.

GREY AND BRITAIN'S STRATEGIC INTERESTS

By 1914, Sir Edward Grey—aged fifty-two—had already served longer as foreign secretary than any of his European counterparts. The youngest member of Parliament in 1885, Grey had been under-secretary for foreign affairs from 1892 to 1895. A Liberal Imperialist, he had supported the Conservative government during the Boer War (1899–1902), in which British troops eventually defeated the Dutch settlers in South Africa to gain complete control of the country. When the Liberals returned to power in December 1905, Grey was chosen to be foreign secretary. By 1914, he had become one of the most influential members of the Liberal government. Many shared King George's view that Grey was the leading statesman of his time and irreplaceable (Figure 12).

Despite his record of achievement and his political stature, Grey remained an aloof figure, seldom seen in public. Yet he enjoyed the company of army friends, ardently supported women's suffrage, and was a two-time English tennis champion. He and his wife, Dorothy, had a childless and, by all accounts, platonic marriage. Her accidental death in February 1906 prematurely aged Grey, whose affection for her can be seen in his account of his decision to take office in the fall of 1905.[2] (This is the only mention of her in his memoirs.)

**Figure 12.
Edward Grey**
A strong supporter
of France, the British
foreign secretary's
failure to be more
assertive in the July
crisis owed much to
the Irish question,
which dominated
British politics. A
skilled speaker, he
could be very eco-
nomical with the
truth when publicly
discussing Anglo-
French military and
naval arrangements.
Getty Images.

EDWARD GREY

Memoirs

1925

It will be understood . . . that the decision [to become foreign secretary]
brought no joy either to my wife or myself; it meant exile again from
home, life in London, and a number of those social functions which Sir
George Cornewall Lewis had in mind when he said that "life would be
tolerable if it were not for its amusements." Probably my wife's com-

ment had much to do with the decision. "If we had refused office," she said, "we could not have justified the decision to the constituency." It was the constituency that had kept us in public life. They had returned me to Parliament at the age of twenty-three, a young and untried man; for twenty years they had continued their confidence; giving me generously freedom to indulge individual views even when these differed from those of the majority of the party. . . .

. . . My wife had done much to found and encourage Liberal Associations, not so much for party purposes as from a belief that such Associations were good for women. She thought that to take an intelligent interest and an organized part in public affairs broadened outlook and enlarged life. Her views had met with response and co-operation, and she had made many friends. Thus we were conscious of the responsibility to a number of earnest people, who had a right to expect me to do my best in Parliament. . . . Now suddenly I was asked to take one of the highest offices in public life, and when my wife said that refusal could not be justified to the constituents, I felt that this was indeed the truest and decisive judgment on the matter.[3]

After Dorothy's death, his hobbies were simple: fishing, bird-watching, and escaping London for his fishing retreat in Hampshire or his estate in the north of England. Not until April 1914 would Grey travel abroad as foreign secretary, on that occasion accompanying George V on a state visit to France. Subsequent critics have attacked Grey's parochialism, castigated his inflexible approach to policy matters, and assailed him for his lack of imagination during the July crisis. But his contemporaries also commented on his tenacity and his refusal to allow his key subordinates to control him.

The assumptions of Grey's foreign policy from 1905 on can be quickly stated. German navalism and militarism posed the greatest threat to British interests and must be contained, whatever the costs. The entente with France was of paramount importance, and France could not be left to face Germany alone. The agreement with Russia was also central. But Britain would not become a formal ally of the French and the Russians. This aversion to alliances, often blamed on radicals in the Liberal cabinet whom Grey would have had to convince, was actually shared by Grey. Binding alliances were not in keeping with Britain's tradition of remaining aloof from the Continent. Indeed, recent British reluctance to join the European Common Market and to accept the Eurodollar as a common currency springs from this same attitude. Grey, like his predecessors, wanted to be free to judge the question of commitment to the Continent on its merits, not by a binding, written obligation. Instead, under Grey, Britain continued to pursue a balance of power approach to world politics.

Grey's performance during the July crisis was far more sharply influenced by strategic and military dimensions than he perhaps realized then, or than later commentators have noted. From January 1906 to July 1914, the foreign secretary had sanctioned the secret military (and later naval) conversations between British and French staff officers. At each point when the cabinet sought to end or curtail the staff conversations, Grey fashioned a compromise that satisfied radical critics without restraining the actual planning.

Grey also participated in all of the significant strategic discussions. For example, during the greatest tension of the Second Moroccan Crisis in August–September 1911, he met often with Haldane, Wilson, Asquith, and Churchill to review military plans for possible British intervention in a continental war. At the time and later, Grey claimed to know little of the plans or their implications, but this may have been part of a deliberate effort to hide his own participation in such decisions.

In spring 1914, for example, the Russians wanted to open naval conversations with London. Although Grey could see no benefit to Britain, he did not want to offend the French, who pressed strongly on the point when he made his first visit to Paris. Clearly, the French wanted to use the secret talks to create a de facto alliance arrangement. As we saw in Chapter 4, a German spy in the Russian embassy in London informed Berlin of the proposed naval conversations with Saint Petersburg. Not surprisingly, Grey faced questions from Germany and in Parliament on the matter. His statement to the House of Commons and his later memoir account help to explain the subsequent postwar criticisms of the foreign secretary for his less-than-honest answers.

Statement to the House of Commons

June 11, 1914

Mr. King asked whether any naval agreement has recently been entered into between Russia and Great Britain, and whether any negotiations, with a view to a naval agreement, have recently taken place, or are now pending, between Russia and Great Britain.

Sir William Byles asked the Secretary of State for Foreign Affairs whether he can make any statement with regard to an alleged new naval agreement between Great Britain and Russia; how far such agreement would affect our relations with Germany; and will he lay papers?*

Sir E. Grey: The Hon. Member for North Somerset asked a similar question last year with regard to military forces, and the Hon. Member for North Salford asked a similar question also on the same day as he has done again to-day. The Prime Minister then replied that, if war arose between the European Powers, there were no unpublished agreements which would restrict or hamper the freedom of the Government, or of Parliament, to decide whether or not Great Britain should participate in a war. That answer covers both questions on the paper. It remains as true to-day as it was a year ago. No negotiations have since been concluded with any Power that would make the statement less true. No such negotiations are in progress, and none are likely to be entered upon, as far as I can judge. But, if any agreement were to be concluded that made it necessary to withdraw or modify the Prime Minister's statement of last year, which I have quoted, it ought, in my opinion, to be, and I supposed that it would be, laid before Parliament.

* *Lay papers:* provide a written explanation.

EDWARD GREY

Memoirs

1925

The answer given is absolutely true. That criticism to which it is open is, that it does not answer the question put to me. That is undeniable. Parliament has an unqualified right to know of any agreements or arrangements that bind the country to action or restrain its freedom. But it cannot be told of military and naval measures to meet possible contingencies. . . .

. . . Political engagements ought not to be kept secret; naval or military preparations for contingencies of war are necessary, but must be kept secret. . . .

[As to Germany and the talks, he then added:] German intelligence agencies, especially the military, must have become aware that the relations between the two staffs were intimate. The disposition of the British and French naval forces—the latter being in the Mediterranean, leaving all the north coast of France exposed to the German Fleet— was evidence that there were some arrangements between British and French naval authorities. There must have been frequent speculation at Berlin as to whether we were committed to an alliance; whether in the event of war with France and Russia, England was certainly to be reckoned with. . . . If Germany had not invaded Belgium, she would not have had to reckon with Britain, at any rate not at the outset of war.[4]

Grey's statement confused the German government as well as many in his own party, who remained woefully ignorant of the military conversations he used to appease repeated French demands for a British alliance. Were Grey's attitudes those of a democratic statesman or more like those of a minister from an aristocratic, militaristic society? And did these secret staff conversations constitute a breach of civil-military relations, taking from the cabinet the power of strategic decisions?

GREY'S INITIAL RESPONSE TO SARAJEVO

Although the deaths at Sarajevo did not long divert British attention from the Irish question, Grey initially paid more attention than others did. He duly conveyed the official regrets of the British government to Vienna and privately wrote the Habsburg ambassador, Count Mensdorff, about his sympathy for Emperor Franz Joseph. Yet beyond an official statement and this private communication, Grey had no further contact with the Habsburg ambassador until July 23—the day the Austrian ultimatum was delivered in Belgrade. Grey's failure to be more assertive toward Austria–Hungary is especially puzzling given the alarming information that he was receiving from Vienna. But this lack of assertive diplomacy perfectly reflected Grey's entire performance in July 1914. He focused almost exclusively on Berlin as the controller of Habsburg policy, and thus of the crisis, despite the recent Balkan War experience, which suggested otherwise.

On July 6, Grey saw German Ambassador Prince Lichnowsky, who had just returned from Germany. The prince reported that there was "pessimism" in Berlin over the death of Franz Ferdinand. He added that he "knew for a fact" that Vienna would take action. The ambassador wanted Grey to calm Saint Petersburg, and the foreign secretary pledged to try. On July 8, he saw Count Benckendorff, the Russian ambassador. Grey's account of this meeting in a letter to Sir George Buchanan, Britain's ambassador to Russia, sums up his assessment of the European situation eleven days after the assassinations.

EDWARD GREY

Letter to Saint Petersburg

July 8, 1914

Speaking to Count Benckendorff quite unofficially to-day, I expressed the apprehension that the Austrian Government might be forced by the strength of public opinion in Austria to make some *démarche* with regard to Servia. . . . The circumstances were such that the position of Count Berchtold was weak, and the Austrian Government might be swept off their feet.

Count Benckendorff said that he was aware of the strong feeling in Austria, but he did not see on what a *démarche* against Servia could be founded.

I said that I did not know what was contemplated. I could only suppose that some discovery made during the trial of those implicated in the murder of the Archduke—for instance, that the bombs had been obtained in Belgrade—might, in the eyes of the Austrian Government, be foundation for a charge of negligence against the Servian Government. But this was only imagination and guess on my part.

Count Benckendorff said that he hoped that Germany would restrain Austria. He could not think that Germany would wish a quarrel to be precipitated.

I said that my information was that the authorities in Berlin were very uncomfortable and apprehensive. They had got into their minds that Russian feeling was very adverse to Germany. They had obtained information somehow from Paris or St. Petersburg, founded upon the conversations between the Russian and British naval authorities, and they no doubt imagined that there was much more in these conversations than actually existed. All of this might lead the German authorities to think that some *coup* was being prepared against Germany, to be executed at a favourable moment. Of course, there was no foundation for such a thought. I told Count Benckendorff what I had said to reassure Prince Lichnowsky.

[The Russian ambassador did not think Germany would act.]

I [Grey] said that it would be very desirable that, in whatever way the Russian Government could best do it, they should do all in their power to reassure Germany, and convince her that no *coup* was being prepared against her. I often thought, in these matters, that things would be better if the whole truth were known. The difficulty was to tell people the truth, and make them believe that they really knew the whole truth. They were apt to think that there was a great deal more than they had been told.[5]

When Grey saw Lichnowsky the next day, he also warned that Vienna should not demand too much if it wanted Russian tolerance. London for its part would continue to work, as it had during the Balkan crises, to preserve the peace. But for the next ten days, Grey's promises did not translate into any significant action. Despite alarming information from Vienna and even Saint Petersburg, he did not meet with the principal ambassadors until mid-July, by which time the situation had grown far more threatening. He told Lichnowsky on July 20 that the prospect of the great powers being dragged into a war by Serbia was "detestable." The next day he told Paul Cambon, the French ambassador, that he hoped that Berlin would moderate Vienna's demands. A day later, he urged a reluctant Benckendorff to press for direct conversations between Vienna and Saint Petersburg. Then, with the presentation of the Habsburg ultimatum on July 23, Grey came face-to-face with the full scope of the dangers to European peace.

While Grey struggled to discern Vienna's intentions in mid-July, his cabinet colleagues wrestled anew with the Irish question. Desperate to prevent a possible civil war, George V had convened a conference at Buckingham Palace on July 21 to address the Irish question. But no solutions emerged. Then on Sunday, July 26, tensions over Ireland mounted still higher when British troops in Dublin fired upon a crowd of Irish nationalists, killing four. Not surprisingly, the cabinet continued to devote its chief attention to the Irish question, even as late as

Monday, July 27, when signs of a European war were increasingly evident. The press, too, remained fixated on Ulster and home rule and the conference hosted by the king.

THE TIMES
A Fourth Day
July 24, 1914

Conference to Meet This Morning
Gloomy Forebodings

WORLDWIDE SUPPORT FOR THE KING

The Conference of Party leaders met yesterday for the third time at Buckingham Place and sat for two hours. It is to meet again to-day.

In the fact that it has not yet broken up is to be found the one ray of hope in a dark situation. On almost every hand it is gravely feared that agreement has been found impossible. . . .

[The *Times* editorial added the following:]

The sole object of the Conference was to find a way by which civil war might be averted. That was the single item upon its programme. It had nothing to decide about the general government of Ireland. It was only asked to dispel, if it could, the approach of internal strife. The actual issue was very narrow. It concerned the question of area, and nothing else. All the members of the Conference were agreed that some portion of Ireland, greater or less in extent, was to be excluded from the operations of the Home Rule Bill. The question was—how much?

THE TIMES
Grave News from Ireland
July 27, 1914

The grave news which we publish this morning from the European capitals is accompanied, we are sorry to say, by very serious intelligence from Ireland. An attempt at gun running by the National Volunteers near Dublin yesterday morning resulted in collisions between the Volunteers, the public, the police, and the military. Four persons were killed and some sixty injured, of whom several are not expected to live. The excitement in Dublin is intense. The incident is from every point of view deplorable; but it is emphatic testimony to the true position of affairs across the Irish Channel. The nation to which a Liberal Administration was to bring a message of peace is mobilized for an internal war. The past week has seen one more hope of a settlement vanish in thin air. One spark, struck from such a momentary collision as that in Dublin yesterday, may serve, when and where we least expect it, to set in train the long-dreaded conflagration.[6]

Ireland remained the major British political issue until Thursday, July 30. By then, Austria had declared war on Serbia, and the Russians were about to mobilize. Would a more attentive cabinet, less distracted by the Irish issue, have been able to assist Grey in preventing war? However judged, the Irish question severely handicapped Grey's ability to focus on maintaining the European peace.

GREY AFTER THE HABSBURG ULTIMATUM

When Grey finally saw Count Mensdorff on July 23, his worst fears were confirmed: Vienna was sending an ultimatum to Serbia. Despite Grey's warning, Mensdorff insisted that any "possible consequences" depended on Russia and not Austria–Hungary. Even Grey's grim description of a European war involving the four great powers failed to shake the Habsburg aristocrat. On the other hand, Grey asserted that Britain might not be involved in such a war, even a Franco-German war.

The Foreign Office received a copy of the ultimatum the next day. It was immediately taken to 10 Downing Street, where Grey was listening to still another cabinet debate on Ireland. At its conclusion, he informed his colleagues of Vienna's demands. In his later account of the war, Winston Churchill, then first lord of the admiralty, describes the scene.

WINSTON CHURCHILL

The World Crisis, 1911–1914

1923

The Cabinet was about to separate, when the quiet grave tones of Sir Edward Grey's voice were heard reading . . . the Austrian note to Serbia. He had been reading or speaking for several minutes before I could disengage my mind from the tedious and bewildering debate which had just closed. We were all very tired, but gradually as the phrases and sentences followed one another, impressions of a wholly different character began to form in my mind. This note was clearly an ultimatum; but it was an ultimatum such as had never been penned in modern times. As the reading proceeded it seemed absolutely impossible that any State in the world could accept it, or that any acceptance, however abject, would satisfy the aggressor. The parishes of Fermanagh and Tyrone faded back into the mists and squalls of Ireland, and a strange light began immediately, but by perceptible gradations, to fall and grow upon the map of Europe.[7]

Still, the cabinet did not discuss the matter that day, but rather adjourned for the weekend. Before departing, Grey saw a series of ambassadors and dealt with the increasingly frantic telegrams from the other European capitals. On that Friday he had the first of his tense discussions with French ambassador Paul Cambon, as his letter to the British ambassador in Paris, Sir Francis Bertie, revealed.

EDWARD GREY

Letter to Paris

July 24, 1914

M. Cambon said that, if there was a chance of mediation by the four Powers, he had no doubt that his Government would be glad to join in it; but he pointed out that we could not say anything in Saint Petersburg till Russia had expressed some opinion or taken some action. But, when two days were over, Austria would march into Servia, for the Servians could not possibly accept the Austrian demand. Russia would be compelled by her public opinion to take action as soon as Austria attacked Servia, and therefore, once the Austrians had attacked Servia, it would be too late for any mediation.

I said that I had not contemplated anything being said in Saint Petersburg until after it was clear that there must be trouble between Austria and Russia. I had thought that if Austria did move into Servia, and Russia then mobilised, it would be possible for the four Powers to urge Austria to stop her advance, and Russia also to stop hers, pending mediation. But it would be essential for any chance of success for such a step that Germany should participate in it.

M. Cambon said that it would be too late after Austria had once moved against Servia. The important thing was to gain time by mediation in Vienna. The best chance of this being accepted would be that Germany should propose it to the other Powers.[8]

That same Friday, Grey pressed Lichnowsky on the desperate need for Berlin to help with Vienna. Saying he "felt helpless as far as Russia was concerned" because of the Austrian action, the foreign secretary implored Germany to restrain Austria–Hungary.

These conversations make clear that Grey wholly failed to see the implications of mobilization, a perspective that characterized his subsequent actions throughout July, as he always believed that the situation might be rescued even after the mobilizations began. He never understood that if Russia mobilized, the Germans would respond — and far more disastrously. Despite his experience, he did not grasp that mobilizations on the Continent could create a chain reaction, and he failed to realize the dynamics of alliance relationships and the interconnectedness of the mobilization timetables. His mental images were limited to naval mobilization, where operations could still come later, instead of a more comprehensive approach.

Grey finally left for his fishing retreat late on Saturday, July 25, still believing that peace might be preserved. But his comments also suggest that he now thought that if war came, Britain might be drawn into the fray. To avoid this possibility, he and his advisers had discussed proposing a four-power mediation effort. On Sunday, July 26, he authorized Permanent Undersecretary Sir Arthur Nicolson to make such a proposal when he met with Ambassador Lichnowsky. A laconic Grey later wrote on that fateful Sunday, "My usual weekend was curtailed, but things were not yet so critical that it was unsafe to be out of town even for a Sunday, and I left Nicolson in charge that day, July 26."[9]

WILSON FINALLY SEES A CHANCE FOR WAR

Sir Edward Grey had worried about the ramifications of the Sarajevo murders from early July. By contrast, the director of military operations (DMO), Major General Henry Wilson, only turned to the crisis on Saturday, July 25. The explanation for this gross inattention comes from his passionate involvement in the Irish question.

Henry Wilson was representative of the sizable presence of Anglo-Irish officers in the British army, men whose families had land holdings in Ireland but whose family ties were English and not Irish. His family had modest estates in County Longford and near Dublin. But unlike many future army officers, Wilson had had a French governess as a child, spoke fluent French (Grey could barely express himself), often traveled to Europe, and had become an avid skier and an indefatigable cyclist on the Continent. Commissioned in 1882, he had served in Burma, attended the Staff College at Camberley, and then gone to South Africa for the Boer War. Arrogant, bright, tirelessly energetic, with a sharp tongue, Wilson worked hard at being a soldier (Figure 13). As head of the Staff College from 1906 to 1910, he had relentlessly pressed the younger officers to prepare for a future continental war.

Wilson became DMO in August 1910, responsible for all mobilization plans and intelligence assessments. From then until July 1914, he worked to prepare British military forces for a continental mission. He exploited the precedent of the staff conversations with Paris to arrange detailed plans with the French general staff. During the Second Moroccan Crisis, Wilson gained grudging acceptance from the Asquith government that if war came and Britain intervened, his plan for continental intervention would prevail.

Supremely confident of his abilities as an officer and a strategist, Wilson was constantly conspiring. Already in 1904, Sir John French thought he ought to have his "wings" clipped. An ardent conservative and a proponent of conscription, Wilson consorted openly with those who vigorously opposed Liberal defense policies, and he was vehemently contemptuous of Liberal politicians. Like many military officers then and later, he doubted whether any political leader could

Figure 13.   Henry Wilson with Winston Churchill

A zealous conservative general who plotted against the Liberal government over the Irish question even in July 1914, Wilson once correctly received a postcard addressed to the "ugliest man in the British Army." Churchill, though a Liberal minister, worked well with Wilson, and together they helped bring Britain to the Continent in 1914.

Imperial War Museum.

truly understand military affairs. His diary was full of vitriolic rants against political figures. Of Grey, he wrote that he "seemed to me to be an ignorant, vain and weak man, quite unfit to be the foreign minister of any country larger than Portugal. A man who knows nothing of policy and strategy going hand in hand, a man incapable of understanding the German and French positions and their respective points of view." And he dismissed the Liberal cabinet ministers as "dirty, ignorant curs."[10]

The general had, moreover, established contacts to ensure that he knew the details of Liberal policy. He cultivated Sir Arthur Nicolson, whose own dislike of Grey steadily increased after 1912. The permanent undersecretary thus became a valuable source of intelligence on Liberal foreign policy. And in 1912, Wilson met Andrew Bonar Law, the new leader of the Conservative Party. Thereafter, the two were in almost constant contact, so much that no military decision of any consequence was kept from the Conservative leadership.

Most important, Wilson's intrigue over the Irish question saw him engage in very questionable behavior. He stirred the passions of his fellow Anglo-Irish officers and even gave aid to the Ulster counties to arm a militia to resist his own army. Paradoxically, at the very time he proclaimed the need for Britain to prepare itself to intervene on the Continent, his own divisive actions within the British army could easily convince Berlin that the British Expeditionary Forces (BEF) should not be considered seriously. His diary entries at the end of the Curragh mutiny reflect the serious divisions within the senior ranks of the military over this issue and illustrate Wilson's own dubious behavior.

HENRY WILSON

Diary

March 29, 1914

"I telephoned to Sir John [French] at 9 A.M. and told him of the result of my mission to the Staff College yesterday. Charlie Hunter* came to say that Milner† had said to him yesterday: "They talk a lot about Gough,*

---

* *Charlie Hunter:* another senior officer.
† *Alfred Milner:* a senior Conservative leader.

but the man who saved the Empire is Henry Wilson." This, of course, is much too flattering. I lunched at Bonar Law's house, only Carson† there. We talked about the situation in all its bearings. . . .

At 5 o'c. I went up to Sir John at 94 Lancaster Gate. I was much upset to find he was still havering. He had been for hours with [Richard] Haldane who had produced another letter to square the circle again. I read this letter carefully several times. It was to Sir John from Asquith. It sets out that Sir John had conceived that, by giving Hubert [Gough] the assurance, he was only carrying out the instructions of the Government, that the idea of any soldiers dictating to the Government was just as distasteful to him and to every soldier as to the Cabinet, and that they never have done so. . . .

There followed a paragraph to which I took grave exception, and which Sir John cut out in consequence—it said that Asquith's statement on Friday last had satisfied Sir John and, he thought, all others. It wound up by saying that he believed it was the Government intention not to coerce public opinion in Ulster, nor to initiate any movement which would result in active operations there, and that the whole incident might be considered as closed. So no action would be taken against Hubert and the letter which he held.

The idea then is that Asquith should read this letter out to the House of Commons to-morrow, and that then Sir John and [Sir Spencer] Ewart should withdraw their resignations. Provided this is done, and the obnoxious paragraph is cut out, I should be inclined to agree.

Gwynne‡ is to see Sir John at 7 P.M. At 9 P.M. I rang up Gwynne and he told me Sir John was resigning. He said that he saw Sir John and saw the letter, and even with the obnoxious paragraph cut out, he objected in *toto*. On this Sir John told him he might announce that he had resigned. This is splendid."

[The following is omitted from the published version.]

"Rang up B. L. [Bonar Law] and told him [that Sir John would resign] and added that it was now his business to drive the wedge deep into the Cabinet by causing the downfall of [John] Seely, Morley§ and Haldane. A good day's work."[11]

* Hubert Gough: the leader of the mutiny.
† *Carson:* the leading Ulster politician.
‡ *H. A. (Taffy) Gwynne:* editor of the *Morning Post.*
§ *John Morley:* the senior radical minister.

Wilson's less-than-discreet actions in March 1914 raise a fundamental issue, which will be discussed in more detail later: Why did the Liberal government refuse to discipline the general? Who or what protected him? What does this say about the status of civil-military relations in the one country usually taken as the norm for the civilian control of the military?

If Wilson's loyalties could raise doubts, so could his strategic judgments, especially when he finally turned his attention to the European crisis. The general bent every energy to the task of helping France. His plan was simple: Immediate British intervention would rescue the French and protect British interests. This continental strategy enjoyed broad support in the British army but equally strong opposition from British naval leadership. It represented, furthermore, a major shift from Britain's traditional strategy of depending first on the navy and only later intervening on the Continent. The full consequences of this shift were, of course, only apparent after the Great War got under way.

Wilson strongly resisted any evidence that contradicted his premise of continental intervention. At a meeting of the Committee of Imperial Defence on August 23, 1911, he insisted that British help would be decisive in assisting France. (The Committee of Imperial Defense, or CID, chaired by the prime minister, considered issues of British security.) Asserting that the Germans would violate Belgian neutrality and stay below the Meuse-Sambre line, he showed the location on a map of British divisions on the extreme western edge of any German sweep. But his analysis depended on Germany's failure to use reserve troops. He never conceded then or later that Germany might deploy more troops and thus swing much farther westward, a point that Churchill had argued in a more prescient memorandum on August 13, 1911. As it happened, in August 1914, British troops found themselves confronting nearly two German armies.

Nor did Wilson provide for a second line of British troops in case of a stalemate. Had he admitted the need for more troops, of course, then the six British divisions would not have been enough, thus undermining the case for intervention. To be sure, he advocated conscription as the real solution for Britain's strategic position, yet he was never honest enough in the strategic discussions to concede this need for fear of thwarting his intervention scheme.

Furthermore, while Wilson frequently talked of the need for Britain's simultaneous mobilization with France, he never assessed whether a British cabinet would or could act promptly. Nor does he appear to have studied the linkages between any Russian or French mobilization and a likely German response. Wilson, like Grey, apparently believed that peace could be preserved even if the Russians mobilized, a view the French staff did not share. In any event, the chances for peace were much diminished when General Wilson finally conceded that Europe was more important than Ireland. Or did he see Europe as a way to abort the Irish question?

GREY, CABINET POLITICS, AND THE MILITARY POLITICIAN

The surviving records permit only a partial reconstruction of the interaction between Grey and Wilson during the July crisis and indicate only a few meetings between the two. While Wilson and Grey did not agree on much, in July 1914 they shared a common goal: Britain would not abandon France. Otherwise, their views were often contradictory, not least because Wilson scornfully disagreed with Grey's patient consensus building for British intervention.

Grey's efforts for peace had clearly failed by July 29–30. His proposals for a four-power conference, for mediation, and then for direct Vienna–Saint Petersburg talks came to naught; none of the continental powers would take the risk. Then on July 30, Grey flatly rejected Germany's blatant attempt to secure British neutrality. This provocative German step, coupled with the absence of any German commitment about Belgian neutrality, effectively ended Grey's peace efforts. His single goal now became ensuring that Britain would join France if Germany actually attacked.

As Grey's mediation efforts faltered, he, Asquith, Churchill, and the cabinet moved to protect Britain's basic strategic position. The first moves were naval, and Grey still hoped they might sway Berlin to reconsider its support of Vienna. On Sunday, July 26, Churchill ordered the first and second fleets to remain together as they had been since the completion of the recent naval maneuvers; the government then worked to see that the British press signaled this deliberate naval move to Germany, while the British armada sailed from its Channel stations through the Dover Straits into the North Sea. Churchill's letters give a full account of the decisions.

WINSTON CHURCHILL

Letter to George V

July 28, 1914

During the last few days the Navy has been placed upon a preparatory & precautionary basis. The First Fleet will sail secretly tomorrow for its preliminary Northern station. The Second Fleet will assemble in Portland as soon as its men return in the ordinary course of leave on Friday. The Patrol flotillas have been raised to full strength and are moving in succession to their war stations. The two Irish blockades have been abandoned and all vessels engaged in them will conform to the general dispositions. The aircraft are collected at and around the estuary of the Thames to guard against airship attack. All vulnerable points such as oil tanks & magazines were last night guarded by the army against aerial attack (the air guns being manned) & against *sabotage*. It is possible that all East coast lights & guns will be manned tomorrow.

The reserves of oil & the coal arrangements are satisfactory. The reserves of ammunition show large surpluses. The torpedo reserve is complete. There will be no deficiency of officers on a complete mobilization & we shall have at least 20,000 Reservists for whom no room can be found on any ship fit to send to sea.

A variety of other precautions & measures have been taken with wh I will not trouble Your Majesty.

It is needless to emphasize that these measures in no way prejudge an intervention or take for granted that the peace of the great powers will not be preserved.

WINSTON CHURCHILL

Letter to Mrs. Churchill

July 28, 1914, Midnight

My darling one & beautiful,

Everything tends toward catastrophe & collapse. I am interested, geared up & happy. Is it not horrible to be built like that? The preparations have a hideous fascination for me. I pray to God to forgive me for such fearful moods of levity. Yet I wd do my best for peace, & nothing would induce me wrongfully to strike the blow. I cannot feel that we in this island are in any serious degree responsible for the wave of madness wh has swept the mind of Christendom. No one can measure the consequences. I wondered whether those stupid Kings & Emperors cd not assemble together & revivify kingship by saving the nations from hell but we all drift on in a kind of dull cataleptic trance. As if it were somebody else's operation.

. . . You know how willingly & proudly I wd risk—or give—if need be—my period of existence to keep this country great & famous & prosperous & free. But the problems are vy difficult. One has to try to measure the indefinite & weigh the imponderable.

I feel sure however that if war comes we shall give them a good drubbing.

. . . Ring me at fixed times. But talk in parables—for they all listen. Kiss those kittens [his children] & be loved for ever only by me.

Your own,

W[12]

General Wilson, meanwhile, spent his time seeing members of the French embassy, visiting Nicolson at the Foreign Office, and considering various mobilization schemes. To his surprise and satisfaction, the Liberal government on July 29 ordered "the Precautionary Period," but the next day Grey refused to give the French any firm guarantee of intervention, pledging only that the cabinet would continue to discuss the matter. Wilson's diary accounts chronicle how his views about the probability of war changed rapidly during the last days of July.

HENRY WILSON

Diary Entries

July 26 to August 1, 1914

JULY 26, 1914

"Went to see Sir A. Nicolson and found a lot more dispatches, all warlike. Austria, Russia, and Serbia seem to be going to mobilize, but, so far, no news of Germany moving. Until she moves there is no certainty of war. The Serbians have agreed to almost all the Austrian terms, making it difficult [for] Austria and Germany to have a European war. My own opinion is that if Germany does not mobilize to-day there will be no war."

JULY 27
"A lot of dispatches in all day, but no sign of Germany mobilizing, so I think there will not be any war. Meanwhile, after some fuss about gun-running at Howth yesterday, 2 companies K.O.S.B.s* were mobbed in the streets of Dublin and fired on the mob, killing 3 and wounding 40. This is a further upset for this Government. Panouse† told me this afternoon that the Austrian Ambassador in Paris had told the French Foreign Minister that the Austrians would move to-morrow."

JULY 28
"Went to the Foreign Office and had a long talk with Arthur Nicolson, which was interrupted by Asquith walking in. I presume now the Austrians will take Belgrade. There may then be a pause, but further advance will mean a mobilization in Russia, and then impossible to say what will follow."

JULY 29
"The Russians have ordered the mobilization of 16 Corps. The Austrians are mobilizing 12 Corps. The Germans and French remain quiet. At 3 P.M. a note came to Douglas from Asquith ordering the 'Precautionary Period.' This we did. I don't know why we are doing it, because there is nothing moving in Germany. We shall see. Anyhow it is more like business than I expected of this Government."

JULY 30
"The news is all bad to-day and war seems inevitable. Sazonov and the German Ambassador fell out last night, and the German went to Sazonov's house at 2 A.M. this morning in tears and said all was over. The Germans asked us to guarantee neutrality. Grey answers, 'Wait and see.' Nicolson, whom I saw several times, expects German mobilization to-morrow. I confess it looks like it. Panouse to-night brought me a paper which Cambon gave Grey this afternoon, showing German preparations."

JULY 31
"No news when I called for my usual visit to Arthur Nicolson at 9 A.M. Later (11 A.M.) the Cabinet met. Later we began to suspect that the Cabinet was going to run away.

"Later, 5 P.M., Eyre Crowe came to see me and told me that Germany had given Russia 12 hours to demobilize. Russia's answer was an order for 'General Mobilization.' Germany was going to order mobilization to-night, followed by France; and we were doing nothing. Later Johnnie

---

K.O.S.B.s: King's Own Scottish Borderers was a British regiment stationed in Ireland.
† *General Vicomte Louis de la Panouse:* the French military attaché.

Baird* came in. I told him of the state of affairs and got him to write to Bonar Law, who had gone to Wargrave, begging him to come up and see Asquith to-night.

"Later I saw Panouse and advised him to get Cambon to go to Grey to-night and say that, if we did not join, he would break off relations and go to Paris. An awful day.

"No C.I.D. has been held, no military opinion has been asked for by this Cabinet, who are deciding on a question of war."[13]

*Johnnie Baird: a leading Tory/Unionist political figure.

The British press reflected the sudden change of focus from Ireland to the prospect of a European war. The editorial columns of the *Times* convey this shift and the near hysterical tone that now dominated coverage of the approach of war.

THE TIMES

Lowering Clouds

July 30, 1914

The very briefness of the Prime Minister's statement, like the silence of the House as it was made, shows the growing danger of the European crisis. It proclaims the "extreme gravity" of the situation actually existing at this moment. It declares that nothing further can be said with advantage, save that the King's Government are not relaxing their efforts to "circumscribe the area of possible conflict." That is a task which it may exceed all the wisdom of diplomacy to accomplish. Once the passions of the nations become kindled, protocols and "conversations" can do little to arrest their fatal course. The manifesto which the Emperor Francis Joseph has addressed to his peoples is calculated to stimulate these passions, not in the Dual Monarchy alone. In its tone, and in not a few of its phrases, it recalls, as so much recalls besides, a former occasion when, in an access of exasperation, he rashly drew the sword. The charges which it makes against Servia now closely resemble those levelled against Piedmont fifty-five years ago. Then, as now, the Hapsburg Monarchy possessed a large measure of European sympathy in her legitimate grievances, until she forfeited it by flinging restraint and prudence to the winds. Then, as now, this country spared no exertions to maintain the peace of Europe.

Waning Hopes

July 31, 1914

Again the House of Commons has had to listen to Ministerial statements of the most ominous kind. The Prime Minister withdrew his motion giving precedence to the Home Rule Amending Bill, and explained that he took this course because the House was meeting under conditions of gravity which were almost without a parallel. Accepting the view which common sense and patriotism dictate, as we observed yesterday, he declared that, at a moment "when the issues of peace and war are hanging in the balance," it is in the interests of the whole world that England should "present a united front," and be able to "speak and act with the authority of an undivided nation." His words acquire double weight because this unprecedented step was taken with the full consent and the hearty approbation of the Unionist Party, and, as Mr. Bonar Law was careful to add, of Ulster besides. Sir Edward Grey was obliged to inform the members yesterday that he could not say the situation was less grave than it had been the day before. He had nothing to add to what was already [a] matter of public knowledge, but the words "so far as our information goes," with which he safeguarded the announcement that up to the hour when he spoke no other Power had taken any corresponding steps in answer to the partial mobilization ordered by Russia, show how very near the brink of the precipice we stand. We are still working for "the one great object of preserving European peace." With that end in view we are keeping in close touch with other Powers, and so far have not experienced any difficulty in this. That is the one faint ray of comfort that can be detected in what he had to say.

Interests and Duty of Great Britain

July 31, 1914

The Position Analyzed

One question is to-day on all lips: What course shall England pursue should a general European war break out? Prejudice, passion, or ignorance of the fundamental conditions of our national freedom inspire divergent answers. It is therefore necessary to consider in the cold light of historical fact and of reason the actual terms of the problem before making up our minds as to the course to be pursued.

At the moment of supreme peril nations, like individuals, are best guided by the impulse that is strongest in human beings—the instinct of self-preservation. It is well that this should be so; for none but interests instinctively recognized as vital can carry a people through a life-and-death struggle.

Dangers of Isolation

The first principle of all British foreign policy is recognition of the fact that England, though an island, forms part of Europe. Forgetfulness of this simple fact has in the past had disastrous consequences. Without reverting to the war of 1870, when England, by abandoning France to her fate, allowed her to be dismembered, and has ever since paid the cost in the growing burden of international armaments, it is necessary only to remember the position held by Great Britain at the end of the South African War. The policy of the late Lord Salisbury had been one of "splendid isolation." When disaster overtook us in South Africa we were without a friend on the Continent, and were only saved from attack by a European coalition because the Empire of Russia declined to sanction such a policy, and because the question of Alsace-Lorraine formed an insuperable obstacle to military and naval cooperation against us by Germany and France. . . .

Britain's Vital Interests

A vital British interest is therefore at stake. This interest takes two forms—the general interests of European equilibrium, which has been explained, and the more direct interest of preserving the independence of Holland, and particularly Belgium. The Franco-German frontier along the Vosges has been so formidably fortified on both sides that a German or French advance across it seems improbable. The point of contact between the German and French armies would probably lie in or near Belgium. But a German advance through Belgium into the north of France might enable Germany to acquire possession of Antwerp, Flushing, and even of Dunkirk and Calais, which might then become a German naval base against England. This is a contingency which no Englishmen can look upon with indifference.

Europe in Arms

August 1, 1914

Europe was rapidly arming last night, as was foreshadowed by the exceedingly grave disclosures made yesterday by the Prime Minister. He
said that the Government had just heard—not from Saint Petersburg,
but from Germany—that Russia had proclaimed a general mobilization
of her Army and Fleet, and that in consequence martial law was to be
proclaimed in Germany. It was understood, he added, that mobilization
would follow in Germany if the Russian mobilization continued. . . .

Even at this late moment, we need not wholly despair of averting the
supreme catastrophe. Mobilization does not inevitably lead to actual
warfare. . . . We fear, however, that the hopes of peace, or rather of localization of the limited conflict already begun, have grown very faint
indeed.[14]

Grey, meanwhile, continued his efforts to sway his cabinet colleagues, but successive meetings saw him fail to convince his colleagues for a more assertive policy. Despite the maladroit German bid
for British neutrality, the cabinet on July 31 still refused to let Grey
warn Berlin that a violation of Belgian neutrality would bring British
action. Instead, he was authorized to demand that France and Germany pledge to respect Belgian neutrality, a commitment quickly
given by Paris and evaded by Berlin.

The impact of the Belgian issue on Britain's road to war merits
additional comment. At least since 1911, Grey, Asquith, Churchill, Haldane, and others had accepted Wilson's prediction that Germany
would attack France through Belgium, which remained a focal point
of strategic planning. Yet surprisingly, Grey did not immediately
seize the Belgian issue in 1914. Rather, Grey continued to insist on
the preservation of the entente, perhaps fearing that if he played the
Belgian card too early, the Germans might agree to respect neutrality, thereby leaving France truly exposed. In any event, not until
August 1 and the conspicuous German silence on the neutrality issue
did Grey move to exploit the emotional possibilities of Belgium. His
failure to argue the Belgian issue earlier may have hurt the chances

for European peace. But it also kept open the chances for British intervention. Wilson might fret, but Grey was managing slowly to ensure British intervention.

But Henry Wilson could not know this. Thus, as the diary extracts have already shown, on July 31 Wilson reverted to his conspiratorial activity, urging Conservative leaders to push for war, behavior that continued relentlessly until August 6 and final cabinet approval for dispatch of the BEF to France. On August 1, Wilson's efforts intensified, with his home at 7 Draycott Place the headquarters of an effort to pressure the Liberal government to go to war. This was, to say the very least, an unusual civil-military dimension to the July crisis. Wilson met with Conservative leaders, talked with newspaper editors, and in short acted like a parliamentary whip and not a general.

The first task of Wilson's campaign was to gather the Conservative leadership, bringing some leaders back to London from their weekend. By 11 P.M. that Saturday, August 1, Bonar Law and others had drafted an emphatic letter to Asquith, pledging Conservative support for intervention on the side of France and Russia.

While Wilson conspired to push the Liberal government to war, Asquith struggled to keep the cabinet together and to help Grey with a desperate last-minute bid to save the peace. He described this effort in a letter to his young female friend.

HENRY ASQUITH

Letter to Venetia Stanley

August 1, 1914

When most of them had left, Tyrrell* arrived [the night before] with a long message from Berlin, to the effect that the German Emperor's efforts for peace had been suddenly arrested & frustrated by the Czar's decree for complete Russian mobilization. We all set to work ... to draft a personal appeal from the King to the Czar, & when we had settled it I called a taxi & in company with Tyrrell drove to Buckingham Palace at about 1:30 A.M. The poor King was hauled out of his bed, & one of my strangest experiences (& as you know I have had a good lot) was sitting

---

* *Sir William Tyrrell:* private secretary to Edward Grey.

with him—he in a brown dressing gown over his night shirt & with copious signs of having been aroused from his first "beauty sleep"—while I read the message & the proposed answer. All we did was to suggest that it should be made more personal & direct—by the insertion of the words "My dear Nicky"—and the addition at the end of the signature "Georgie"! I got home again about 2 A.M. and tossed about for a little on my couch—(as the novelists say)—but really I didn't sleep badly, and in that betwixt & between sleeping & waking, thank God the vision of you kept floating about me and brought me rest & peace.

You see I can't expel you, if I would—and wouldn't if I could.

There was really no fresh news this morning. We had a Cabinet wh. lasted from 11 to half past 1. It is no exaggeration to say that Winston occupied at least half of the time. We came, every now & again, near to the parting of the ways. . . . Ll. George—all for peace—is more sensible & statesmanlike, for keeping the position still open. Grey, of course, declares that if an out & out uncompromising policy of non-intervention at all costs is adopted, he will go. Winston very bellicose & demanding immediate mobilisation. . . . The main controversy pivots on Belgium & its neutrality. We parted in a fairly amicable mood, & are to sit again at 11 to-morrow (Sunday) an almost unprecedented event.

I am still *not quite* hopeless about peace, tho' far from hopeful. But if it comes to war I feel sure (this is entirely between you & me) that we shall have *some* split in the Cabinet. Of course, if Grey went I should go & the whole thing would break up.[15]

BELGIAN NEUTRALITY BECOMES THE BREAKING POINT

The turning point in Britain's path to war came on Sunday, August 2. When the group of ministers finally left Downing Street after two long sessions, the major decisions for Britain's entry into the war had been made. The mobilization of the continental armies, Germany's declaration of war on Russia and its seizure of Luxembourg, and Berlin's continuing failure to promise to respect Belgian neutrality—each event reinforced the prospect of a European war that endangered British interests. In these circumstances, shifts in the alignments within the badly divided cabinet were inevitable. Asquith moved cautiously, keeping his eye on David Lloyd George, the one person who could provide the leadership for a peace party and who remained a holdout until the end.

In these Sunday cabinet meetings, Grey played the Belgian card aggressively. At the same time, he exploited his own political position and reputation within the government. Since Friday, he had left few doubts that he would leave the government if the cabinet failed to back the French entente. His departure would almost certainly topple the Liberal government; at best, it would mean the formation of a coalition regime. The Conservatives' letter of support of that Sunday simply buttressed this threat.

Once more, Asquith's indiscreet letters offer the best summary of the situation. He conveyed the anguish of the moment to Venetia.

HENRY ASQUITH

Letter to Venetia Stanley

August 2, 1914, Mid-afternoon

I had a visit at breakfast time from Lichnowsky, who was very *émotionné* and implored me not to side with France. He said that Germany, with her army cut in two between France & Russia, was far more likely to be "crushed" than France. He was very agitated poor man & wept. I told him that we had no desire to intervene, and that it rested largely with Germany to make intervention impossible, if she would (1) not invade Belgium, and (2) not send her fleet into the Channel to attack the unprotected North Coast of France. He was bitter about the policy of his Government in not restraining Austria, & seemed quite heartbroken.

Then we had a long Cabinet from 11 to nearly 2, which very soon revealed that we are on the brink of a split. We agreed at last (with much difficulty) that Grey should be authorised to tell Cambon that our fleet would not allow the German fleet to make the Channel the base of hostile operations. John Burns at once resigned, but was persuaded to hold on at any rate till this evening when we meet again. There is a strong party including all the "Beagles"* and reinforced by Ll. George Morley & Harcourt who are against any kind of intervention in any event. Grey of course will never consent to this, & I shall not separate myself from him. Crewe, McKenna, & Samuel are a moderating inter-

---

Beagles: one of the terms that Asquith used to describe the less important members of the cabinet.

mediate body. B Law writes that the Opposition will back us up in any measure we may take for "the support of France & Russia." I supposed a good three quarters of our own party in the H. of Commons are for absolute non-interference at any price. It will be a shocking thing if at such a moment we break up—with no one to take our place.

Happily I am quite clear in my own mind as to what is right & wrong. I put it down for you in a few sentences.

(1) We have no obligation of any kind either to France or Russia to give them military or naval help.

(2) The despatch of the Expeditionary Force to help France at this moment is out of the question & wd. serve no object.

(3) We mustn't forget the ties created by our long-standing & intimate friendship with France.

(4) It is against British interests that France sh. be wiped out as a Great Power.

(5) We cannot allow Germany to use the Channel as a hostile base.

(6) We have obligations to Belgium to prevent her being utilized & absorbed by Germany.

This is all I can say for the moment. If only you were here my beloved! How I miss you—in this most critical of crises. Think of me & love me & *write.* Every day I bless & love you more.[16]

At the end of the second long session, the cabinet—now faced with the prospect of four resignations—resolved that Grey would inform the House of Commons the next day of one simple, overriding principle: Germany must respect Belgian neutrality. If the cabinet did not actually make Belgian neutrality a *casus belli,* it had de facto done so. Berlin simplified Grey's position later that same Sunday evening by presenting the Belgian government with an ultimatum that the Belgian leaders subsequently rejected. When the cabinet met Monday morning, Germany's military intentions were unmistakable. Lloyd George now backed steps that would assuredly lead Britain to war.

Late that Monday afternoon, Grey gave a crowded House of Commons an account of the failed efforts to save the peace, including disclosures about the Anglo-French military and naval conversations. After giving full coverage to the Belgian issue, Grey asserted in closing that Britain would suffer little from intervention in a continental war—an unmistakable suggestion that the navy would bear the burden of the fighting. This assertion, which Grey surely knew to be false, continued his record of parliamentary deception. Nonetheless, the speech was a resounding success. The next day, after the Germans had actually entered Belgium, Grey and Asquith ordered Berlin to withdraw. The German government refused to do so. At 11 P.M. London time, August 4, 1914, Britain went to war with Germany.

THE BEF TO THE CONTINENT: WILSON CONTINUES HIS POLITICAL CAMPAIGN

The German move only ensured that Britain would be at war. It did not guarantee British intervention on the Continent. So just as he had pressured the government to support France, Henry Wilson now lobbied to send the BEF to a predetermined (by Wilson) location in France. In this, he had not only the government to convince, but some of his own senior military colleagues. Once again, his diary reveals much about the politics of the situation and even more about the conspiratorial general.

HENRY WILSON

Diary Entries

August 2 to August 5, 1914

AUGUST 2

Wilson saw Arthur Nicolson before breakfast and learned of the German move into Luxembourg. Nicolson reported that Grey had told him after the cabinet [on August 1] that "we have decided not to send the E.F." Nicolson had retorted, "But this is impossible. You have over and over again promised M. Cambon that if Germany was the aggressor, you would side with France." Grey had replied, "Yes, but he has nothing in writing." [From Wilson MSS.]

"Leo Maxse and Amery to breakfast, and much telephoning to Bonar Law, Austen, and others. Panouse in at 10 A.M. Office all day. Two Cabinet meetings with quite indecisive results. I believe that a note has been sent to the French to say that, although we were not going to take part in the war, we would not allow the Germans to descend on the French coast. Was ever anything heard like this? What is the difference between the French coast and the French frontier? The German light troops were over the frontier today, and some fighting took place.

Crowds outside the Palace 10 P.M. cheering. We have got permission to send troops back to peace quarters."

AUGUST 3

"Usual 9 A.M. visit to Nicolson, no decision yet to mobilize. . . . At 1.9* P.M. [the private secretary to the Chief of the Imperial General Staff] came to my room to show me order for mobilization. Great crowds in streets and opposite Buckingham Palace. Saw M. Cambon in Arthur Nicolson's room. He held out both hands to me. So different from day before yesterday."

AUGUST 4

Wilson went to the French Embassy early on the 4th to discuss the question as to what changes of plans would be necessary owing to our delay in mobilizing. He, also, had long discussions with Sir J. French and Sir A. Murray with regard to the Expeditionary Force. He, moreover, had interviews during the day with Lord Milner, Mr. Amery, Sir J. Baird, Mr. Maxse, Lord Lovat, and other prominent Conservatives. These were busy making arrangements to bring the full force of Conservative opinion to bear upon the Government so as to ensure an immediate utilization of the Expeditionary Force. It was on this day apparently that an old friend of his who came upon the D.M.O.† in a passage in the Admiralty building found him in tears at the delay in deciding to employ that force! . . . "Grey's delay and hesitation in giving orders is sinful," Wilson wound up his diary for the day. Such procrastination as there had been in taking up a firm stand had, however, been the fault of the Cabinet as a whole. Several members of that body had at first been opposed to making the quarrel ours, and three of them had resigned when the right decision was at length taken. At 11 o'clock that night the country was at war.

AUGUST 5

"Asquith said he had summoned the great soldiers at the earliest possible moment. Then a lot of platitudes on the situation and strategy generally. . . .

"Churchill said the Dover Straits now completely sealed. Jimmy Grierson spoke up for decisive numbers at the decisive point. Sir John urged we should go over at once, and then decide destination later. I mentioned the flexibility of French railway system for switching. Haig asked questions and this led to our discussing strategy like idiots.

"Johnnie Hamilton plumped for going to Amiens as soon as possible. Then desultory strategy (some thinking that Liège was in Holland) and idiocy. Lord Kitchener plumped for Amiens, but wanted to get in closer

---

*The published diaries record the visit as coming at "1.9 P.M.," which must be a misprint; a visit at 1 P.M. seems quite logical.

†Wilson, the Director of Military Operations.

touch with French; suggested that they should send over an officer. Sir John urged we should order the transports to be fitted at once. Decision taken to order transports for all 6 divisions at once.

"Question then arose what strength the E. F. should be. Winston in favour of sending 6 divisions, as naval situation most favourable owing to our having had time to prepare. . . . Decision was taken that we should prepare at once for all 6 divisions. Lord Kitchener said one division should be ordered from India to Egypt. All agreed. Slight discussion on Colonial and Ulster contingents, but no decision reached.

"An historic meeting of men, mostly entirely ignorant of their subject."[17]

The decisive moment came on August 5, though Wilson had several scares along the way—chiefly from his military colleagues. At the Army Council that morning, he urged the immediate dispatch of the entire BEF (six infantry divisions and one cavalry division). But General Douglas Haig, slated to be the commander of the I Corps, opposed Wilson, insisting that their move be delayed until more manpower would be available. The DMO retorted that the war would be over before any additional forces would be ready. Moreover, it would disrupt all of the arrangements with the French. His views eventually and fatefully prevailed.

These same points Wilson made to the War Council when it met later that same day. In the session that Wilson described as "an historic meeting of men, mostly entirely ignorant of their subject," he won agreement to send the BEF to a prearranged point near Maubeuge. Despite senior military opposition, Wilson had once again prevailed. He did so because he had all of the arrangements settled and could insist—without fear of contradiction—that the French wanted this response. Wilson's persuasive skills and the fact that everything else seemed (and was) ad hoc helped his case. A triumphant Wilson had attained his goal: British intervention in a European war at a destination that he and the French general staff had selected. In the end, as Churchill wrote later, those who "spoke for the War Office know their own minds and were united."

The staff conversations with France had entangled the British government in a set of arrangements that, once under way, were more thorough than those of the Dual Alliance. Those "unofficial" talks had not formally committed London to intervention, nor indeed compelled it. Nonetheless, the talks and Wilson's role as military planner and conspiratorial military politician had severely curtailed the cabinet's freedom of action. The military in Britain had not forced the decision, nor had they indeed elsewhere in Europe; the statesmen and rulers in each instance made the final decisions. Yet in the British case, the ministerial and monarchical options were as sharply limited as they were in Germany, Austria–Hungary, and Russia by the actions of some of the military subordinates.

There were many reasons for London's decision to join the war. Entente diplomacy, the German naval threat, and the web of Anglo-French military and naval arrangements were among them. When the crucial moment came, a Liberal government—even though more ministers initially favored nonparticipation—committed the country to war. How did the interplay of civil-military relations affect that outcome? And what does this interplay suggest about the validity of the assertion that British governments since Oliver Cromwell in the seventeenth century have been in firm control of the military establishment? Considering this assertion calls into question traditional assumptions of constitutional practice in Britain, assumptions widely shared as normative in the United States.

First, however much Wilson might fail to credit the Liberal government with any strategic achievements, the basic military and naval response to an ambitious Germany remained a product of successive Liberal ministries. The radicals in the cabinet and in Parliament disliked the naval expenditures and especially the Russian entente, but they could not ignore Germany's maladroit international activity, which continually undermined their own arguments against the Triple Entente.

Grey's thorough domination of the British foreign policy process also contributed to this outcome. It could be argued that it was a measure of his importance to the government that he figured so prominently in Henry Wilson's constant diary diatribes. And if the foreign secretary and the DMO interacted only in time of crisis, Grey never forgot Wilson's key role in the talks with France and their importance for the entente.

Henry Wilson also helped to shape Grey's understanding of

Britain's strategic options. But the July crisis revealed that neither man appreciated the interlocking mechanisms of the mobilization schedules and the degree to which Russian mobilization would alarm the Germans. The Russian moves robbed Grey of time, and possibly opportunities, to intervene for peace. Grey's failures in the summer of 1914 stemmed not a little from his narrow conception of military matters.

Henry Wilson's myopia was different. So determined for intervention, he failed to develop several deployment options; only luck and heroic fighting at Mons and later would save the BEF from this neglect. And although Wilson cannot wholly be blamed for the great discrepancy between the forces prepared for France and those actually required, he can be faulted for failure to discuss honestly the contradictions between his strategy and the larger manpower needs.

Wilson's political intrigues rank him with Apis and Conrad among the 1914 leaders, although their actions were more blatant and possibly more fateful. Although Wilson had manipulated and maneuvered throughout his career, the friendship with Bonar Law that developed after 1912 gave him unparalleled access to the senior Conservative leadership. Wilson's interference in domestic political issues was virtually unprecedented in British history.

We turn finally to two questions posed earlier: Why did the Liberal government fail to discipline Wilson, and what does that failure say about civil-military relations in the Britain of 1914? The following points merit mention. Wilson's success with the French staff conversations made him an indispensable figure and to remove him would thoroughly disrupt matters. Nor could Wilson's own genuine abilities be ignored. Wilson worked, thought, slept military affairs. Equally important, to have moved against him would have prompted immediate negative reactions from the French and called the entire entente policy into question. For Grey, this constituted an unacceptable outcome; hence his willingness to tolerate Wilson. Furthermore the Liberals would risk a Conservative onslaught if Wilson were summarily ousted.

What, finally, does the Grey-Wilson relationship say about pre-1914 Britain? First, it emphasizes the degree to which Germany dominated much of the international agenda and thus created the agenda for British strategic policy. The German threat made France and military-naval affairs far more important to London than they had been for nearly a century. As successive American governments discovered during the cold war, a formidable antagonist can frame in large measure the strategic debate. Second, the failure to control Wilson demonstrated the inherent parliamentary weakness of the Liberal government after 1910. While Wilson worked to overthrow the Asquith regime, the cabinet's weakness made it difficult to challenge him, especially since his actions were reinforcing the government's own foreign policy. Wilson had simply become too important to sacrifice.

Closely linked with this would, of course, be the explosive Irish question, an issue about which the British army remains strongly ambivalent. Asking the army to move against its Protestant allies in northern Ireland would have been difficult even if all of the political forces in Britain and the king had been in agreement. They were not, and Wilson had an opportunity to maneuver.

The civil-military tensions so evident in the summer of 1914 in London carried over into the war. The prime ministers, Asquith and later David Lloyd George, never felt strong enough to deal effectively with the generals' manifest failures. Wilson prospered, finally becoming chief of the imperial general staff in early 1918 and retaining that position until early 1922. He then retired and was immediately elected to Parliament on an anti-Irish platform. The Irish Republican Army (IRA) assassinated him in front of his house on June 22, 1922.

Sir Edward Grey stayed in office until 1916. Exhausted and with failing eyesight, he spent much of his retirement defending his actions in the summer of 1914. He returned again and again to the question of what he might have done differently. Each time, he concluded that Britain had no other course of action in 1914. His memoirs reflect this valedictory: "The tragedy was great, but it was for Britain the least of the immense perils with which the time was fraught."[18]

NOTES

[1]Michael Brock and Eleanor Brock, eds., *H. H. Asquith: Letters to Venetia Stanley* (Oxford: Oxford University Press, 1982), 62. (Hereafter cited as *Asquith Letters.*)

[2]Keith Robbins, *Sir Edward Grey: A Biography of Lord Grey of Fallodon* (London: Cassell, 1971), 28–29.

[3]Viscount Grey of Fallodon, *Twenty-five Years, 1892–1916,* 2 vols. (New York: Frederick A. Stokes, 1925), 1:61–63.

[4]Ibid., 1:279–80, 285.

[5]*British Documents on the Origins of the War, 1898–1914,* vol. 11 (London: His Majesty's Stationery Office, 1926), no. 39. (Hereafter cited as *BD.*)

[6]*The Times,* July 24 and 27, 1914.

[7]Winston S. Churchill, *The World Crisis, 1911–1914* (London: Butterworth, 1923), 193.

[8]*BD,* no. 98.

[9]Grey, *Twenty-five Years,* 1:305.

[10]Taken from the Wilson Diaries, Aug. 9, 1911, and Nov. 16, 1911, which are in the Imperial War Museum, London. The published set of the diaries is also helpful; see Charles E. Callwell, *Field-Marshal Sir Henry Wilson: His Life and Diaries,* 2 vols. (London: Cassell, 1927). On army politics, see Hew Strachan, *The Politics of the British Army* (Oxford: Clarendon Press, 1997).

[11]In this and subsequent Wilson entries, the exact diary citations are marked by quotation marks, whether from the published diaries or the actual diary in the Imperial War Museum. The rest of the comments are those of Callwell, the editor of the published diaries; Callwell, *Wilson,* 1:144–45.

[12]Randolph S. Churchill, *Winston S. Churchill,* vol. 2, *Companion,* part 3, 1911–1914 (London: Heineman, 1969), 692–95.

[13]Callwell, *Wilson,* 1:151–55, with additional material from the original diary.

[14]*The Times,* July 30–31, Aug. 1, 1914.

[15]*Asquith Letters,* 139–40.

[16]Ibid., 146–47.

[17]Callwell, *Wilson,* 1:155–59, with additional material from the original diary.

[18]Grey, *Twenty-five Years,* 2:47. For a recent study that strongly criticizes British intervention in the First World War, see Niall Ferguson, *The Pity of War: Explaining World War I* (New York: Basic Books, 1999). Compare Samuel R. Williamson Jr., *The Politics of Grand Strategy: Britain and France Prepare for War, 1904–1914* (Cambridge, Mass.: Harvard University Press, 1969; rev. ed. London: Ashfield, 1990).

Epilogue

In July 1914, no military leader made his civilian-political colleagues go to war. Some generals, like Conrad and Moltke, may have pressed for action. At least one leader, Apis, bore responsibility for having created the crisis through the assassinations, and one general, Wilson, conspired against his government for his own political and strategic ends. But in every instance, the political leadership set the terms, controlled the final policies, and made the fateful decision to mobilize. To be sure, some leaders, such as Berchtold and Sazonov, made decisions based on misplaced hopes engendered by their military advisers. Such hopes misled all the participants about the chances for success. They also prompted decisions—such as the Russian general mobilization—that set in motion actions by other powers that were bound by the hard, iron logic of their war plans. It was this fateful interaction between civilian hopes and expectations and the grim reality of military war plans that caused the escalatory decisions and the final, disastrous outbreak of the First World War.

What lessons should students, the public, even policymakers glean from these experiences? Certain conclusions appear unchallengeable, even enduring. First, in a crisis, a state must be sure it understands the risks of the action proposed by its ally. Wishful thinking or respect for the other power does not excuse the failure to probe all of the options. Bethmann's and Moltke's failure to demand an exact timetable from Conrad and a clear sense of his intended strategy left them exposed strategically when he moved against Serbia and not Russia. In that sense, a country's own ally can be as dangerous as its enemy.

Second, experienced statesmen who have labored through many crises will, almost invariably in their decision making, rely too heavily on assumptions based on past experience. Three times since December

1912, the Habsburg leadership had considered going to war and believed they knew the risks. But in July 1914, they failed to ask themselves what might have changed since the previous tension with Russia in the winter of 1912–13. The British in 1914 talked publicly as if a naval war would be the main British contribution, when in fact since the Second Moroccan Crisis of 1911 some type of continental intervention had been expected. Both sets of leaders had become captives of their own previous crisis experience, deciding more often by historical remembrance and misplaced assumptions than by a thorough examination of their current options. Leaders often tend to assume that they understand the present crisis because they survived the last one.

Third, military values and attitudes are not confined to uniformed service officers. Indeed, militarized civilians like Berchtold and Churchill and the cohort of Habsburg leaders who accepted a social Darwinian view of the world, do not need any pressure from their military associates. Their views might come from their own military experiences or, more probably, from association with the rhetoric and the actions of their senior military associates. In these circumstances, no civilian wants to appear fainthearted or unwilling to take action.

Fourth, military leaders who have experienced long periods of peace are less likely to be realistic about the costs of war than those more familiar with it. Peacetime generals like Joffre and Conrad may well be unwilling to recognize that war is the great "leap in the dark" and, like civilians, may fear being dubbed cowardly. Even those with recent fighting experience, like Wilson, may minimize the risks of engagement if they are anxious to fulfill lifelong ambitions of military glory.

Fifth, control of the armed forces constitutes an unending problem for political leaders. It remains an area in which there are no firm "givens" and no lasting solutions. For civilian-political leaders to control the instruments of force effectively, they must realize the need for mutual respect, must have the courage to say no to the beribboned generals (and admirals), even if this carries some political risk, and must possess a genuine understanding of how war plans are implemented. Before July 1914, Berchtold had successfully resisted the efforts of Conrad to bring Austria–Hungary to war with Serbia; in Berlin, Bethmann had also resisted both the generals and the admirals on more than one occasion before July 1914.

In all decisions for peace or war, constitutional frameworks provide structures for debate and for accountability. The reader may, by now, have reached some conclusion about whether monarchical, absolutist systems make decisions for militant action more likely than parliamentary systems. Certainly, the governments in Vienna, Berlin, and Saint Petersburg acted without extensive consultation. By contrast, the leaders in Paris and London knew that they had to convince their elected colleagues of the correctness of their actions, and they moved more cautiously. They knew they would be held accountable, while their counterparts elsewhere had more freedom to maneuver—and to make mistakes.

The events of July 1914 provide the historian with ample examples of the role of contingency in human affairs. If Princip had missed the archduke or had killed only his wife; if Pašić had jettisoned Apis; if Wilhelm II had already departed on his North Sea cruise before Hoyos arrived; if Tisza had continued to resist Berchtold; if the Italian indiscretions about Habsburg actions had become public; if Poincaré had been more restrained in his enthusiasm for Russia; if the Russians had worried less about Pan-Slavism and more about the future of the Romanovs; or if actual civil war had broken out in Dublin—any one of these possibilities could have changed the situation dramatically.

Furthermore, it is important to note the significance of personalities as contingent factors. If any one of these leaders had acted differently (save Cadorna), he might well have interrupted the slide to war: if, for example, Pašić had exposed Apis and accepted a Habsburg investigation into the assassinations; or if Berchtold had pressed Conrad to seize Belgrade but go no further; or if Bethmann had reversed course when the Habsburgs delayed so long in their move against Belgrade and warned Vienna to rethink its policies. But in July 1914, there was a fateful convergence of personalities with other factors. Opportunities, fears, egos, constitutional arrangements, past crises, Darwinian attitudes, passionate advocacy, wishful thinking, possibly even romance—all combined to bring Europe to war.

Ultimately, it may be impossible for any state, including a democratic one, to avoid armed conflict. The events at the World Trade Center and the Pentagon on September 11, 2001, have shown that a superpower can have war thrust upon it. Yet even in the conduct of such a war on terrorism, it remains the responsibility of the civilian-military leadership to ensure that decisions to employ force are coherent and that the military goals are reasonably achievable. Moreover, there has to be a clear realization that the military action will touch on the security interests of other governments and that different points of view, even among allies, will almost surely emerge.

At the start of the new millennium, and after September 11, 2001, there is an urgent need for civilian understanding and control of the military forces of the state. Yet paradoxically, this need comes at a time when very few civilians in western society have had any direct experience in the military, either as members of the uniformed services or as students of strategic issues. Conversely, recent studies also show that many in the military have little appreciation of the American traditions of civil-military relations and even of the assumed tenets of civilian control.

The lessons of July 1914 remain valid in a new era of global tension about terror, along with the traditional issues of national security. Some who read this study may bear some future responsibility for decisions that carry the risk of war; our hope is that they will remember that declaring war is the most momentous act of statesmanship and that things can and do go wrong. As members of the great democratic electorate, we must ensure that our leaders—political and military—understand the dangers of militarism and the imperative for civilian control of the decisions for war or peace.

A Chronology of the Main Events Leading to the First World War (1870–1914)

1870– Franco-Prussian War: German Empire emerges from French
1871 defeat and annexes French provinces of Alsace and Lorraine, poisoning Franco-German relations thereafter

1877– Russo-Turkish War: Russia makes large gains in the Balkans
1878 under the Treaty of San Stefano

1878 Congress of Berlin overthrows San Stefano settlement and readjusts Balkan balance; Austria–Hungary gains right to "administer" Bosnia-Herzegovina

1879 Austria–Hungary and Germany sign alliance treaty

1882 Italy joins the Austro-German alliance; it becomes the Triple Alliance

1894 Franco-Russian alliance agreements exchanged

1894 French Army Captain Alfred Dreyfus charged with treason and unjustly convicted; pardoned in 1899

1899– Anglo-Boer War
1902

1902 Anglo-Japanese alliance

1904 Russo-Japanese War; Anglo-French entente

1905 First Moroccan Crisis

1907 Anglo-Russian entente; together with the Anglo-French entente it becomes the Triple Entente

1908 Austria–Hungary announces annexation of Bosnia-Herzegovina; crisis ensues

1911 Second Moroccan Crisis over Agadir; Italy attacks Turkey in Tripoli (Libya)

1912 *October:* Start of First Balkan War; Russia keeps third-year troops on active duty; Austria–Hungary mobilizes some troops

December: German crown council allegedly plots war; Austria–Hungary decides not to attack Serbia

1913 *May:* Austria–Hungary issues ultimatum to Montenegro over Scutari; Treaty of London ends First Balkan War

June: Second Balkan War begins

August: Treaty of Bucharest ends Second Balkan War

1914 *March:* Russo-German press war

June: Kaiser Wilhelm II visits Archduke Franz Ferdinand

June 28: Archduke Franz Ferdinand and wife, Sophie, assassinated at Sarajevo

July 1: Italian Chief of Staff Pollio dies

July 5–6: Hoyos mission to Berlin; Austria–Hungary receives "blank check" from Germany for action against Serbia

July 7: Habsburg Common Ministerial Council favors war with Serbia: Hungarian Premier Tisza opposes

July 19: Habsburg Common Ministerial Council approves terms of ultimatum

July 20–23: French President Poincaré and Premier Viviani visit Saint Petersburg; French reaffirm their diplomatic support of Russia

July 23: Austria–Hungary gives forty-eight-hour ultimatum to Serbia

July 25: Serbian reply does not accept demand for an outside (Habsburg) investigation of conspiracy; Austria–Hungary breaks diplomatic relations with Serbia; Serbia orders mobilization; Russia takes some steps preliminary to mobilization

July 26: British Foreign Secretary Sir Edward Grey proposes mediation; it is rejected by Vienna

July 28: Austria–Hungary partially mobilizes and declares war on Serbia

July 29: Scattered Austro-Hungarian shelling of Serbian territory; Germany attempts to win British neutrality

July 30: Russia orders general mobilization; Britain rebuffs German overtures on neutrality

July 31: Germany demands that Russia cease its mobilization; Austria–Hungary orders general mobilization

August 1: France refuses to bow to German demands of neutrality in event of Russo-German war; France and Germany mobilize; Germany declares war on Russia

August 2: British Cabinet gives limited assurance to France on defense of its northern coasts; Germany invades Luxembourg; Italy declares neutrality

August 3: Germany invades Belgium; Germany declares war on France

August 4: Britain declares war on Germany

August 6: Austria–Hungary declares war on Russia

Key Participants in the July 1914 Crisis

Asquith, Herbert Henry   British prime minister, 1908–16

Berchtold, Count Leopold Austro-Hungarian foreign minister, 1912–15

Bethmann Hollweg, Theobald von   German chancellor, 1909–17

Cadorna, Luigi   Chief of the Italian general staff, 1914–17

Cambon, Paul   French ambassador to London, 1898–1920

Churchill, Winston S.   First lord of the admiralty, 1911–15

Conrad von Hötzendorf, Baron Franz (later Count)   Chief of the Austro-Hungarian general staff, 1906–11, 1912–17

Dimitrijević, Dragutin (nicknamed "Apis")   Head of Serbian military intelligence; major figure in the Black Hand

Franz Ferdinand   Austro-Hungarian archduke and heir to the throne

Franz Joseph   Emperor of Austria and king of Hungary, 1848–1916

Grey, Sir Edward (later Viscount Grey of Fallodon)   British foreign secretary, 1905–16

Hoyos, Count Alexander   *Chef de cabinet* of the Austro-Hungarian Foreign Ministry, 1912–17

Isvolski, Alexander   Russian foreign minister, 1906–10; Russian ambassador to Paris, 1910–17

Jagow, Gottlieb von   German foreign minister, 1913–16

Joffre, Joseph C.   Chief of the French general staff, 1911–16

Lichnowsky, Prince von   German ambassador to London, 1912–14

Lloyd George, David   British chancellor of the exchequer, 1908–16

Messimy, Adolphe   French war minister, 1911; July crisis 1914

Moltke, General Helmuth von   Chief of the Prussian general staff, 1906–14

Nicholas II   Tsar of Russia, 1894–1917

Nicolson, Sir Arthur   British ambassador to Saint Petersburg, 1906–10; permanent undersecretary of the Foreign Office, 1910–16

Paléologue, Maurice   French ambassador to Saint Petersburg, 1914–17

Pašić, Nikola   Frequent Serbian prime minister (1906–18); also Serbian minister of foreign affairs, July 1914

Poincaré, Raymond   French prime minister and also minister for foreign affairs, 1912–13; president of the French Republic, 1913–20

Pollio, Alberto   Chief of the Italian general staff, 1910–14

Princip, Gavrilo   Bosnian-Serb assassin of Franz Ferdinand and his wife, Sophie

Rasputin   Siberian mystic with close ties to the Russian royal family

Salandra, Antonio   Italian prime minister, 1914–16

San Giuliano, Marquis Antonino di   Italian minister for foreign affairs, 1910–14

Sazonov, Serge   Russian foreign minister, 1910–16

Schlieffen, General Alfred von   Chief of the Prussian general staff, 1891–1905

Sukhomlinov, General Vladimir A.   Russian minister for war, 1909–15

Tirpitz, Admiral Alfred von   German naval minister, 1898–1916

Tisza, Count István   Hungarian premier, 1913–17

Viviani, René   French premier, 1914–15; also minister for foreign affairs, June 13– August 3, 1914

Wilhelm II   Emperor of Germany and king of Prussia, 1888–1918

Wilson, Henry   British director of military operations, 1910–14; later chief of the imperial general staff

Yanushkevich, Nikolai   Chief of the Russian general staff, 1914–15

Selected Bibliography

The following general works in English provide excellent introductions to this topic.

Albertini, Luigi. *The Origins of the War of 1914*. Trans. and ed. Isabella M. Massey. 3 vols. London: Oxford University Press, 1952–57.

Berghahn, Volker. *Militarism: The History of an International Debate, 1861–1979*. Leamington Spa, England: Berg, 1981.

Cohen, Eliot A. *Supreme Command: Soldiers, Statesmen, and Leadership in Wartime*. New York: Free Press, 2002.

Evans, R. J. W., and Hartmut Pogge von Strandmann, eds. *The Coming of the First World War*. Oxford: Clarendon, 1988.

Ferguson, Niall. *The Pity of War: Explaining World War I*. New York: Basic Books, 1999.

Geiss, Imanuel, ed. *July 1914: The Outbreak of the First World War— Selected Documents*. New York: Charles Scribner's Sons, 1967.

Herrmann, David G. *The Arming of Europe and the Making of the First World War*. Princeton, N.J.: Princeton University Press, 1996.

Herwig, Holger H. *The Outbreak of World War I: Causes and Responsibilities*. 6th ed. Boston: Houghton Mifflin, 1997.

Huntington, Samuel P. *The Soldier and the State: The Theory and Practice of Civil-Military Relations*. Cambridge, Mass.: Harvard University Press, 1957.

Joll, James. *The Origins of the First World War*. 2d ed. New York: Longman, 1992.

Kagan, Donald. *On the Origins of Wars and the Preservation of Peace*. New York: Doubleday, 1995.

Keegan, John. *The First World War*. New York: Alfred A. Knopf, 1999.

Keegan, John. *An Illustrated History of the First World War*. New York: Alfred A. Knopf, 2001.

Kennedy, Paul. *The War Plans of the Great Powers*. Boston: Allen and Unwin, 1985.

Martel, Gordon. *The Origins of the First World War*. New York: Longman, 1987.

Miller, Steven E., ed. *Military Strategy and the Origins of the First World War.* Princeton, N.J.: Princeton University Press, 1985.

Snyder, Jack. *The Ideology of the Offensive: Military Decision Making and the Disasters of 1914.* Ithaca, N.Y.: Cornell University Press, 1984.

Stevenson, David. *Armaments and the Coming of War: Europe, 1904–1914.* Oxford: Clarendon, 1996.

Strachan, Hew. *The First World War.* Vol. 1, *To Arms.* Oxford: Oxford University Press, 2001.

Strachan, Hew, ed. *The Oxford Illustrated History of the First World War.* Oxford: Oxford University Press, 1998, 2000.

Vagts, Alfred. *A History of Militarism: Civilian and Military.* Rev. ed. New York: Free Press, 1959.

Wilson, Keith, ed. *Decisions for War, 1914.* New York: St. Martin's Press, 1995.

For specific works on each of the great powers and Serbia, see the following titles.

AUSTRIA–HUNGARY

Bled, Jean-Paul. *Franz Joseph.* Trans. Teresa Bridgeman. Oxford: Blackwell, 1992.

Bridge, F. R. *The Habsburg Monarchy among the Great Powers, 1815–1918.* New York: Berg, 1990.

Fellner, Fritz. "Austria–Hungary." In *Decisions for War, 1914.* Ed. Keith Wilson. New York: St. Martin's Press, 1995.

Herwig, Holger H. *The First World War: Germany and Austria–Hungary, 1914–1918.* London: Arnold, 1997.

Jelavich, Barbara. "What the Habsburg Government Knew about the Black Hand," *Austrian History Yearbook,* no. 22, 1991.

Leslie, John. "The Antecedents of Austria–Hungary's War Aims." In *Archiv und Forschung: Das Haus-, Hof-, und Staatsarchiv in seiner Bedeutung für die Geschichte Österreichs und Europas.* Ed. Elisabeth Springer and Leopold Kammerhofer. Vienna: Verlag für Geschichte und Politik, 1993.

Morton, Frederic. *Thunder at Twilight: Vienna, 1913–1914.* New York: Charles Scribner's Sons, 1989.

Palmer, Alan. *Twilight of the Habsburgs: The Life and Times of Emperor Francis Joseph.* New York: Grove, 1994.

Rothenberg, Gunther. *The Army of Franz Joseph.* West Lafayette, Ind.: Purdue University Press, 1976.

Sondhaus, Lawrence. *Franz Conrad von Hötzendorf: Architect of the Apocalypse.* Boston: Humanities Press, 2000.

Tunstall, Graydon A., Jr. *Planning for War against Russia and Serbia: Austro-Hungarian and German Military Strategies, 1871–1914.* Highland Lakes, N.J.: Atlantic Research and Publications, 1993.

Williamson, Samuel R., Jr. *Austria–Hungary and the Origins of the First World War.* New York: St. Martin's Press, 1991.

BRITAIN

Ash, Bernard. *The Lost Dictator.* London: Cassell, 1966.

Asquith, Herbert H. *H. H. Asquith: Letters to Venetia Stanley.* Selected and edited by Michael and Eleanor Brock. Oxford: Oxford University Press, 1982.

Callwell, Charles E. *Field-Marshal Sir Henry Wilson: His Life and Diaries.* 2 vols. London: Cassell, 1927.

Cannadine, David. *The Decline and Fall of the British Aristocracy.* New Haven, Conn.: Yale University Press, 1990.

Churchill, Winston S. *The World Crisis, 1911–1914.* London: Butterworth, 1923.

Grey, Viscount of Fallodon. *Twenty-five Years, 1892–1916.* 2 vols. New York: Frederick A. Stokes, 1925.

Hinsley, F. H., ed. *British Foreign Policy under Sir Edward Grey.* Cambridge: Cambridge University Press, 1977.

Robbins, Keith. *Sir Edward Grey: A Biography of Lord Grey of Fallodon.* London: Cassell, 1971.

Steiner, Zara. *Britain and the Origins of the First World War.* London: Macmillan, 1977.

Strachan, Hew. *The Politics of the British Army.* Oxford: Clarendon, 1997.

Trevelyan, G. M. *Grey of Fallodon: The Life and Letters of Sir Edward Grey, Afterwards Viscount Grey of Fallodon.* Boston: Houghton Mifflin, 1937.

Williamson, Samuel R., Jr. *The Politics of Grand Strategy: Britain and France Prepare for War, 1904–1914.* Cambridge, Mass.: Harvard University Press, 1969; rev. ed., London: Ashfield, 1990.

Wilson, Henry Hughes. *Diaries.* Imperial War Museum, London.

Wilson, Keith M. *The Policy of the Entente: Essays on the Determinants of British Foreign Policy, 1904–1914.* Cambridge: Cambridge University Press, 1985.

Wilson, Trevor. *The Myriad Faces of War: Britain and the Great War, 1914–1918.* New York: Blackwell, 1986.

FRANCE

Andrew, Christopher. "France and the German Menace." In *Knowing One's Enemies: Intelligence Assessment before the Two World Wars.* Ed. Ernest R. May. Princeton, N.J.: Princeton University Press, 1984.

Berenson, Edward. *The Trial of Madame Caillaux.* Berkeley: University of California Press, 1992.

Burns, Michael. *France and the Dreyfus Affair: A Documentary History.* Boston: Bedford/St. Martin's, 1999.

Joffre, Joseph J. C. *The Memoirs of Marshal Joffre.* Trans. T. Bentley Mott. 2 vols. London: Geoffrey Bles, 1932.

Keiger, John F. V. "France." In *Decisions for War, 1914.* Ed. Keith Wilson. New York: St. Martin's Press, 1995.

Keiger, John F. V. *France and the Origins of the First World War.* London: Macmillan, 1983.

Keiger, John F. V. *Raymond Poincaré.* Cambridge: Cambridge University Press, 1997.

Porch, Douglas. *The French Secret Services: From the Dreyfus Affair to the Gulf War.* New York: Farrar, Straus and Giroux, 1995.

Porch, Douglas. *The March to the Marne.* Cambridge: Cambridge University Press, 1981.

Stevenson, David. *French War Aims against Germany, 1914–1919.* Oxford: Clarendon, 1982.

Tanenbaum, Jan Karl. "French Estimates of Germany's Operational War Plans." In *Knowing One's Enemies: Intelligence Assessment before the Two World Wars.* Ed. Ernest R. May. Princeton, N.J.: Princeton University Press, 1984.

GERMANY

Berghahn, Volker. *Germany and the Approach of War.* 2d ed. New York: St. Martin's Press, 1993.

Bernhardi, Friedrich von. *Germany and the Next War.* Trans. Allen H. Powles. New York: Longmans, Green, 1914.

Bethmann Hollweg, Theobald von. *Reflections on the World War.* Part I. London: George Butterworth, 1920.

Bucholz, Arden. *Moltke, Schlieffen, and Prussian War Planning.* New York: Berg, 1991.

Clark, Christopher. *Kaiser Wilhelm II.* New York: Longman, 2000.

Craig, Gordon A. *Germany, 1866–1914.* New York: Oxford University Press, 1978.

Craig, Gordon A. *The Politics of the Prussian Army, 1640–1945.* Oxford: Clarendon, 1955.

Farrar, Lancelot L. *The Short-War Illusion: German Policy, Strategy, and Domestic Affairs, August–December 1914.* Santa Barbara, Calif.: ABC-Clio, 1973.

Fischer, Fritz. *Germany's Aims in the First World War.* New York: W. W. Norton, 1967.

Fischer, Fritz. *War of Illusions: German Policies from 1911 to 1914.* Trans. Marian Jackson. New York: W. W. Norton, 1975.

Jarausch, Konrad H. *The Enigmatic Chancellor: Bethmann Hollweg and the Hubris of Imperial Germany.* New Haven, Conn.: Yale University Press, 1972.

Kitchen, Martin. *The German Officer Corps, 1890–1914.* Oxford: Clarendon, 1958.

Meyer, T. H., ed. *Light for the New Millennium: Rudolf Steiner's Association with Helmuth and Eliza von Moltke.* Trans. Heidi Herrmann-Davey, William Forward, and Martin Askew. London: Rudolf Steiner, 1997.

Mombauer, Annika. *Helmuth von Moltke and the Origins of the First World War.* Cambridge: Cambridge University Press, 2001.

Moses, John A. *The Politics of Illusion: The Fischer Controversy in German Historiography.* London: G. Prior, 1975.

Ritter, Gerhard. *The Schlieffen Plan: Critique of a Myth.* Trans. Andrew and Eva Wilson. New York: Praeger, 1958. Reprint, Westport, Conn.: Greenwood Press, 1979.

Ritter, Gerhard. *The Sword and the Scepter: The Problem of Militarism in Germany.* Vol. 2. Coral Gables, Fla.: University of Miami Press, 1970.

Shanafelt, Gary. *The Secret Enemy: Austria–Hungary and the German Alliance, 1914–1918.* New York: Columbia University Press, 1985.

Thompson, Wayne C. *In the Eye of the Storm: Kurt Riezler and the Crises of Modern Germany.* Iowa City: University of Iowa Press, 1980.

Weed, Annie F. "German Student Letters." In *World War I and European Society.* Ed. Marilyn Shevin-Coetzee and Frans Coetzee. Lexington, Mass.: D. C. Heath, 1995.

ITALY

Bosworth, R. J. B. *Italy and the Approach of the First World War.* New York: St. Martin's Press, 1983.

Bosworth, R. J. B. *Italy, the Least of the Great Powers: Italian Foreign Policy before the First World War.* Cambridge: Cambridge University Press, 1979.

Giolitti, Giovanni. *Memoirs of My Life.* Trans. by Edward Storer. London: Chapman and Dodge, 1922.

Gooch, John. *Army, State, and Society in Italy, 1870–1915.* London: Macmillan, 1989.

Gooch, John. "Italy before 1915: The Quandary of the Vulnerable." In *Knowing One's Enemies: Intelligence Assessment before the Two World Wars.* Ed. Ernest R. May. Princeton, N.J.: Princeton University Press, 1984.

Halpern, Paul G. *The Mediterranean Naval Situation, 1908–1914.* Cambridge, Mass.: Harvard University Press, 1971.

Palumbo, Michael. "Italian-Austro-Hungarian Military Relations before World War I." In *Essays on World War I: Origins and Prisoners of War.* Ed. Samuel R. Williamson Jr. and Peter Pastor. New York: Columbia University Press, 1983.

Renzi, William A. *In the Shadow of the Sword: Italy's Neutrality and Entrance into the Great War, 1914–1915.* New York: Peter Lang, 1987.

Smith, Denis Mack. *Italy and Its Monarchy.* New Haven, Conn.: Yale University Press, 1989.

Sullivan, Brian R. "The Strategy of the Decisive Weight: Italy, 1882–1922." In *The Making of Strategy: Rulers, States, and War*. Ed. Williamson Murray, MacGregor Knox, and Alvin Bernstein. Cambridge: Cambridge University Press, 1994.

Whittam, John. *The Politics of the Italian Army, 1861–1918*. London: Croom Helm, 1977.

RUSSIA

Alekseev, Michael. *Military Intelligence Service of Russia: From Rurik to Nicholas II*. Moscow: Russian Intelligence Service, 1998.

Fuller, William C., Jr. *Civil-Military Conflict in Imperial Russia, 1881–1914*. Princeton, N.J.: Princeton University Press, 1985.

Fuller, William C., Jr. *Strategy and Power in Russia, 1600–1914*. New York: Free Press, 1992.

Gatrell, Peter W. *Government, Industry, and Rearmament in Russia, 1900–1914: The Last Argument of Tsarism*. Cambridge: Cambridge University Press, 1994.

Lieven, Dominic C. B. *Nicholas II: Twilight of the Empire*. New York: St. Martin's Press, 1994.

Lieven, Dominic C. B. *Russia and the Origins of the First World War*. New York: St. Martin's Press, 1983.

Rogger, Hans. *Russia in the Age of Modernization and Revolution, 1881–1917*. New York: Longman, 1983.

Sazonov, Serge. *Fateful Years, 1909–1916*. New York: Frederick A. Stokes, 1928.

Stone, Norman. *The Eastern Front, 1914–1917*. London: Hodder and Stoughton, 1975.

SERBIA

Cornwall, Mark. "Serbia." In *Decisions for War, 1914*. Ed. Keith Wilson. New York: St. Martin's Press, 1995.

Dedijer, Vladimir. *The Road to Sarajevo*. New York: Simon & Schuster, 1966.

Dragnich, Alex N. *Serbia, Nikola Pašić, and Yugoslavia*. New Brunswick, N.J.: Rutgers University Press, 1974.

Lampe, John R. *Yugoslavia as History: Twice There Was a Country*. Cambridge: Cambridge University Press, 1996.

MacKenzie, David. *Apis, the Congenial Conspirator: The Life of Colonel Dragutin T. Dimitrijević*. Boulder, Colo.: East European Monographs, 1989.

MacKenzie, David. "Serbian Nationalist and Military Organizations and the Piedmont Idea, 1844–1914." *East European Quarterly*, 16 (Sept. 1982).

Acknowledgments (continued from page iv)

Reprinted with the permission of Scribner, an imprint of Simon & Schuster Adult Publishing Group, from *Origins of the World War,* Vol. I by Sidney B. Fay. Copyright © 1928 by The Macmillan Company; copyright renewed © 1956 by Sidney Bradshaw Fay.

Extract from *War of Illusions* by Fritz Fischer, published by Chatto & Windus. Used by permission of The Random House Group Limited.

Fuller, William C., Jr. *Civil-Military Conflict in Imperial Russia 1881–1914.* © 1985 by Princeton University Press. Reprinted by permission of Princeton University Press.

Geiss, Imanuel. *Juli 1914: Die europäische Krise und der Ausbruch des Ersten Weltkriegs* [*July 1914: The Outbreak of the First World War*]. English Edition by Charles Scribner's Sons, New York. © 1965 Deutscher Taschenbuch Verlag, Munich, Germany.

Excerpts from Vladimir I. Gurko. Edited by J. E. Wallace Sterling, Xenia Joukoff Eudin, and H. H. Fisher, *Features and Figures of the Past: Government and Opinion in the Reign of Nicholas II.* © 1939 by the Board of Trustees of the Leland Stanford Jr. University; renewed 1967.

Hantsch, Hugo. *Leopold Graf Berchtold: Grandseigneur und Staatsmann.* 2 vols. (Verlag Styria, 1963). II, 558.

Copyright © 1990 by M. E. Sharpe, Inc. from Sidney Harcave, ed. and trans., *The Memoirs of Count Witte* (Armonk, N.Y.: M. E. Sharpe, 1990), pp. 702–3. Reprinted with permission.

Herwig, Holger H. *Luxury Fleet: The Imperial German Navy 1888–1918* (1980). Reprinted by permission of the author.

Jelavich, Barbara. "Documents: What the Habsburg Government Knew about the Black Hand." *Austrian History Yearbook,* 22 (1991). By permission of the Center for Austrian Studies and the editors of *The Austrian History Yearbook.*

From *Apis: The Congenial Conspirator: The Life of Dragutin T. Dimitrijević,* by David MacKenzie. © 1989 Columbia University Press. Reprinted with the permission of the publisher.

Massie, Robert K. *Nicholas and Alexandra.* Originally published by Atheneum, 1967. Reprinted by permission of the author.

Meyer, Henry Cord, ed. *The Long Generation: Germany from Empire to Ruin, 1913–1945* (Harper & Row, 1973). Reprinted with permission of Helen Grove Meyer, widow of Professor Emeritus Henry Cord Meyer, University of California, Irvine.

Mombauer, Annika. *Helmuth von Moltke and the Origins of the First World War* (2001). Reprinted with the permission of Cambridge University Press.

Montgelas, Max, and Walter Schücking, eds. *Outbreak of the War: German Documents Collected by Kaul Kautsky* (Oxford University Press, 1924).

Poincaré, Raymond. *Au Service de la France: Neuf années des souvenirs,* Vol. IV: *l'Union sacrée.* Librairie Plon 1927.

© Vandenhoeck & Ruprecht, Kurt Riezler. *Tagebücher, Aufsätze, Dokumente,* ed. Karl Dietrich Erdmann, Göttingen, 1972, pages 181–84.

Ritter, Garhard. *The Schlieffen Plan: Critique or a Myth.* Translated by Andrew and Eva Wilson (1979). Reprinted with Permission from Berg Publishers. All rights reserved.

Seldes, George. *Sawdust Caesar.* Reprinted by the permission of Russell & Volkening as agents for the author. Copyright © 1935 by George Seldes, copyright renewed 1963 by George Seldes.

Index